Doing RESEARCH in SOCIAL WORK and SOCIAL CARE

SAGE was founded in 1965 by Sara Miller McCune to support the dissemination of usable knowledge by publishing innovative and high-quality research and teaching content. Today, we publish over 900 journals, including those of more than 400 learned societies, more than 800 new books per year, and a growing range of library products including archives, data, case studies, reports, and video. SAGE remains majority-owned by our founder, and after Sara's lifetime will become owned by a charitable trust that secures our continued independence.

Los Angeles | London | New Delhi | Singapore | Washington DC | Melbourne

CATHERINE FLYNN
FIONA MCDERMOTT

Doing RESEARCH in SOCIAL WORK and SOCIAL CARE

THE JOURNEY FROM STUDENT TO PRACTITIONER RESEARCHER

Los Angeles | London | New Delhi
Singapore | Washington DC | Melbourne

Los Angeles | London | New Delhi
Singapore | Washington DC | Melbourne

SAGE Publications Ltd
1 Oliver's Yard
55 City Road
London EC1Y 1SP

SAGE Publications Inc.
2455 Teller Road
Thousand Oaks, California 91320

SAGE Publications India Pvt Ltd
B 1/I 1 Mohan Cooperative Industrial Area
Mathura Road
New Delhi 110 044

SAGE Publications Asia-Pacific Pte Ltd
3 Church Street
#10-04 Samsung Hub
Singapore 049483

Editor: Mila Steele
Assistant editor: Alysha Owen
Production editor: Tom Bedford
Copyeditor: Camille Bramall
Proofreader: Andy Barter
Indexer: David Rudeforth
Marketing manager: Camille Richmond
Cover design: Shaun Mercier
Typeset by: C&M Digitals (P) Ltd, Chennai, India
Printed and bound by CPI Group (UK) Ltd,
Croydon, CR0 4YY

First published 2016

Library of Congress Control Number: 2016935865

British Library Cataloguing in Publication data

A catalogue record for this book is available from
the British Library

ISBN 978-1-4739-0661-7
ISBN 978-1-4739-0662-4 (pbk)

At SAGE we take sustainability seriously. Most of our products are printed in the UK using FSC papers and boards.
When we print overseas we ensure sustainable papers are used as measured by the PREPS grading system.
We undertake an annual audit to monitor our sustainability.

Contents

Acknowledgements

Many thanks are due to our generous practitioner and student researchers, who kindly shared the ups and downs of their research journeys in their contributions; to Ellie Fossey for many robust discussions and feedback on early chapters; and to Niamh Clarke for her patience in editing the final reference list. It is also important that we acknowledge all of the students and practitioners we have both worked with over the years, who were and continue to be a wonderful source of ideas and intellectual stimulation. As ever, we would be keen to hear your feedback as you read and use this book.

Introduction

Why this book?

We have been motivated to write this book for a number of reasons:

- We have both been seeking a professionally relevant and accessible text that locates research clearly within the ethical and value base of social work
- We wanted a text that bridged the gap between 'students' and 'practitioners': we do not see these as distinct groups, but rather the same group at different places on the professional journey
- We wanted a text that acknowledged both the real world and individual experience.

The guiding framework for this book

This book is therefore shaped by a pragmatist approach. When we say this we do not mean we focus only on 'how' to do research and a simplified account of 'what works'. Rather, we are of the view that pragmatism requires us to consider why we do research in particular ways, as well as what difference it makes to do our research in one way rather than another (Morgan, 2014). This ensures that the focus is clearly on our research goals, and the desired practical application of our research.

We agree with the view of classical pragmatist William James that

> the world of everyday life is 'multitudinous beyond imagination, tangled, muddy, painful, and perplexed', continually presenting us with ambiguities and complexities, confusions and contradictions ... (1907/1975, pp. 17-18). Our explanatory systems offer but a 'summary sketch, a picture of the world in abridgement, a foreshortened bird's eye view' of the immediacy and particularity of real life (1909/1967, p. 8). (Borden, 2013: 261)

To work with such uncertainty and contingency requires us to engage in and seek knowledge and responses to problems in pluralist ways. This is a clear feature of the social work profession (Borden, 2013), which involves both developing meaningful goals and using appropriate methods (Morgan, 2014).

Aims of this book

We hope that this book will be a 'companion' for you on your journey to practitioner researcher in the fields of social work and social care. To encourage and support your learning, you will see that this text is grounded in professional practice and built around relevant case examples, from a range of perspectives and disciplines. These cases provide concrete illustrations of research, showing how problems can be approached and studied differently, depending on the research context or the research aim; the case studies also provide real examples of how research aims can be achieved and made use of in practice. Use of such examples provides you with 'hangers' for key methodological concepts so you can integrate these with your existing knowledge (Csiernik et al., 2010). Because we have framed this book as a companion for your journey, we also make use of the experiences of a group of social work practitioner researchers and students (we call them 'the chorus'). All have been engaged in their own research journeys over the past few years. Along the way they have questioned, reflected on and analysed the research process, recording their experiences with a view to using them to assist other novice researchers. We will use their insights and comments as the research process unfolds in the book, providing 'snatches' of their conversations as they worked with the challenges, surprises and successes of their first ventures into researching their practice issues. (You will hear their voices in the quote text boxes throughout the book.)

It is important to note at this point that although being a 'good' social work and social care professional means being both a consumer and producer of research, our primary focus in this book is on developing the skills to be a research producer. We believe that these skills will also give you the tools to read and understand other people's research (we discuss reading and reviewing others' work in Chapter 4).

Structure of this book

Pragmatism shapes not just the ideas within, but the layout and approach of the book: drawing on case examples; making links between research goals and appropriate methods; and the use of the chorus, who provide contextual information, sharing their learning experiences about the messiness of research and the importance of experiential and collaborative learning.

We present this book in a largely linear fashion, walking you through the steps of the research process. The book consists of three parts:

1. Preparing for research (Chapters 1-4): attending to the varying contexts in which we do research, the frameworks that shape how we approach research, and the ethical and intellectual requirements for engaging in inquiry.
2. Doing research (Chapters 5-9): covering the more practical aspects of research - establishing your study, deciding on a sample and deciding on appropriate methods.
3. Making use of research (Chapters 10-12): focusing on working with your data and ensuring that knowledge dissemination is part of your overall research plan.

We hope that you find our approach helpful and even enjoyable as you join us on the journey to being a skilled and research-minded researcher, practitioner and practitioner researcher.

PART 1
Preparing for Research

1

Research in the Professional Practice Context

In this chapter you will learn about

- Defining research
- Evidence based practice
- Your role as a researcher – perhaps student or practitioner – and the impact of the research context on your role and activities
- Insider and outsider research
- The importance of self-reflection and self-awareness, as well as some tools to assist you to develop these skills.

Introduction

This chapter begins by introducing you to the idea of research, particularly within a climate of evidence based practice (EBP). What follows is a definition of research, specifically related to research in the social work and social care fields. Given that researchers in these fields are often concerned that their research will 'make a difference' and generate useable knowledge in practice, we have included (in Chapter 2) a description of pragmatism as offering a valuable philosophical basis for such research. But, to begin, this chapter 'sets the scene' by outlining the types of research in which we as professionals are engaged. We focus on practitioner researchers and the importance of evidence informed practice, to student research on placement or as graduate and postgraduate researchers. Given that a commitment to reflective practice and ongoing self-awareness is a key expectation of professional practice, in this chapter (and indeed throughout the book) we pay particular attention to this idea and explain how it also 'fits' with research. We provide guidelines on *how* to be self-reflective and what this might mean in different contexts and with different epistemological orientations (and we will definitely define all words like this!). We focus on the different expectations and constraints when research takes place in varied contexts such as organisations and agencies, as well as in clinical and community settings. We discuss, for example, researchers as 'insiders' and 'outsiders', time pressures, as well as issues of ethics, power and researcher roles.

Real-world examples will be given, outlining the researcher's location and position alongside the role of reflection. Links will be made here to Chapter 2 with regard to the frameworks that underpin our research practice, as well as how self-awareness assists with conducting the research, and at what points.

Research

It's very hard not to do research! In fact, every time we go shopping or go to work or just engage in the usual activities of everyday life, we do research. We can't avoid making observations, remembering previous experiences when we did something similar, making comparisons such as which shampoo to buy; in fact without using our 'research faculties' we would rarely be able to participate in, let alone enjoy, life. Perhaps what differentiates this 'everyday research' from research as a formal activity, is the fact that the latter requires a systematic approach to the identification, collection and analysis of data, and the sharing of the outcomes or results of that process with the wider community (see also Charles, 1997).

Evidence based practice

In contemporary times in many countries, service managers and increasingly service users expect that professional practice is built upon an evidence base, with social workers engaged in what is usually referred to as evidence based practice (EBP). The need for EBP is recognised as central to the development of social work's professional credibility amongst other professions (Berger, 2010; Edmond et al., 2006: 377). EBP is credited with a potentially powerful and vital role of translating research findings into practice interventions and initiatives, thereby giving it a key role as a focus for reflective practice, so prized by social work practitioners (Adams et al., 2009: 168). Indeed the potential that EBP activities hold for integrating theory and practice requires greater recognition (Edmond et al., 2006: 380) and, when combined with practice wisdom, will enhance practitioner skill and expertise. As Rubin and

Parrish (2007: 409) comment, 'instead of ignoring clinical expertise and client values and expectations, the EBP process requires practitioners to extend themselves beyond the realm of practice wisdom and combine these elements with the best evidence'.

There has been criticism of EBP (perhaps rather unfairly) as providing students and practitioners with a cookbook approach to interventions and decision-making, thereby decreasing the need and subsequently the capacity for critical thinking (Adams et al., 2009). Despite this, practitioners in social work and social care are nevertheless expected to have the skills and knowledge to be able to analyse the evidence presented in the research of others to inform and better serve their clients, as well as carry out research into their own practice.

Rubin and Parrish (2007: 407) offer a definition of EBP useful to social workers and social care workers:

> a process in which practitioners attempt to maximise the likelihood that their clients will receive the most effective interventions possible by engaging in the following four steps:
>
> 1. Formulating an answerable question regarding practice needs
>
> 2. Tracking down the best evidence available to answer that question
>
> 3. Critically appraising the scientific validity and usefulness of the evidence
>
> 4. Integrating the appraisal with one's clinical expertise and client values and circumstances and then applying it to practice decisions.

(For variations on this definition, see also Adams et al., 2009; Berger, 2010; Edmond et al., 2006.)

It has been noted that both qualified and practising social workers, as well as social work students, demonstrate reluctance with regard to doing research (Unrau and Grinnell, 2005), perhaps indicative of their lack of confidence in their abilities to read and understand research or to develop strategies to incorporate it into their practice. This book may help to address this problem.

Defining research

There are many definitions of research. Alston and Bowles (2012: 9) describe *social research* as 'the systematic observation and/or collection of information to find or impose a pattern, to make a decision or to take some action', and that, further, social work research 'implies action, pursues social justice and collects systematic information in order to make a difference in people's lives' (see also Dominelli and Holloway, 2008; Shaw, 2008). In addition, McDermott (1996) emphasises the importance of having a theoretical understanding of a problem in its broader social context. She also notes (p. 6) that social work research should '[enable] the participation of the researched, the poor, the vulnerable, the oppressed and those who interact with them'. From this perspective, social work research might be considered to be characterised by a focus on:

- Conceptualising problems in their social context
- Seeking a multi-dimensional understanding of problems
- Seeking change and an action-orientation to so doing
- Meeting the broad aims of social work: human rights, social justice, respect, integrity, empowerment and participation.

How these ideals translate into the practice of research across the broad area of social care might include:

- An interest in practical knowledge, or the application of knowledge and understanding to practical problems
- A social justice orientation, motivated by the potential that their research might lead to changes or improvements to or demonstrate the benefits of remaining with the status quo
- An interest in human rights, such as enabling groups like sex workers or Indigenous peoples whose experiences are rarely in the public domain to be heard
- Work as part of a team of other professionals, which could include community workers, policy-makers, service users and consumers of services
- Work across sectors: health, mental health, alcohol/drug and child and family services.

The researcher

Our aim with this book is to provide a map and signposts for doing research from the start of your journey as a student in social work/care to becoming a practitioner. As we will discuss, while the particular tasks and activities that researchers perform may be generic, the role of the researcher will be different depending on where one is along this pathway.

Role difference has implications for how generic tasks may be carried out, for example, with regard to the degree of autonomy that the researcher has.

What questions about social work practice do you have? Are there concerns or injustices you'd like to see addressed? Have you observed gaps in services that you think need to be resolved?

Case study

The research environment

Research environments: Geoffrey, a researcher who is employed by an organisation to do research, may have minimal choice about the questions he will research but perhaps some autonomy with regard to the methods used; Annie, a self-funded PhD student, may appear to have complete autonomy in relation to the research area chosen, but may encounter constraints which limit autonomy in the form of ethical factors, or feasibility issues, or access to research participants because of student status.

All researchers like Geoffrey and Annie share contexts that are complicated and complex. It should also be clear to you that these concerns are shaped by a broad pragmatic philosophy, notably with regard to a commitment to social justice, and a focus on creating knowledge for practical application.

Complexity does not only refer to the web of systems and players involved in delivering services, but can also include the diverse and sometimes conflicting ways in which issues and problems are defined, recognised and understood.

Take, for example, the very different ways in which 'risk' and 'vulnerability' are understood by doctors, social workers, physiotherapists, patients and families (McDermott, 2014) in the following example.

 Case study

Understanding risk

Discharge of an older patient is being considered; the physiotherapist may be concerned about the risk that the patient may fall should she go home; the social worker may place greater emphasis on risk to the patient's right to autonomy and independence; the carer may be concerned at the pressure on him to monitor the patient's health while being anxious about risks to his own emotional wellbeing; the patient herself may be currently assessed as having moderate rather than severe dementia and hence believe that others making decisions for her risks her ability to express her freedom to choose where she wishes to live; the neuropsychologist may believe that the patient's dementia is at risk of worsening and hence admission to a facility rather than a return home is warranted sooner rather than later.

This example highlights the variety of ways in which the concept of risk might be understood, indicating that a researcher researching such a concept will need to be clear how he himself is going to define the term. It also draws attention to the context, for example, is a 'health risk' different from a 'child protection risk'? And from what position or location is the researcher defining 'risk', for example, as a health practitioner or a policy-maker? Thus, the researcher will need to identify from which vantage point, or within which context, he is viewing the issue or problem. This positioning will be significant with respect to the way in which the research question is formulated, the literature reviewed, and the research design and methods chosen.

Although we go on to discuss these issues in greater detail in Chapter 2, it is important here to acknowledge that all of us have views that shape how we see the world and how we think we can see the world; this is known as our *epistemological* position.

When we translate our interest into a research question, the question we arrive at will reflect that position, but more of that in the next chapter.

The context

This takes us to a key principle in doing social research: that of understanding the importance of context. Social workers bring to their research a perspective which emphasises the context-bound nature of human action. Importance is placed on understanding the person within their environment. Environment is conceptualised very broadly as including many 'levels' of action: intrapsychic, interpersonal, organisational, environmental and structural. Particular interest in the experiences of vulnerable people, structural barriers to service access, impact of stigma or prejudice might characterise research questions in the social work and social care fields.

In the case example below you will see how Fiona and colleagues in a health setting studied the ways in which their social workers understood the concept of 'complexity' as it referred to their clients in sub-acute settings (McAlinden et al., 2013). They positioned their research in the context of a hospital, identifying the various 'levels' at which the research question was relevant. The methods chosen reflect the 'level' at which data were sought and the rationale for this.

 Case study

Understanding complexity in a hospital environment

Fiona McA, Fiona McD and Jo (the study team) wanted to understand the factors influencing the service social workers were delivering to patients. Their intention was to use the findings to support and improve the capacity of social workers to work with patients identified as complex. They approached the study questions from a social work perspective, influenced by the conceptual framework of person-in-environment. They wanted to capture understanding of complexity that resonated at micro, meso and macro levels.

At the micro level, structured interviews were used to identify the perspectives of social work practitioners across all sites of the hospital regarding the nature of 'complex cases'. The research team's interpretation of these data included analysis of both workforce and organisational issues relevant, at the meso level, to perceptions of complexity and social workers' responses to complex casework practice. In drawing out the implications of these findings, the analysis included consideration of macro level factors relating to training and workforce policies including recognition of the complicated social, economic and legal context in which their work and their organisation is embedded.

Earlier, we introduced the idea of epistemology (and more of that later!). Suffice to say here, epistemology relates closely to our consideration of context because the way we understand context will be influenced by our epistemological orientation. For example, how does our understanding of the context in which we are researching influence how the phenomena we wish to understand are defined and expressed within that context? Do we look at context as in some way responsible for the way phenomena become known, and then responded to?

Where researchers do research in direct (clinical) practice settings such as hospitals, community mental health services, correctional/probation services or family support agencies, the contextual issues that require recognition are often also ethical issues. For example, if you have questions relating to the needs or experiences of your own patients/clients, or the agency's service users, you will be alert to the possible power differentials in your relationships with them, and the importance of ensuring that they are free to participate, or not, without pressure in any research you propose. If your interest lies in researching the policies and programmes of your own organisation, there may be issues to manage regarding your own position within the organisation and how comfortable your peers or superiors will be with participating in research, given that some issues may be sensitive. While the topic of ethics in research will be discussed fully in Chapter 3, it is important to note here that the extent to which confidentiality and anonymity can be preserved in 'in-house' research will also require consideration.

These examples of the ways in which attention to context will shape research highlight some of the issues that context-focused research generates. In later chapters in this book we will explore them in greater detail. What they do raise, however, is the question of who the researcher is and where the researcher situates or locates themselves.

The researcher in context: insiders and outsiders

Another key principle in getting started with your research, is to think about 'who the researcher is'; that means, do they enter the research context as an *insider* or an *outsider*, as a student, as a practitioner, as a member of a cross- or inter-disciplinary team?

Insider (sometimes referred to as 'emic') research generally refers to research that is carried out by a researcher who is located 'inside' the organisation which is the site and focus of the research. It can also refer to a researcher who belongs to a group that is itself experiencing a problem or concern which the researcher decides to study; for example, they may themselves be a carer for a person with a disability and decide to research how others in the same situation experience this. An *outsider* (sometimes referred to as 'etic') researcher generally does not belong to the organisation or community which is being researched, nor do they personally experience the problem or issue being studied.

The advantages of being an 'outsider researcher' are considered to be the researcher's objectivity and neutrality, whilst an 'insider researcher' brings personal knowledge and understanding of the research question or issue, and with this may come increased trust from research participants. But 'insiders' may be criticised for lacking the necessary objectivity in data interpretation, while 'outsiders' may be criticised for not gaining sufficient 'entry' into the world of participants and hence having limitations on their access to data and information. For a critique and analysis of some of these issues, see Shaw and Faulkner (2006), Dwyer and Buckle (2009), and Humphrey (2013).

Importantly, however, as Kerstetter (2012) points out, it is more often the case that insider/outsider positioning occurs on a continuum, with researchers rarely being either/or. Indeed, some community based research, especially that which is participatory and action-oriented, may proceed from the basis that researchers, when they are 'outsiders', may move, over time, to becoming 'almost insiders'. Dwyer and Buckle (2009) reflect on their movement along the insider/outsider continuum, with one researcher being drawn more closely 'inside' the research, whilst the other became more clearly positioned as an outsider by the research participants.

Leigh's (2014) research provides an interesting ethnographic case study of a researcher alternating between a carefully chosen insider and outsider positioning. In her study of child protection, she adopted the dual role of 'insider' observing the work of her own social work team, and 'outsider' observing another team in another child protection setting, intending that taking these dual roles would enhance her reflexivity. In her paper she identifies the personal and professional dilemmas that complicated her 'intimate insider' role, in particular issues of boundaries in relationships with colleagues in her own organisation. While it was emotionally demanding and at times unsettling, Leigh was able to use her capacities to reflect, enhanced by her 'outsider' role in the second agency, assisting her to process and work with the challenges of studying the impact of personal relationships that she was a part of, and their influence on the social work role.

Participatory Action Research (PAR) is an important form of research, especially in community settings, which often leads to (and may even instigate) the differences between insiders and outsiders overlapping. There are two main strands in participatory research: one is rooted in action research and a second more critical, and openly emancipatory strand, originates in concerns with issues of oppression, marginalisation and resource inequities (Pyett, 2002; Wallerstein and Duran, 2003; Khanlou and Peter, 2005). Drawing on the work of Paulo Freire and others in Latin America, PAR has transformed thinking about research relationships: instead of communities being objects of research, community members become partners in inquiry (Wallerstein and Duran, 2003). Such participatory approaches have strongly influenced approaches to health research (Wallerstein and Duran, 2003; Baum et al., 2006). Feminist perspectives have also enriched participatory approaches through questioning how difference, power issues and representation of others are accounted for in the research process and in the knowledge produced (de Koning and Martin, 1996).

If you are engaged in a study currently, or are considering doing so, here are some issues to reflect on:

Are you an insider or an outsider ... or perhaps a bit of both?

What are the advantages and disadvantages to your position?

Does your research question reflect your insider/outsider status?

What does it feel like to be in your position (as insider or outsider)? Do you think you have a different view of the research issue than if you were in the 'opposing' position? How is your view different?

How can you make best use of your status in answering your research question?

If you are starting out or already beginning your research, or refer back to the issue you noted earlier, there are some important questions to ponder in the box above.

Student researchers

Student researchers, whether undertaking graduate or postgraduate study, by virtue of their status *as* students, are faced with a number of issues for consideration. They are more likely to be 'outsiders', not only because they are generally not employed by the organisations they are researching, but also with regard to their position in structures of power and influence. Thus, much of what was earlier noted about 'outsider researchers' is relevant here, for example, the benefits of neutrality and objectivity, and the challenge of working towards achieving the acceptance and trust of research participants. In addition, however, we are used to thinking of researchers as being in more powerful positions than research participants and hence the necessity of designing research to minimise any harm to those who may be vulnerable. But student researchers are often in less powerful positions, particularly if they are researching organisations, policies or programmes provided by professionals. From the student point of view, we may say that in these circumstances, they are researching 'up' and they themselves may experience feelings of anxiety and vulnerability. Ways of addressing this power imbalance might take the form of working to a reference group or steering committee which can guide and mentor them. The availability of good, supportive and easily accessed supervision is a key factor in minimising anxiety and building confidence. Harvey (2011) provides some practical guidelines to interviewing 'elites', those in senior managerial positions in organisations or highly skilled professionals. Such issues as being aware of the need to gain the interviewee's trust, coming to the interview well-prepared, being flexible with availability to fit with the interviewee's commitments and the advisability of asking open-ended questions are useful to consider.

Being a student however, also confers a particular kind of identity that may be derived from social class, educational attainment and economic status. These factors might set a student apart from some of the groups that they are researching, particularly if participants come from more marginalised backgrounds. To such groups, student researchers may be perceived as outsiders and again they may face the challenge of building trust and acceptance with those whom they are researching.

Practitioner researchers

As discussed in the introduction, social work and social care practitioners are, by definition, those whose primary role is to provide a service of some kind to those who are service users of their organisation or agency: to work with those experiencing difficulties in their day-to-day lives. Practitioner research is therefore a particular form or kind of research. Within social work it exemplifies the very kind of research that we might consider to be synonymous with social work itself – research which occurs within, is mediated by and is reflective of its social context. Mitchell et al. (2010: 13), in reviewing practitioner research studies, noted that 'most studies reflected the service delivery context in which practitioners operated ...'. This is what we might expect, for, above all, social work practice is *contextualised* practice, summed up in social work's recognition of the defining significance for the profession of person-in-environment. In this sense then, practitioner research derives its legitimacy and imperative *because* it informs the context where social workers are practising.

There are a number of definitions of practitioner research in the literature (Epstein and Blumenfield, 2001; Wade and Neuman, 2007; Lunt et al., 2009; Mitchell et al., 2010; Bawden and McDermott, 2012; Harvey et al., 2013; Marshall, 2014). The Salisbury Statement on Practice Research (International Practice Research Conference, 2008: 2–3) defines it as:

> [involving] curiosity about practice. It is about identifying good and promising ways in which to help people; and it is about challenging troubling practice through the critical examination of practice and the development of new ideas in the light of experience ... It is an inclusive approach to professional knowledge that is concerned with understanding the complexity of practice alongside the commitment to empower, and to realise social justice through practice.

Given this definition, we see that the kinds of research questions which *practitioner researchers* (those practitioners who undertake research in or on their own practice), address focus on the issues, problems and situations that they encounter in their day-to-day practice which challenge, surprise or perplex them. For example, McAlinden et al.'s study (2013) began with wondering about social workers' practices with complex patients and resulted in a study to examine the meaning of complexity. Practitioner researchers also undertake evaluations of the impact of their practice or the programmes they develop (see, for example, Green et al., 2015). Importantly, they may focus on identifying the evidence that supports or challenges their practice, perhaps prompting change in that practice. These activities are often in response to the increasing emphasis being placed on practitioners working from an evidence based or evidence informed position. With this comes an expectation that practitioners be familiar with the evidence supporting their practice or be active in contributing to this evidence by researching their own practice (Caldwell et al., 2007; Fox et al., 2007; Mullen et al., 2008; Rubin and Parrish, 2007; Arnd-Caddigan, 2010; Berger, 2010; Rubin and Bellamy, 2012; Bellamy et al., 2013).

Practitioner researchers are primarily 'insider' researchers, working from the basis of their 'practical' or 'tacit' knowledge, that rich store of understanding that they (perhaps almost intuitively) bring to bear on the situations and problems of everyday practice. Tacit knowledge might be thought of as providing their 'theory in use' (Argyris and Schon, 1974); that is, their knowledge about how to 'go on' in order to achieve the outcomes they want in particular situations. Doing research can provide an opportunity to bring such tacit or practical knowledge to light, and in this way advance the practitioner's understanding and critique of what they do and why. Importantly, doing practice research provides a ready-made opportunity to critically reflect on their actions and their impact on service delivery.

Studies undertaken by practitioner researchers are typically small in scale and in timeframe. Usually practitioners design and develop their own studies, often adopting a variety of methods (Lunt et al., 2009; Mitchell et al., 2010), such as data mining (Epstein and Blumenfield, 2001), surveys, interviews and focus groups. Very importantly, research conducted by practitioners on their own practice can become a vital way of translating research findings into practice interventions and initiatives, a translation that is often very difficult to achieve from other approaches (see Gray et al., 2015). It is thus a key pathway towards ensuring practitioners work from an evidence or knowledge informed base.

Doing research as a practitioner brings with it many challenges. From the outset, their role as a practitioner signals their 'insider' status, which, as we've noted earlier, requires close attention to identifying, recognising and working with the potential biases that may influence the design process and analysis of data collected. As we have also noted, ethical issues around access to research participants, anonymity and confidentiality need to be attended to.

Collaborative research

Social workers and other social care practitioners as well as students often join with colleagues from a range of disciplines and locations, as well as with service users and consumers in order to do research. This then becomes a collaborative and/or cross-disciplinary approach.

 Case study

Benefits of collaborative research

Laura, who was a student writing her social work Honours thesis, worked with a group of allied health practitioners who wanted to explore both the characteristics of patients admitted to hospital as 'social admissions', and the role social workers played in the multidisciplinary team making discharge plans for such patients. The student was supervised and guided by the multidisciplinary team, and data gathering involved interviews with various allied health workers. This was a situation of mutual reward! The student had access to patient records and data as well as very good supervision from the team; the team had the disciplined contribution of an Honours student with a thesis to write within a tight timeframe. Everyone blossomed! The thesis was completed on time; the team proceeded to build on the research with a further research question; the findings were presented at several conferences, and an article has been written by the team.

Researching with others has advantages and disadvantages. As seen with Laura's example above, such projects can bring together researchers from a variety of locations, perspectives, skills and interests, with differential access to resources, data and information. Importantly, different stakeholders will by definition have different stakes and interests in how the question will be framed, the methods to be used, and how the findings or results can be analysed and interpreted. Our earlier example of how risk is defined differently amongst health service providers highlights this point. Given the range of potential definitions and understandings which a multidisciplinary team represents, the first step is likely to be that of achieving common ground amongst the team of researchers. And this may require a shift in thinking, concepts and methods, where different discipline-specific knowledge is shared and discussed in order for the team to arrive at a collective understanding of the phenomena being studied (see Lawrence and Despres, 2004: 401).

All teamwork, and this is what cross-disciplinary research is, poses the challenge of learning to communicate and understand across disciplinary and consumer/provider divides. As Newhouse and Spring (2010: 315) note, one challenge may be that the team members 'need to learn to communicate, understand each other's language, ideally develop a shared language, and learn to coordinate their actions as a team'.

A collaborative cross-disciplinary approach to research is one important way of integrating discipline-specific and practice knowledge. Hadorn et al. (2010: 13–16) highlight the value of such integration. They identify five core areas for a cross-disciplinary team to attend to in order to facilitate team integration. These are: shared systems based thinking, attention to problem framing and to shared values, an acceptance of uncertainty and understanding that collaboration rests on the team's capacity to harness difference.

Problem-solving in a multidisciplinary collaborative research team depends on the extent to which those involved contribute their knowledge and information to the discussion. The more unshared knowledge (that is, disciplinary knowledge) which is not known to all, is included in the debate, the more comprehensive will be the solution to the problem (Godemann, 2008: 631). The team's collaborative work encourages a focus on the process of working together. This might require self-examination through cycles of self-reflection. It might throw up hunches or hypotheses for consideration. For example, the kinds of questions researchers might ask themselves and one another could be: What is it that we are observing? How are we observing? What do we know? And what do we know because of our observations? In this way, the team encourages the ongoing and continuing critical analysis of members (Wolf-Branigin, 2013: 7). Importantly, however, issues of power and influence within the team are also an important focus of analysis. In these ways, what emerges from the interaction of the team itself can become a source of insight for reflection-on-practice and reflection-in-practice (Wolf-Branigin, 2009: 122).

Having sketched the centrality of context and the importance of researcher positioning and identity in social work and social care research, we can bring these two 'principles' together through addressing another important principle, that of the importance of self-reflection and self-awareness to the research project.

Self-reflection and self-awareness

Self-reflection and self-awareness are closely related concepts, with the former (self-reflection) usually being the pathway to the latter (self-awareness). Knowing who the researcher is means knowing from what position in the social world they are approaching their research; for example, as an insider or an outsider, as a service provider or as a student. More importantly, it means knowing how this social location influences what can be seen and known, and how social structures of age, gender, ethnicity and power influence the way we all look at the world. What is difficult is realising that the influence of such aspects, which may be outside our awareness, works to filter and bias what we see and understand.

These characteristics of a researcher – both structural and individual – provide researchers with what we might think of as 'windows' through which to view the social world, making some aspects visible and others opaque.

The challenge is to tease out and recognise their influence rather than to dispense with it; for, in an important sense, our 'biases' can become very valuable sources of knowledge and understanding, in much the same way that a psychoanalyst uses transference and counter-transference to assist their therapeutic interventions. Here is an example of a social work practitioner who wanted to evaluate her practice by seeking input from patients in the pallia-tive care ward where she worked about how they understood her role.

Case study

Reflecting on our own practice – reflecting on ourselves

Miriam is a palliative care social worker. Her patients, completing a self-administered survey placed in a box anonymously on the ward, almost unanimously praised her for her care and support. While Miriam was initially very pleased, if not flattered, by the response, she began to reflect and ask: Why are these comments so positive? Who is making them? What are patients wanting to convey by providing such pos-itive comments? In this self-reflective approach, the social worker learned something about the patients' anxiety for care and support, for not being rejected despite their neediness in the face of life-threatening illness.

As a researcher, she began to consider that their strong tendency to provide 'positive' comments might have concealed other underlying feelings, which were difficult to acknowledge.

Qualitative researchers who gather data using structured and unstructured interviews are, in an important sense, the 'data gathering instrument', their personal characteristics having the chance to influence what data are gathered.

Two student researchers early in their research journey make just this point, highlighting their developing understanding of themselves as researchers and of the role of self-reflection and self-awareness in conducting research.

Student researchers

From the time I began to consider this research, it was clear that I needed to think about it (not being neutral) and manage my own subjectivities and personal biases. (Marc)

Another measure I took to manage subjectivities was my effort to 'get the full story'. I attempted to achieve this by including consumer, carer and worker perspectives, programme and policy evalu-ations and a cost perspective in my research. (Amy)

How can we develop self-awareness?

One way of developing self-awareness, which several novice practitioner researchers in a large health network adopted, was through forming a small research group. This group met monthly as the practitioners developed, refined and carried out their projects.

Participating in the group provided a key resource, which not only spurred the social workers on towards completing their projects, but also was seen as supportive and helpful.

Using peers, who could be other practitioners, or class mates, or fellow postgraduate students, can be an excellent way of ensuring researchers adopt a reflective and reflexive mindset. In much research, qualitative in particular, the researcher's challenge is to capture her own perspective so that it can be 'bracketed out' and used to assist with making interpretations rather than clouding the process. Of course this is a bit like one hand clapping: is it truly possible to understand and interpret one's own perspective at the same time as understanding the perspectives of others?

Practitioner researchers at a health service

Group meetings are important, supportive and interesting: different perspectives to bring and different questions to ask ... good to bounce off each other.

... the group model has been really supportive - been good to talk things out, get other opinions: helps you reflect.

Good to come from different areas of work - helps with objectivity.

... leave here feeling so motivated.

Peer researchers are the most helpful allies in this challenge: they can take on the task of asking critical questions about the existence and nature of our assumptions (see Gerstl-Pepin and Patrizio, 2009).

How to 'do' self-reflection

The task confronting the reflective researcher is that of ensuring that his or her research results or findings are the 'best possible' interpretations of the data; that is, that the findings can be relied upon to be trustworthy and authentic accounts of what has come to be known through the research process. As we will discuss in Chapter 2, researchers come to do research holding different world views, or understandings of the nature of social reality. We refer to these as holding different epistemological positions. These will influence how research findings are arrived at and interpreted. Different ways of knowing require different research methodologies and methods, and with these come different standards for determining the accuracy or 'truthfulness' of the findings. So, when reflecting on research processes and findings, the researcher's epistemological position may direct him or her to asking and answering different questions.

On the next page are the kinds of questions that reflective researchers might ask as they set out on their research journey.

See the comment from Amy, a student researcher, which highlights the positive impact of attention to self-awareness on the research process.

Keep a journal or research diary

This can become a repository for those thoughts, feelings and decisions that can easily be forgotten. Diaries and journals comprise the written reflections of the researcher who charts their research journey and in so doing reflects, critiques and, importantly, records the process. Because reflection emerges out of the process of writing, it can provide opportunities for clarifying one's view of the world by noting answers to questions such as: What do I know? Why do I know this? How do I know this?

Engin (2011) writes about her use of a diary as she undertook her PhD. She highlights its role in assisting her personal development and learning about how to be a researcher as well as its role in demonstrating how she was going about the process of constructing her (ethnographic) research. Indeed, she notes that her diary became an important emotional support as she encountered the challenges, set-backs and dynamics of her research. Engin (2011: 301–3) organised her diary under these headings: *questions to self*, for example, how she planned to manage potentially different scenarios arising as she collected data; *justifications for decisions made*, for example, why she chose to interview a participant in a particular time or place; *noticing*, here she recorded comments on things that seemed to surprise or perplex her in the data collection; *dialogue with expert other*, the 'expert other' being other writers and researchers whose work she was reading and analysing in relation to her own emergent findings.

Many researchers, perhaps particularly qualitative ones, find that it can be a good idea to use a journal or diary frequently, structuring the diary by posing specific questions, such as those to the right.

While few researchers use their journal entries as a data gathering method (though they may be used for this), those who do make use of journals

Why am I researching this question? Whose question is it? What difference does it make who has formulated or raised this question?

Who am I as a researcher; for example, am I a student, a practitioner, an insider, an outsider?

What are my personal attributes and characteristics? What do I bring to the research and how might this influence what I see and what I do?

What is my world view?

How might my world view influence my research?

Amy, student researcher

By remaining mindful of my world view I was able to appreciate both the strengths and weaknesses of previous attempts at reform in relation to my topic.

Where policy and programmes were inconsistent with my perspective, I was more able to acknowledge their goals and success by 'suspending initial judgements'.

What have I learned today?

What has surprised me today?

What are three questions I now have?

consider that they are an intrinsic part of the research process, often filling an important role as part of enhancing the rigour of data analysis. This is particularly so in research relying on qualitative thematic analysis where (as we will see in Chapter 9) it is essential to stand back and review and interrogate the themes arrived at to ensure their trustworthiness and authenticity. The diary may be most effectively used to record this process, the insights gathered along the way, the support found for those asserted and the play made with engaging rival explanations to challenge them with.

Supervision

As a research student or a social work and social care practitioner, ensuring you have access to a research supervisor can be important. The role of the research supervisor is to provide you with the guidance, support and useful criticism to enable you to progress on your journey. Doing research whether as a student or practitioner is a big undertaking! As we see throughout this book, there are complicated decisions to be made, issues to be considered, skills to learned (often including how to use supervision); and research supervision provides a place for working with these issues throughout the journey.

Choosing a supervisor is rarely done lightly. Most researchers seek to work with a more experienced researcher with whom they are personally compatible, share a research interest and who is reasonably accessible. If you are a student, your supervisor is likely to be an academic within your school, department or faculty. Supervision is generally a core activity of academic staff, forming an important part of their role.

For social work and social care practitioners, you may need to search out a research supervisor. Some large agencies or organisations may have staff who are suitably qualified to provide research supervision. If this is not the case, many practitioners make links with a university or academic department where staff are available to supervise. It might also be worth considering whether enrolment in a postgraduate course will include access to research supervision. Such a decision can not only provide rewards in the form of further qualifications, but can also offer the structure and support to do research. And some employers offer incentives such as study leave for staff enrolled in higher degree studies.

It's a good idea when you first meet with your supervisor to map out how you propose to work together, for example, how often you will meet, whether the supervisor wants to read your work in advance of meeting, whether, if articles are written from your study, they expect to be acknowledged or included as a co-author. Supervisors generally provide suggestions and feedback on your work-in-progress. They may assist you in analysing your data, ensuring added rigour in data interpretation. Above all, they have 'been there before' and know from personal experience those moments of frustration, confusion and exhilaration that the journey brings.

Feedback from research participants

A great source of feedback and prompts to reflection and self-awareness can come from those who participate in your research. As we noted earlier, the question of whether a student researcher is perceived as 'more powerful' than they actually believe themselves to be, is one better answered in discussion with participants. Of course, the extent to which participants are contributors to the reflective research process depends on the kind of research they are doing. Cossar and Neil (2015), in their research on post-adoption support, provide an excellent example of service user involvement in research. They include reflections from birth parent consultants, particularly about how research is and should be conducted, noting time, respect, care and trust as vital. Similarly, PAR is characterised by the formation of partnerships with the researched and clearly their contributions are intrinsic to all aspects of it. By way of contrast, clinical research, such as a randomised controlled trial, makes every effort to exclude participant influence on the research in order to avoid any potential source of bias.

One important strategy used by participatory action researchers is to establish a project steering group of key community members or stakeholders, which can be a space for shared listening, learning and decision-making (Wadsworth and Epstein, 1998; Viswanathan et al., 2004). Yoland Wadsworth (1991) has argued for what she termed the 'critical reference group' to be central. Critical reference groups are made up of people who may be users of services or members of self-help groups, or others whose interests are critical to the research in question; they are sources of 'literally critical things to say about' the question (Wadsworth, 2001: 56). In participatory projects, these group members bring critical perspectives on the issues and may also undertake a range of researcher roles. For instance, Warr and Pyett (1999) described working with a critical reference group of women with experience of the sex industry in planning, recruiting and interviewing female sex workers, and in interpreting the findings to understand the complexity of meanings attached to sex work and intimate relations for these women.

Whilst other research approaches are less driven by the interests of stakeholders, many qualitative interpretive research designs provide opportunities for participants to comment on research findings by, for example, reviewing transcripts of interviews or meeting in a focus group to review the findings. For example, a researcher was studying the parenting experience of people who had been adopted. After extensive interviews with a number of participants, she analysed these data into broad themes. She then invited participants to comment on her interpretations as part of the process of arriving at the 'best possible' interpretations of the data.

Benefits of self-awareness and self-reflection

These are many. But perhaps of great significance is that self-reflection enables us to develop awareness of the nature and influence of our own intellectual and personal qualities and how these can contribute to improving lives and opportunities. Self-reflection also helps us to see something of our own limitations, the barriers and impediments that disadvantage us in our relationships with others and hence in our understanding of others. It is sometimes thought that doing research is 'easier' in the social work and social care fields than in direct practice because researchers are shielded from dealing with the difficult realities of other people's everyday lives. Nothing could be less true: the reflective, reflexive and self-aware researcher is more accurately understood as a front-line worker whose job it is to listen, think, grapple with, understand and motivate change through the power and practice of research.

Chapter summary

We have begun this book by concentrating on the context in which you will conduct research, examining the factors that will impact on your observation of and connection to the problem and your autonomy. We outlined strategies for ensuring self-awareness throughout the research process. In the next chapter we address the frameworks underpinning research in social work and social care, including epistemology and participant driven research, which we have introduced in this chapter.

Key take-home messages

How we approach the doing of research will be shaped by our position as insiders/outsiders, our role (student, practitioner, etc.), the context in which we are conducting our study and the interaction amongst these factors. Self-reflection and self-awareness are vital to understanding this interplay and ensuring methodical and transparent research.

Doing research in the social work and social care fields may, as the examples in this chapter identify, be best understood as a strategy for solving problems in a pragmatic way. The knowledge generated by research can provide the means to do so.

Additional resources

Hallowell, N., Lawton, J. and Gregory, S. (2005) *Reflections on Research: the Realities of Doing Research in the Social Sciences*. Milton Keynes: Open University Press/McGraw-Hill Education. This book is a great read as an orientation to doing social science research. It contains the stories of 20 researchers who have all contributed stories about the pleasures and pains of doing research. There are lots of vignettes and tips about carrying out research as well as more serious accounts of dilemmas and challenges along the research path.

Twitter has a collection of hashtags for researchers, which can provide a good way to connect and share the research journey. See, for example, Piirus Voice Chat, which hosts guest bloggers and researchers' comments on a wide range of research issues in diverse fields, including the social sciences – www.piirus.com.

A good companion as you learn about and develop your research understanding and skills might be The Social Research Update: http://sru.soc.surrey.ac.uk. It is published quarterly by the Department of Sociology, University of Surrey, Guildford, UK, and provides helpful explanations and information on many research topics and issues.

A useful discussion of how to work reflectively as a researcher can be found at the Participation Research Cluster, Institute of Development Studies, supported by the Swiss Agency for Development and Cooperation: www.participatorymethods.org/method/reflective-practice.

2

Frameworks Underpinning Research

In this chapter you will learn

- The difference between ontology, epistemology and theory in research and the influence these have on how we understand the world and build knowledge
- About pragmatism as a centralising concept in research in social work and social care
- About basic ethical requirements for research (before covering this in detail in the next chapter)
- To reflect on your own 'position'; as a researcher and how this also has an impact on how you construct your research.

Introduction

So far in our research journey (Chapter 1) we have emphasised the importance of understanding the context where research takes place. You may be working as students, practitioners or colleagues, and this places you in different roles, for example, insiders or outsiders, each position providing you with different access to information and understanding. We also highlighted the importance of you being critical observers and analysts of your research practice, increasing your awareness of yourself and what you bring to the research task, personally and professionally. In this chapter our focus is on understanding 'research underpinnings', i.e. the theoretical, ontological and epistemological bases that are the building blocks of research.

These key terms will be defined and the relationships between them clarified. You will be encouraged to consider the role and application of such concepts in your research context. We will continue to use case examples from research to highlight these concepts and their impact on decision-making and outcomes in the research process. The chapter will conclude with links to readings that we have found useful.

The role of theory in the research process

Theoretical knowledge derived from the range of social science and social work theories is essential to research. Theories provide an explanation about why things (actions, beliefs, behaviours) are as they are. They provide us with the conceptual tools to go beyond and make meaning of what we observe or what might at first appear self-evident. They direct us towards considering the presence of forces or factors that, even if they are outside our awareness, may be impacting on us, influencing what happens or does not happen to us. They might be thought of as providing coherence and/or meaning to the complexity we encounter as social beings, or as offering a causal explanation for what might otherwise appear perplexing or irrational.

Interestingly, it would seem that the relationship between theory and research is not well articulated in the scholarship of social work research. A quick flick through some recent social work research texts shows that it has little place in the thinking about or writing about research. This discussion is much more evident in broader 'social research' texts, such as sociology. Perhaps this has something to do with what Armstrong (2014) describes as a fundamental difference between critique and action – with social work having a lesser focus on analysis and theorising and a more substantive focus on solutions. This interest in seeking solutions to social problems is, as we noted in Chapter 1, one of the reasons why pragmatism (which we will explore a little later in this chapter) has considerable appeal to social work and social care researchers.

And yet, in the context of research, theory plays a vital role in assisting us to formulate our research questions, highlighting what might be pertinent aspects of the phenomena we are interested in. In our interpretation of research data, theory points us towards identifying factors or elements that are noteworthy or of significance. Theory offers us ways of using language and defining terms so that we can communicate with others holding a similar theoretical perspective. It offers us signposts or frames for reflection and critical appraisal, and importantly, may direct us towards seeking rival explanations or understandings of the meaning or relevance of what we discover. In fact, research may be driven by a wish to prove or demonstrate or refute a particular theory, or even reveal understanding that enables us to generate new theory.

Theory, put simply, is an organised set of concepts and ideas that can play a number of roles in social work and social care research, either as an 'input' or as an 'output'. Grbich (1999) describes research as being either theory driven or generating (as per Glaser and Strauss, 1967) (see Figure 2.1).

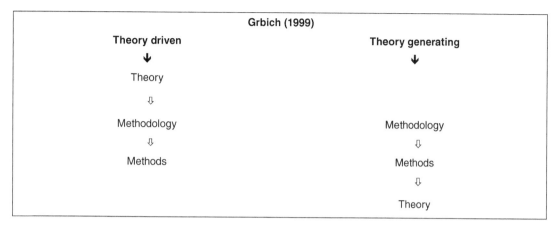

Figure 2.1 The role of theory in the research process

According to Grbich's (1999) perspective, research that is driven by theory has, at its foundation, a clear theoretical framework, and a knowledge base, which shapes the view of knowledge generated, the design of the study, and the questions or hypotheses developed. So, as researchers, we can examine a problem through a particular theoretical lens. It shapes how we see, what we see and what we propose. This type of research approach is much more likely to be conducted in an academic setting.

Case study

An academic study with a theoretical framework

As an Honours student, Catherine completed a small study, which was a feminist investigation of women's addiction to benzodiazepines. This study was conducted in the 1980s – a time when thinking about addiction was developing, as was critique of dominant medical ideas. This research was in response to these debates and sought to specifically utilise a feminist theoretical framework by examining the impact of social role expectations in benzodiazepine dependence. A feminist critique of women's social roles formed the lens through which the problem was defined and examined.

More recently a less deterministic approach to theory as an input has been described: theory-oriented research. This approach is one that begins intentionally with an overt theoretical or ideological viewpoint, but the degree to which this orientation will influence the research process varies, as you can see with the example of Alexis' study below.

If you have a topic you are considering or working on now, are you aware of any theoretical discussions/constructions of this?

Case study

Theory-oriented research

Alexis, a student researcher, was preparing for a study of women's experiences of hospital treatment after miscarriage. In her review of previous research she found that this had typically relied on quantitative data that 'hid' the voices of participants. In response, she developed and utilised a feminist-informed methodology and sought to gather qualitative data solely from women about their views and experiences of their miscarriage treatment. In this case the theoretical orientation shaped the development and implementation of the study, but did not bring a theoretical analysis to the research focus or the resulting data (see McLean and Flynn, 2013).

We would describe this as theory that provides the scaffolding for the research. To take the building analogy a step further, whilst scaffolding is not central to the building itself, it is needed to do the work, and has an impact on how the building (or in this case, the research) takes place.

Research can also be theory generating; and to a degree, all of us are engaged in this process – developing concepts for broader application. Perhaps the most influential and well known approach is *grounded theory*, first posed by Glaser and Strauss (1967), and then taken on divergent paths by these researchers individually (and developed by scholars such as Charmaz, 2006). From this general viewpoint, the research journey begins from a point of 'not knowing', and endeavours to enter the field relatively clear of preconceptions or expectations, with the aim being to build theory upon fresh observations. Patton identifies the foundational question of this approach as: 'What theory emerges from systematic comparative analysis and is grounded in fieldwork so as to explain what has been and is observed?' (2015: 109). The focus, therefore, is on constructing theory, not comparing to, or proving or disproving existing theoretical constructs. A major criticism of this type of approach suggests that without ongoing reflection, it can serve to merely reaffirm the researcher's own biases and unacknowledged assumptions.

Social work theory: understanding social problems

Social work has evolved a wide range of theories, many of them borrowed from other social science disciplines because of their capacity to shed light on and to strengthen understanding and practice. For example, social constructionist theory has informed narrative interventions, while strengths based practice relies on theories of human development from biology and psychology. But social work's foundational perspective of person-in-environment has proved vital to the profession's development as well as useful to other disciplines. Person-in-environment draws on systems theory in order to account for the ways in which individual human lives both shape and are shaped by social phenomena and social structures. In relation to social work research, it directs our attention to research designs that incorporate multiple methods to gather data at micro, meso and macro 'levels'.

Contemporary developments of systems theory have led to the emergence of complexity theory (CT), which constitutes a new way of thinking about the world, holding particular resonance for social work as well as other areas of social practice. This is evident in the work of, for example, Byrne (1998), Green and McDermott (2010), Sanger and Giddings (2012), Pycroft and Bartolas (2014), McDermott (2014) and Wolf-Branigin (2009). With regard to social work, Wolf-Branigin (2009: 124) has noted: '[a]pplying complexity is about developing our knowledge, skills, and ability to understand the interconnectedness and exigencies present within our clients' systems'. CT is particularly valued by researchers because it provides mental models and strategies for working collaboratively and purposefully across disciplinary divides, and in partnership with service users. Trans- or cross-disciplinary approaches differ from multidisciplinary perspectives in that they propose the transcending of traditional disciplinary boundaries in order to find new and innovative solutions that integrate knowledge from the social, natural and biological sciences (Choi and Pak, 2006; Leavy, 2012), as well as that contributed by service users (Abma et al., 2009; Truman and Raine, 2001). As CT is an explanatory theory, explaining the changing construction of different systems identified and studied within the natural, biological and social sciences disciplines, it is a theoretical perspective that holds promise for providing a shared theoretical basis for social science and trans-disciplinary research, with the potential to extend our understanding of the world and the way it works (Green and McDermott, 2010).

Ontology and epistemology

Central to what the researcher brings to the task is a perspective on or understanding of the social world. As we noted above, social work and many other social-science-based professions recognise that human life is embedded in and shaped by what we might think of as many 'spheres' of reality, impacting at the micro, meso and macro 'levels'. The undoubted complexity of the interactions of these human, social and natural ecological systems, co-evolving and adapting whilst simultaneously creating that context, challenges any researcher who 'dares' to study it! Sometimes we know about these impacts, and sometimes we are unaware of them, but whether or not we are aware of them they are influencing all aspects of our lives, and in turn we are influencing them whether or not we are aware of so doing.

So, we can start by asserting that as researchers we are aware that we are working in a complex, multi-dimensional and always-interacting world. But in order to study this world and the people in it, we need to decide exactly *what* it is we are studying, and from this basis *how* we propose to research it. This takes us on a brief excursion into ontology and epistemology, which we introduced in Chapter 1.

Ontology is the science of being; that is, the study of what it means to *be*. In the social sciences in particular, researchers are for the most part studying humans as social beings, asking all kinds of questions about the nature of human experience and the ways in which social reality influences, changes and mediates human life and behaviour. Starting out to do research provides a somewhat rare opportunity to think about what we consider characterises a 'human being'. One way to tease out our own understanding of this fundamental question is to pose it. You might want to take a bit of time now to brainstorm a response to the question to the left.

What do you think are the defining characteristics of human beings?' or

What do you think it is to be human?

There are varied responses to questions like these, e.g. you may see that being a person is to be: a meaning-maker; a creative problem-solver; not much different from a laboratory rat; rational; irrational; having an unconscious and a conscious mental life; being determined; having free will; shaped by social, political and historical forces; having no foundational essence; and so on.

In answering this question, you will have begun to formulate a position that will shape the way you might go about your research. For example, if your interest is in the role of carers, and you notice that in the exercise above you have placed emphasis on the meaning-making character of human beings, your question might be in relation to the personal experience and meaning of being a carer. Or if you found yourself more acutely focused on the way in which human life is constrained by the social and political context, then you might want to design your research to explore issues of gender as they relate to the caring role.

Ontology is closely connected with epistemology. *Epistemology* refers to the theory of knowledge itself. As researchers we start out wanting to know something, or about something. How we go about knowing suggests that we hold a particular perspective on what constitutes knowledge, and hence how we might go about acquiring more or different knowledge about phenomena. This perspective reflects a paradigm, a set of beliefs and/or world view held together by consensus amongst the community of scientists. Paradigms encompass:

- A view of the world, that is, a view of what constitutes reality
- A human construction, hence able to be changed
- A view of human nature - what it is to be a person
- A view of methodology - how we go about finding out what we believe can be known.

Let's now explore each of these elements:

- A view of the world, that is, a view of what constitutes reality.

You might ask yourself: what do I mean by 'reality'? Is the world primarily a material object 'out there', or is reality knowable only through metaphors and analogies, such as 'a level playing field', 'a jungle of people jostling for survival'?

- A human construction, hence able to be changed.

Here you might ask yourself: Have I always held the same view of the world, of what constitutes reality? Does everyone share the same view of the world as me? For example, do I see the material world as created by God and kept in motion and existence by Him? Do I see it as primarily a political reality, in which some prosper and some don't? Do I see the world as a planet in a galaxy made of gases and matter, some elements of which we can observe and study, and other elements which we so far lack the technology to observe and study?

- A view of human nature – what it is to be a person.

A little earlier we explored this question. Now it might be interesting to reflect on whether you find congruence or contradiction between your views on human nature and your understanding of the world.

- A view of methodology – how we go about finding out what we believe can be known.

Depending on how you have answered these earlier questions, you will, logically speaking, adopt different approaches; for example, you might want to measure different material elements, or pray, or talk to people. But a fuller discussion of methods comes a little later. Let's move on to a discussion of *paradigms for research*.

Paradigms for research

It is generally accepted that there are three different paradigms characterising research in the social sciences: the traditional or positivist, the interpretive or social constructionist, and the critical (see Neuman, 2014).

Positivist

The traditional or *positivist* paradigm holds that, ontologically speaking, there is an objective reality to be found; it exists and can be known through the use of the scientific method. According to this position, human beings behave in ways that are determined by causal laws and the purpose of research is to discover these laws and the structures which determine them. The theories which underpin positivism, such as structural functionalism, reflect this perspective. The researcher is seen as a neutral, scientific expert for whom human beings are the objects of research; as such, effort is required to limit any biases through the development of research designs that ensure reliability, validity and thereby enable research findings to be generalised. For these reasons those methods that enable researchers to quantify data such as test–retest designs, surveys and the use of standardised scales are used. Research is considered, at its best, to be a value-free technological tool.

In contemporary times however, the positivist approach has undergone critique and revision and has come to be characterised more by a focus on methodological (quantitative) than on philosophical issues. The theoretical development of critical realism in the work of sociologists such as Bhaskar (2008) and Sayer (2000) argues for a more process-oriented approach to observing and studying the relationship between cause and effect. See the case example below.

Case study

Seeking to understand cause and effect

PhD student Angel was studying the problem of falls amongst elderly people, both in hospital and in the community. Her argument was that there was a relationship between the provision of education and falls prevention behaviour amongst this population. To study this phenomenon, she used a range of methods including: conducting a systematic review; pre- and post-testing of people, both those who had fallen and those who had not fallen, following a falls prevention intervention; and surveys of health service providers in hospitals and in the community. In drawing together the findings from all these methods, Angel was able to develop a conceptual model that depicted information flow between healthcare providers and older adults on falls prevention during and after hospitalisation. From these results she made recommendations for future clinical practice (Lee et al., 2015).

Interpretive or social constructionist

Within this paradigm, it is the subjective and meaning-making aspects of people's experiences that are the focus of research (Berger and Luckman, 1966). Human beings act purposefully and intentionally, and thus not always predictably. *Phenomenology* (the study of people's perceptions, meanings and interpretations of their experiences), *hermeneutics* (the study of the interpretation of texts) and *symbolic interactionism* (the study of the language and symbols we use in communication and how we act in relation to them) provide a theoretical basis for interpretivist research, the purpose of which is to explore experience and explain the ways in which people make meaning of their experiences, and in so doing, shape their own reality. Unlike the positivist researcher, who strives for neutrality and distance, an interpretivist researcher interacts with the researched, drawing on, observing and analysing his or her own values and biases, and involving the participants in exploring the social meanings of their behaviour. As such, interpretivist or social constructionist research is recognised as an imperfect, value-laden process. Instead of using methods that measure or quantify research participants' perceptions and experiences, the interpretivist researcher will use in-depth interviews, and collect narratives and stories from the researched in relation to the question being posed. Here is an example of research within this paradigm.

Case study

Seeking subjective understandings of elder abuse

A social worker, Marilyn, worked with aged patients in a sub-acute hospital. She was interested in how 'elder abuse' was understood by different players within the hospital, recognising that this issue has implications at the policy, treatment, community and individual level. Her first task was to decide which players, at which organisational levels, in which organisations or treatment and rehabilitation settings may have perspectives that would shed light on decisions made for individual patients. In reflecting on this Marilyn realised that she held the view that 'elder abuse' was socially constructed. She began by reading the relevant literature, noting that there were various definitions (or constructions) of 'elder abuse', depending upon whether the author was a researcher or a service provider or a family member or carer. She then decided to interview and ask 'front line' social workers in a large acute and sub-acute hospital for their definitions. Then she surveyed hospital managers for their accounts. Lastly she reviewed patient files to analyse how the term 'elder abuse' was used by health service providers in relation to individual patients. Her approach allowed her to bring all these views and perspectives together in a discussion paper, which she provided to social work managers who were in the process of considering whether a universal risk assessment tool for detecting elder abuse should be introduced.

Post-modernism is a difficult term to define because it has a wide range of meanings. It describes an approach that questions all ideas, and places focus on innovation and experimentation in research, valuing pluralism and an openness to hearing the experiences of all groups, particularly those least often heard. Post-modernism shares ground with the interpretivist and social constructionist paradigm. If we were to consider social constructionism as if on a continuum, then post-modernism would be located at one end and constructionism at the other. Post-modernists assert that there is no reality or real world accessible beyond language, indeed that reality is only constituted in and through language (as discourse) (see the works of Foucault). Language is seen as a system of meaning, but meanings are not fixed, rather they are discursive and plural.

Whilst so-called 'human nature' is not recognised as existing in any foundational sense, the 'self' being understood as decentred and in-process, the researched themselves are seen as self-interpreting. In this sense, subjectivity and reality are both creations of language. The researcher is concerned to become attuned to the various ways in which people interpret themselves and their 'lived realities', identifying the contradictory values expressed and produced through constitutive ideologies of gender, race and class. Thus the methods used in post-modern research reflect these interconnections, including story-telling, narratives, plays, photos and artefacts.

A post-modern perspective proposes that power and knowledge are inseparable, serving simultaneously to enable and to subjugate. Indeed, questioning the foundations and frameworks of knowledge is a focus of post-modernism. The 'truth status' accorded to scientific knowledge itself is seen as one of the effects of power. Human actions are understood as structured through linguistically privileged and coordinated concentrations of power and it is the researcher's task to analyse these power relationships generated through discourse, including those emerging between the researcher and the researched. This explains why a focus of much post-modern research is on enabling the emergence of multiple voices and multiple discourses. Through 'interrogating' these discourses, the relationship between power and knowledge may be exposed. In this way too, voices that are marginalised may be heard, perhaps for the first time. For an example of post-modern research, see Schofield et al. (2012).

Critical

Researchers working within the critical paradigm draw on theories derived from Marxist, feminist and critical sociology perspectives, arguing that, whilst human behaviour is social it is also historic. The structural impact of gender, race, economic position and social class stratify social lives, oppressive for some and liberating for others. Reality is in fact defined by the powerful in order to serve their own interests, and indeed knowledge itself should be seen as a political tool of the oppressor, who may use and shape it to promote the interests of the powerful against the interests of the powerless.

Very importantly, personal distress and social organisation are tightly bound together, for example, in the experience of social exclusion that characterises the lives of those who are poor or stigmatised. Critical researchers see people as active agents, shaping their world but simultaneously they are also being shaped by it, whether or not they are aware of this. For this reason, researchers in the critical paradigm see the purpose of their research as to challenge and change existing oppressive social structures (see Brophy and McDermott, 2013). The researcher is unequivocally on the side of the oppressed, working for their liberation. Research participants may be either objects to be liberated or, as they are in PAR, subjects who work as allies with the researcher. Critical researchers may use a range of quantitative and qualitative methods, for example, surveys, demographic and economic data or consciousness raising groups, amongst other things, in order to demonstrate the structural impacts of social organisation. See the summary of Ralph's research into aged care. In the case study below, we describe Ralph's critical theoretical research into aged care and the challenge this posed to ethics committees more familiar with positivist research. In getting his proposal approved, it seemed that he might have expanded ethics committee members' awareness of other ways of seeing aged residential care residents.

 ## Case study

Bringing a critical view to research in aged care

Ralph, a PhD student asked the question 'What do residents in aged care facilities want?' This researcher held the view that once people entered such facilities they were shut out from mainstream social life, stigmatised as old and useless, and denied a voice in determining the physical conditions of their lives. He sought ethical approval to interview residents and encountered myriad problems and obstacles, principally related to the committees' anxieties over whether the research would 'upset' aged participants living in residential care, and whether they were capable of discussing their experience (see Hampson and McDermott, 2004), but finally received permission to do so, reinforcing both his view of the 'sequestering' of aged people and his commitment to an approach to research grounded within the critical paradigm.

Bringing theory, ontology and epistemology together

So far in this chapter we have outlined the 'building blocks' for research: theory, ontology and epistemology. We can now begin to bring them into dialogue, considering how the question that we arrive at is in fact a reflection and an outcome of the theoretical, ontological and epistemological position adopted by the researcher. Here are some comments from Master's students, describing their thoughts as they work to bring these aspects of their research together.

In Table 2.1 is an example 'worked through' so that it demonstrates how these three elements work together, and in the process directs us towards the research methods, relevant and appropriate to the position advocated.

Let us propose that we are concerned to understand and/or measure depression in women: How are we going to define or conceptualise 'depression'? Is it a biological disorder of the brain? Is it something that emerges as a response to women's place in patriarchal societies? Is it a way some women make meaning of their experiences? Is it all three of these, or something other or additional? Each definition suggests a different perspective on depression and each may reflect a different epistemological position; that is, each refers to and emerges from a different understanding of the nature of knowledge, for example, that depression is an objectively measurable biological condition (positivist), or that depression may be a response to making a particular meaning out of the social realities that a woman might subjectively experience (social

Helen, student researcher

My topic choice (family violence disclosure) also arises by virtue of my gender. As a female observer to the questioning of the agency's clients, I experienced the vulnerability of being interviewed by males. This gave me insight into some power structures operating. In contrast I did not relate to the cultural or socio-economic background of the clients. My critical epistemological approach, however, frames my research question to specifically address this subjectivity.

Alex, student researcher

I have to be aware of my 'image of reality' (Grix, 2002: 177) and thus my approach to the topic (the possible health consequences of increased length of hospital stay for elderly patients) aligns with a constructivist paradigm, where there is not necessarily an objective 'social reality', where complex issues like this can be quantified or encapsulated like the physical sciences. Rather, the social reality of this issue will be shaped by political, economic and social factors, and its meaning or existence will be subject to individual interpretation. As a social work student, I am going to view this issue from a psychosocial lens rather than from a medical or physiological lens. Thus, grasping and understanding the issue may depend on exploring the subjective experiences of those involved, aligning with an interpretivist epistemological position.

constructionism). When we translate our interest into a research question, the question we arrive at will reflect that epistemological position. Table 2.1 shows how we can work through from epistemology to methods, using a specific example of English women aged 18–34 years diagnosed with serious depression in 2014. Importantly, this is an example only and there may be many other theories and methods that are appropriate for a particular question. For example, in both the positivist and critical paradigms, complexity theory may be useful in conceptualising the research and would suggest the use of methods such as a case study in order to capture the influence of factors at micro, meso and macro levels.

Table 2.1 Research paradigms

Question	Paradigm	Relevant theory	Methodology	Methods
In England in 2014 what can we learn about the number, socio-economic position, geographic location, sexual orientation and marital status of women aged 18–34 years diagnosed with serious depression and the causal connection between these factors and the diagnosis of depressive illness?	Positivist	Critical realism	Formulation of hypothesis to test assertion that there is a causal connection between impact of women's structural position and incidence of depression; identify two units of analysis, i.e. women diagnosed/not diagnosed	Collect demographic, socio-economic and health data; compare group 1 and 2; statistical analysis to determine whether hypothesis is supported
In 2014, what do English women aged 18–34 years with serious depression tell us of the impact on them of this diagnosis?	Interpretive, social constructionist, post-modern	Social constructionism, post-structuralism	Qualitative	Purposive sampling and in-depth interviews
Diagnosis of serious depression amongst English women aged 18–34 years in 2014 outnumbers that of men: what can this tell us about the social, economic and emotional location of women in patriarchal society and the likely relationship of these factors to depression?	Critical	Feminist	Mixed quantitative and qualitative	Collection and analysis of national demographic and mental health data; stratified sampling and case study analysis; focus group

Pragmatism: bridging the paradigm divide?

While it is often argued that paradigmatic positions are mutually exclusive, this may be counterproductive, particularly within the social work and social care fields where practical action and a desire for change frequently motivate researchers. Indeed Evans and Hardy (2010: 11) comment that researchers should 'be sceptical of any assertions that there is only one right way to practice, one right form of knowledge for practice'.

Pragmatism as a philosophical – rather than a purely practical 'easy way out' – perspective can offer a bridge between paradigms, allowing the researcher to 'navigat(e) a course between the ideal and the possible' (Evans and Hardy, 2010: 168). For researchers who recognise a need to draw on a range of ways of understanding people in their various social situations, as well as understanding the researcher's own impact on and relationship with the researched, pragmatism can provide a way forward. Goldkuhl (2012: 2) points out that pragmatism is 'concerned with action and change and the interplay between knowledge and action'. As such, those social work and social care researchers whose wish is to *act* rather than 'merely' observe the social world, for example, in finding better approaches to child protection practice, or in seeking the involvement of stakeholders in research such as in Participatory Action Research, hold 'an instrumental view on knowledge; that it is used in action for making a purposeful difference in practice' (Goldkuhl, 2012). As Goldkuhl (2012) points out, the pragmatist's focus on generating useable knowledge means that such an approach, which engages with the researched, may be instrumental in knowledge transfer and knowledge use both within and outside local contexts.

Evans and Hardy (2010: 170–3) describe the essence of the pragmatist position as premised on a belief that knowledge is a vehicle for problem solving in a world characterised by change and complexity, in which uncertainty is something to be solved rather than taken for granted. Pragmatic researchers are reflective researchers, asserting their freedom to change their mind should the situation and their research suggest that. The researcher is an active, engaged explorer, experimenting in the real world. As such, any methods, quantitative and qualitative, which advance the search for solutions can be used.

In Table 2.2, we have sketched a research question that a pragmatic social worker might develop to study the impact of gender on outcomes in a group for women with depression that she facilitates. Her desire is to facilitate a group that provides maximum benefits to participants and she wonders whether a women-only group might do so. After discussing her research question with her current group, she designed a study in which she would recruit for two groups – one women-only and the other a comparative group for both men and women with depression. She would replicate the 12-week group structure she had developed with these two new groups.

Table 2.2 Applying pragmatism

Question	Paradigm	Relevant theory	Methodology	Methods
Is there a relationship between depression scores for female patients with clinical depression aged 18–34 years who attend a women-only 12-week support group?	Pragmatism: not concerned about various epistemological debates but wants to know what works in a gender-specific group	Various: cognitive behavioural theory; psychodynamic theory; developmental theories; theories of group therapy that promote psychological change	The researcher began with discussions in her current group (not part of the study) about the role that gender might play in group dynamics; she then devised a mixed quantitative and qualitative comparative design with matched samples of women attending/not attending a women-only group; 12-week group intervention – group 1: mixed gender group; group 2: women-only group	Quantitative and qualitative: administration of depression scale pre- and post-group; individual interviews with some questions drawn from earlier group discussions; follow-up interviews

A word about ethics

While Chapter 3 will deal in much more detail with ethics, it is important to note that an ethical framework informs all aspects of the research process. Thus, ethics will be relevant from the very beginning, even in the choice of questions to research. Before setting out on your research, it is important to get guidance from your national ethics body, for example, the Health Research Authority in the UK (www.hra.nhs.uk), the Office for Human Research Protections in the US (www.hhs.gov/ohrp), the Panel on Research Ethics in Canada (www.pre.ethics.gc.ca) the National Health and Medical Research Council in Australia (www.nhmrc.gov.au) or the New Zealand Health Research Council (www.hrc.govt.nz/ethics-and-regulatory).

Have a go at writing down a question for your research topic.

Which paradigm does it seem to exemplify?

Now have a go at writing it in order for it to exemplify a different paradigm.

Many health and welfare bodies also have their own institutional ethics committees, which will provide advice, guidelines and permission for researchers and evaluators to proceed.

Two central issues dominate the development and application of ethical principles for research: the minimising of harm to those involved in the research, and the assurance that participants give informed and voluntary consent for their involvement. Although these principles appear relatively straightforward, in practice researchers and evaluators need to think carefully about their implications. There are various forms of potential harm, such as physical, legal, psychological, emotional or social harm, that may be relevant to specific situations.

The reason for being alert to ethical issues early in the research journey is that they are closely intertwined with matters to do with research design and the choice of methods, and these in turn emerge directly out of the epistemological perspective within which your research is framed. For example, if you are working within the critical paradigm, undertaking PAR, then participants are centrally involved with the researcher in driving the study, designing the research and interpreting the findings. By way of contrast, if you are working within the positivist paradigm, conducting a randomised controlled study, then participants have no control over the study and no part to play in its design or execution. The onus is on researchers and evaluators to recognise any potential sources of harm and adopt strategies to minimise them. We will return to these issues in the next chapter.

Chapter summary

This chapter has identified and described the building blocks of the research process – theory, ontology, epistemology and paradigm. The terms themselves often appear difficult and challenging. In essence however, they are about exploring our beliefs and understandings about the nature of the social world and human action within it so that these considerations help us to formulate and frame our research questions. The more we reflect upon and critique what we know and learn, the better equipped we become to identify and work with the complex context that social research presents us with.

Key take-home messages

The methods with which we choose to explore social and material reality are very closely allied with the epistemological and ontological position in which we locate ourselves.

Additional resources

There are a wealth of books relevant to theory, ontology, epistemology and paradigms.

A good place to begin is with Neuman, W.L. (2014) *Social Research Methods: Qualitative and Quantitative Approaches* (7th edn). Harlow: Pearson New International. Especially Chapter 5, where he sets out a range of questions to assist in distinguishing between paradigms and epistemological positions.

For a scholarly and fascinating exploration of issues relating to ontology, epistemology and methodology, see Crotty, M. (2003) *The Foundations of Social Research: Meaning and Perspective in the Research Process.* London: Sage. Crotty challenges readers to focus on the theories of knowledge that underlie methodology and how epistemology informs methodology.

Karen M. Staller's (2013) paper 'Epistemological boot camp: the politics of science and what every qualitative researcher needs to know to survive in the academy', *Qualitative Social Work*, 12 (4): 395–413, sets out to 'make sense of epistemology'. She addresses this question from the point of view of a qualitative researcher and her conclusions (411–12) about why epistemology matters are particularly worth reading.

The internet also offers a range of valuable resources. For example, check out Eddie Chauncy's blog on ontology and epistemology for a quick and easy introduction: http://eddiechauncy.blogspot.com. au/2012/01/what-are-ontology-and-epistemology_12.html.

The PhD Blog – http://doctoralstudy.blogspot.com.au/2009/05/being-clear-about-methodology-ontology.html – offers a good discussion from research students around this (ontology, epistemology, methodology) as well as many other research topics.

3

Researching Ethically

'What You Do Is Important But How You Do It Is More Important'[1]

In this chapter you will learn

- Why we need to think and act ethically when we do research
- About the underpinning ethical principles which guide our practice
- How to conduct ethical research in a social work and social care context.

Introduction

Research in social work and social care is about improving the human condition: understanding problems better, evaluating what we do. Our research is focused on improving outcomes for people who may be marginalised or deemed vulnerable. This means that in the social work and social care field we have to pay particular attention to ethical practice, including research practice. In previous chapters we have talked about where we do research, and the impact of this environment, along with the impact of the frameworks that underpin knowledge. In this chapter 'ethical practice' is presented as another core framework for good research, which needs to be factored in from the outset, when you start planning your project (you could even

---

[1]Quote from an Indigenous Elder, in Isaacs et al. (2011): 55.

begin by asking yourself 'Is my topic ethical?'). In this chapter, we start by sharing ideas about why we need to consider 'ethics'; we make reference to current ethical frameworks and our professional codes. Naturally we focus on researching in the social work and social care context, with attention to important issues such as engaging with disadvantaged groups, working in ways that are culturally competent and enabling consumer participation. We continue to draw on real-world examples to illustrate ethical challenges and possible resolutions. We will also continue to encourage you throughout to reflect on your ideas and engage in self-directed learning. We aim to provide you with clear pointers about decision-making along the way.

But first, a few brief introductory words about 'ethics'

When talking generally, the word 'ethics' typically generates ideas about doing the 'right' thing and/or about having a set of guidelines to ensure that we do the 'right' thing. But when discussing research, the focus is often on having to 'do ethics' (i.e. obtain approval from a formal ethics committee). Guillemin and Gillam (2004) termed this *procedural ethics*, as distinct from *ethics in practice* (or what we might call ethical research practice). Israel and Hay (2006) describe the difference as being regulatory compliance versus ethical conduct. In this chapter, whilst we address procedural or compliance concerns, the discussion is necessarily framed more broadly in terms of ethical professional conduct. Our aim is to encourage you to engage with key ideas about being an ethical researcher, not just meeting ethical requirements.

Why ethics?

To ensure that the research we conduct is ethically responsive, we need to have some awareness of the broader context in which research has and does occur and some of the challenges that need to be confronted. There are at least four key reasons, which we discuss below, why as social work and social care researchers we need and have a process of ethical guidance and oversight: past ethical problems, the nature of research, human unpredictability and the nature of research in the context of social work and social care practice.

Past unethical research

Firstly, ethical oversight of research with people was introduced in response to past highly unethical medical research conducted during World War II, to ensure that such practices were not repeated. Subsequent war crimes trials in relation to such actions, resulted in the development of the Nuremburg Code, which established moral, ethical and legal principles for medical research. This guide had attention to broad issues, such as the need for research to contribute to social good, as well as individual concerns, including avoiding unnecessary mental or physical suffering. It highlighted the need for voluntary consent, protection for research participants, as well as the need for researchers to be adequately qualified. (As a side note, Israel and Hay (2006) remind us that this neatly packaged sequence of events was a little more complicated. If you want to read more, see Chapter 3 of their very useful text. You may be particularly interested in the timeline they present on p. 23.)

Building on the principles of the Nuremburg Code, the Declaration of Helsinki (Ethical Principles for Medical Research Involving Human Subjects) was first made by the World Medical Association in 1964. The Declaration is based on a basic principle of respect for all research subjects whilst being aware of possible vulnerability. Whilst it focuses on clinical research and has medical practitioners/researchers as its primary target, its broader application, providing ethical guidance to those researching with people more generally, has been encouraged and typically accepted. It is now considered the basis of international ethical standards in research with humans; many national ethical frameworks derive from this. However, the biomedical focus of this framework and its applicability to research in social research has been questioned. There are, of course, obvious differences between medical and social sciences. While biomedical studies often involve therapeutic research and invasive procedures, the social sciences typically have a much broader and arguably less (physically) risky focus. Hoeyer et al. (2005) see the over-application of this framework as the result of a combination of history and western influence. They argue simply that '[t]he social sciences hold a shorter history than medicine and a less-established tradition of research ethics' (p. 1743); this is combined with the widespread influence of western concepts such as individualism and individual rights. These authors clearly see that it is the more powerful group which shapes current ethical boundaries and expected behaviours.

Any further debate about the appropriateness of current research ethics frameworks to social science research is, however, beyond the scope and purpose of this chapter. We are right to continue to question and debate the application of a biomedically based set of ethical guidelines to our research in social work and social care. Such debate is welcome and healthy – ethical guidelines are not static, they change over time as issues emerge and need to be accounted for (the Declaration itself is good evidence of this). Research ethics is a changing space in which social work and social care need to be involved. It is useful, however, to remember the shared space: that the purpose of structured ethical oversight is to improve scrutiny and minimise unethical practices, and to ensure knowledge development is balanced against human rights.

What are we asking of research participants?

Another reason for needing and having ethical guidance and oversight is because of what we are asking people to do in research. You will recall, for example, the cases we have referred to in preceding chapters: they typically outline research that focuses on personal issues, covering topics including addiction, adoption, aged care, etc. Guillemin and Gillan (2004: 271) additionally argue that '[i]n the great majority of cases, research involving humans is a process of asking people to take part in, or undergo, procedures that they have not actively sought out or requested, and that are not intended solely or even primarily for their direct benefit'.

Research can be 'invasive' (in the general sense of the word). Some research obviously involves more discomfort and/or longer term impact (e.g. therapeutic research or clinical trials). But it is important here to acknowledge that the people with whom we, as social work and social care researchers, interact are often already burdened by a range of challenges, needs and experiences. And then our research seeks to gather data from them about these troubling experiences. For example, our own research has ranged from asking children to reflect on their experiences when their mother was in prison, to seeking men's views on behaviour change groups intended to address their violent behaviour. A degree of distress and emotion is not uncommon.

If you currently have a topic, think about some of the questions you might need to ask a participant to find the answers you need. You might want to refer back to the issue you identified when reading Chapter 1.

Would you answer these if asked by someone you didn't know well?

Unpredictable events in research

'Research is a step into the unknown. Because it seeks to understand something not yet revealed, research often entails risks to participants and others' (Tri-Council Policy Statement 2 (TCPS2) 2014: 5). We simply cannot anticipate all likely events or predict all risks: this is just a product of human nature and the fluid nature of human interactions.

Any social work and social care research can pose 'risks' (though in our area, this is most likely to be related to emotion, for example, sadness, distress or recalling troubling experiences). While the need to proceed with caution is obvious with some topics (as in the examples of our own research noted above), Davison (2004: 380) reminds us that 'risks are not always so easy to predict. Topics not thought to be especially sensitive can rapidly become so during the process of fieldwork'. Guillemin and Gillam (2004) provide an illustrative example of a female participant being interviewed about women and heart disease, who in the course of the discussion made a disclosure of abuse by her husband against her daughter.

One of the aims of ethical guidance and oversight is to allow us both to pre-empt and respond to ethical challenges in research as best we can. It is likely that these unanticipated disclosures are, at least partly, a result of people not having had a forum for speaking or being asked about this experience previously. People may also not have felt listened to, which leads to our next important point.

The nature of research in the context of social work and social care practice

Previous research indicates that not only will people say unpredictable things in interviews (or via other methods), but that as researchers we need to be mindful of the possible unanticipated consequences of the 'safe' research environment we create, and how this may encourage over-disclosure.

Because of the nature of social work and social care, as professionals we bring highly developed interpersonal skills: the ability to build rapport, to be empathic, to ask difficult questions and hear difficult answers. As outlined in Chapter 1, we seek to shine light on issues and groups that have been ignored or marginalised, with a clear commitment to social justice and participatory approaches. The combination of these can be enlightening and empowering, but can also provide such a safe space that participants may perceive a closer relationship with the researcher, perhaps more like a personal friendship (Oakley, 1981; Kirsch, 1999, both cited in Davison, 2004). This may lead them to say more than they intend to, perhaps revealing intimate and private details of their life, that they later regret.

In her research with women in prison in Western Australia, Dot Goulding (2004) highlights this theme. She advises researchers in settings like this to be aware of the potential for them to unintentionally exploit their participants. This is an excellent reminder of the importance of paying attention to the impact of the external research environment. She says 'the social isolation, which is certainly characteristic of women's experience of imprisonment, can mean that the women may give too much information in the relief of finding a safe space within which to speak' (2004: 15). This concern about over-disclosure is also raised in research with marginalised children and young people (see Curtis et al., 2004; Daley, 2012).

Take a moment to reflect on an area of research interest to you ... might it generate any connected, more hidden, issues that you need to be aware of?

(We do know it is difficult to anticipate the unanticipated, but perhaps you can start by thinking about any issues that are known to co-occur with your topic.)

As researchers we need to be mindful of the environment we create, but as introduced above, we also need to be aware of the likely participants with whom we will be in contact. Gilgun and Abrams (2002: 42) remind us that 'The persons who are social work's constituencies ... are typically disenfranchised and excluded from the political system. Their voices are routinely suppressed within the many arenas in which their fates are debated and shaped'. It is very important that we have our social work and social care 'caps' firmly on our heads at this point, so that we do not just think about this as an issue of protecting those we may see as vulnerable (definitely more to come on this concept later in the chapter). As is the case with many aspects of social work and social care practice, we need to balance what might be seen as competing interests, in this instance 'empowerment' and 'protection'.

Gilgun and Abrams (2002) suggest that social work should be mindful of its professional and privileged position, and should actively engage in research with those who are marginalised, ensuring that the voices of the excluded are not just represented, but included in the debates and decisions that have an impact on their lives. As introduced in Chapter 1, Fiona (McDermott, 1996: 6) similarly emphasised seeking this 'view from below'. We will discuss some specific strategies shortly.

You can see that this aspect of our response to the question of 'why ethics?' is contoured more generally by our professional role and obligations. We think these words from the British Association of Social Workers' Code of Ethics (2012: 5) sum it up succinctly:

Social work grew out of humanitarian and democratic ideals, and its values are based on respect for the equality, worth, and dignity of all people ... [S]ocial work practice [focuses] on meeting human needs and developing human potential. Human rights and social justice serve as the motivation and justification for social work action.

These ideals of respect and dignity, but equally rights and justice, must also shape how we do research and what we do with it. As Shaw summarises: good social work research 'promotes justice, social change and social inclusion' (2007: 665). On this basis we would argue that the value base of social work and social care implies that we have *additional* ethical expectations, beyond protection of people's rights and welfare in the collecting of data. But to frame this discussion about ethical expectations we turn now to a more detailed outline of the current frameworks and processes for engaging in research with humans more generally (we introduced this idea of 'procedural ethics' at the start of the chapter), before we broaden the discussion to examine our professional obligations for ethical research.

What ethics?

As social work and social care researchers, to respond ethically to our participants we are guided by and need to meet the ethical obligations of two independent 'bodies' that govern and guide human research and our profession, as per Figure 3.1.

Figure 3.1 Governing ethical bodies

Human research ethics

In relation to human research, many countries will have an office or department that provides guidance on matters to do with ethical research with people. This 'guidance' is typically both conceptual and practical: involving a statement of ethical research principles (you will recall we provided links to some of this material at the end of Chapter 2) as well as governance of ethics committees. These guiding statements are largely informed by the Declaration of Helsinki discussed earlier in this chapter. While the Declaration needs to be interpreted (Benatar and Singer, 2000) and made relevant to local conditions, there are recurrent themes (Israel and Hay, 2006: 40) in these statements and their origins and aims. A key aim is to maximise benefit whilst minimising harm.

If you want to read more about this, Chapter 4 in Israel and Hay (2006) provides an excellent description and discussion of the development of processes to regulate research ethics in a range of western countries, including Canada, Australia, the USA and the UK.

What is human research?

Human research encompasses a broad range of activities, including data collected directly from people, via interviews, focus groups or questionnaires/surveys, observations of people (overt or covert), accessing existing data held about people (case files, documents, etc.), or body organs, tissues, etc. (although the latter is much less likely in our research in social work and social care!) about a broad range of possible topics. So, you can see that 'research with people' or 'human research' is defined quite broadly. There continue to be debates, however, about what makes an activity either research or its subjects human.

Generally, research is considered to be a systematic investigation to gain knowledge. If you think or look back to what we discussed in our Introduction and in Chapter 1, you will see that there is a clear suggestion that practitioners will be involved in research (McCrystal and Wilson, 2009) that makes a contribution to the body of professional knowledge and practice. How knowledge is defined varies internationally. For example, in the USA (Office for Human Research Protections (OHRP), 2009) and Canada (Tri-council Policy Statement 2 (TCPS2), 2014) for any activity to be deemed research, it must generate generalisable knowledge (this means knowledge that is broadly applicable). Arguably this would not include evaluations of programmes where these are designed to improve practice in that specific environment – these would be seen as quality assurance or quality improvement. Interestingly, in these jurisdictions, even if you intend to publish and share findings from a quality improvement evaluation, this does not automatically indicate that this is research. However, in the UK, the development of publicly available material does imply knowledge generation. There are also differences based on the types of data collected. In the USA, for example, for the activity to be deemed human research, the information gathered must be *about* the person (i.e. personal/private, and not just from them, about other things such as their workplace, policy, professional practice, etc.) and must be *identifiable*. What is interesting here is that if you were conducting research with colleagues about their professional opinions, as we have described, particularly in Chapter 1, it may not be seen to be research with humans in the USA.

The clear 'take-home' message is that as social work and social care researchers, you need to know your own research context. You need to be aware of and become familiar with the relevant human ethics expectations in your location. Make use of your colleagues, peers, supervisor and/or lecturers. Consult those who are doing research, so that you know where your research 'sits' in terms of requirements about ethical oversight.

If you have a current research topic/proposal or something you are considering, or even the issue you selected in Chapter 1, take a few moments to consider if this would be deemed human research in your context.

You will also most likely revisit this after you have formulated your methodology.

Human research: underpinning values

We have talked a bit about the boundaries around human research. We turn now to consider the underpinning values of this research. There are two fundamental and common principles: *respect for people* and *justice* (which focus on the conduct of research); additional values include *merit and integrity* and *beneficence* (which focus more on why we do research). As you can see, there is a connection to broad social work principles.

Respect: This is expressed in the need for you to prioritise participants' (and potential participants') autonomy and welfare. People must have the freedom to choose to participate or not in any research. One issue that arises here is about payment of research participants; it continues to be a vexed issue, with a wide variety of views evident, from payment as coercion/inducement, to payment as a sign of respect and acknowledgment of people's time. There is no specific answer to the question of 'Should I pay my participants?'. Your decision needs to be guided by consideration of how your approach demonstrates respect. Participants must have all relevant explanatory information (in a format that they can understand, mindful of language, stage of development and dis/ability) to make an informed choice; they must not be coerced or induced to participate. If the proposed participants are deemed unable to consent for themselves – infants, young children, those with intellectual disabilities, etc. – then consent must be obtained from their guardian. There is considerable debate about capacity to consent; we provide some additional readings at the end of the chapter. Participants must be able to withdraw from any research without consequence. They must have any of their information treated with respect, with a clear focus on confidentiality and privacy (we discuss this further in our methods chapters). No harm must come to participants; researchers must show how they will manage any anticipated and likely problems.

Justice: You need to ensure fairness in research, with attention to any likely burden: this is particularly important for groups that are over-researched (psychology undergraduate students might fall into this group!); there must be fairness in both the recruitment into and access to the benefits of the research.

Merit and integrity: You need to be able demonstrate that the research you propose is justifiable, that there is a need for this particular research. Has the research question already been answered? Are you and/or your team qualified to do the research and do you have the necessary resources to carry it out? This is a fundamental first principle. If you cannot demonstrate the need for you to conduct this particular research, it is challenging to argue your case to take the project forward, even if how you propose to conduct the research is ethical.

Beneficence: This value is closely related to that of merit. You need to be able to demonstrate not only that your study is needed, but also what the potential significance and benefits are. It needs to be clear how the study will add to and expand upon our current knowledge, perhaps in the management of or response to a particular issue.

Human ethics in action: ethics committee oversight

As indicated above, a key aim of national ethics bodies is to provide both an underpinning structure framing 'human research' as well as oversight of research conducted.

Although Israel and Hay (2006) describe differences across countries in how committees assess and make decisions on research applications, there is a set of common values and a generally similar process. Most will make some distinction between research which is seen to involve minimal/low risk to participants (with an expedited process of oversight) versus that which involves greater risk (this typically is subject to a more extensive review and oversight process).

In practice, obtaining ethical approval to begin your research can be time consuming, particularly if what you are proposing is seen to involve some risk for participants. Whilst this can be frustrating, it is perhaps useful to remember that ethics committees typically comprise a group of people who often come from very different perspectives. It may also be helpful to remember that the aim of this process is not to stop research, it is to ensure that any research proposed reflects core values and will be conducted ethically. Our chorus certainly reflects both a sense of getting the tick of approval, but finding the process time consuming.

The key message again is to refer to the requirements and guidelines of your local context.

You may find yourself researching in an environment where there is no obvious ethical oversight. Again, it is wise to consult with your colleagues, supervisor and other stakeholders about usual processes as a starting point. If you are conducting this research out of your home country as a student,

Practitioner researchers

Be prepared: 'the process can be annoying and daunting …'

'I was determined to get this (frustrating) thing out of the way …'

'I guess the frustrating part of anything that is new is not knowing what is required, however once you pass that part it is generally relatively smooth. The benefit of receiving ethics approval is that you have the option of seeking publication.'

'The positive thing about Ethics for me is knowing that I am proceeding with research that is "formally" supported by the organisation and that is considered "ethical" by the powers that be. That in itself makes it necessary and worthwhile.'

then it is likely that your university will have a requirement that you meet the ethical obligations of the national framework. If you are not associated with a higher education institution, then we suggest you follow the guidelines of your professional ethical code.

Figure 3.2 gives a generic flow chart that shows the typical processes and decision-making points involved in seeking ethical approval for human research. Please note, some projects may involve multiple institutions and ethics committees. It has become more common now for approval processes to be streamlined, with one committee providing the ethical review and other relevant committees endorsing this. You would need to check first with your institution/organisation about any such processes.

We talked earlier of our need to meet the ethical obligations of both national statements and our own profession. Many professions, including social work, have a code of ethics.[2]

---

[2]Although we have grouped social work and social care throughout this text, and there is a code of ethics for social workers in many countries, the concept of social care (workers) has a more limited application, being more typically used in the UK and Ireland. In the UK, there is a code of conduct for social care workers, which is seen to include social workers. For the purposes of discussing general ethical obligations in relation to research, we make no distinction here, but recognise the differing governance issues.

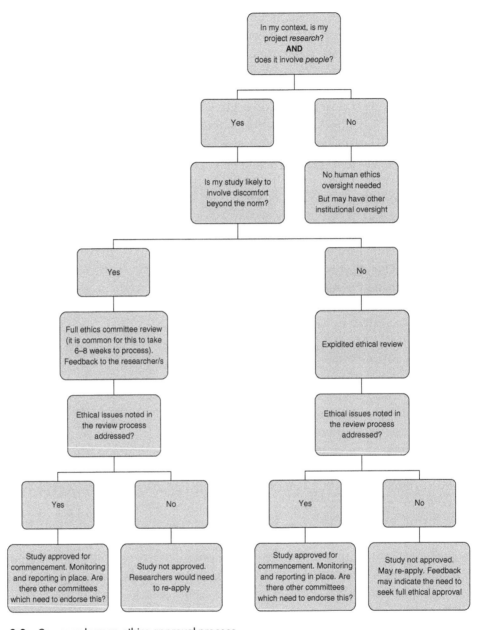

Figure 3.2 Common human ethics approval process

This provides us with a set of guidelines for managing our interactions with service users/research participants, colleagues and organisations. While the 'Global standards on social work education' (International Federation of Social Workers, 2012) indicate that the ability to be both a consumer and producer of research is a key social work practice method, the actual attention given to research varies considerably across the range of countries in which social work operates.

Professional ethical frameworks variably address *why* we need to engage in research (to contribute to knowledge and improved practice) as well as *how* to do this (largely with respect and integrity).

What is your professional code?

What does it say about research generally and your ethical obligations?

How ethics? Researching ethically in a social work and social care context

As is evident in our earlier chapters, we take the view that research in social work and social care must be congruent with the value base and aims of the profession. Therefore, we would argue that ethical research in social work and social care brings further expectations, beyond what is required by procedural ethical processes. In addition to ensuring integrity, showing respect and being mindful of sharing fairly the benefits and burdens of research, we need to bring a commitment to social justice, social change and social inclusion. This requires us as researchers to be self-aware, recognising and responding to inequality, while balancing empowerment/participation with protection. We discuss some strategies to address these issues now.

An awareness of power and inequality

It would be generally accepted that in many situations a power difference exists between the researcher and the researched, with the researcher typically being in a more powerful position. This can have a big impact throughout a study.

Let's take a few moments to think about what might increase this inequality between a social work and social care researcher and a (potential) participant or community.

This could include a range of individual or situational factors, such as:

- Differences as a result of age, gender, socio-economic status, language, dis/ability, etc.
- The participant/community is from a marginalised or stigmatised group
- The participant/community is isolated or has fewer resources or supports available to them
- The research is being conducted in your organisation, on which the participant/community is in some way reliant or dependent for services
- The participant/community is from a group who are 'over-researched'
- The research environment is coercive (e.g. a prison, or a classroom where the teacher hands out a survey for students to complete in class, or even a workplace where your supervisor tells you that you have to participate, or a research situation in which participants were being offered extreme inducements)
- The sensitive or personal nature of the topic of the research, particularly if the participant/community has had a recent experience of this.

Can you think of other situations, perhaps in your professional or academic context?

In social work and social care research, issues of power and inequality may be exacerbated as the research we conduct is often with those who are described as 'vulnerable'. This is a much debated concept. In the arena of procedural ethics, 'vulnerability' is typically attached to groups of people, including children, prisoners and those dependent on medical care. Vulnerability is therefore seen as a characteristic, or as an ongoing circumstance, rather than as situational. We tend to see the potential for vulnerability as being more fluid, accepting that 'vulnerability [is] a varying characteristic of all individuals' (Davison, 2004: 387). This is shaped by an understanding of person-in-environment, with individual factors interacting with the environment, including relationships/interactions, place and time.

The term 'hard to reach' is often used to describe those with multiple disadvantages or complex problems: those more hidden from our understanding, though not necessarily from public view or comment. Think of illicit drug users or those who are homeless; they are often highly visible and generate clear public opinions, although marginalised from the wider community. Arguably this term indicates that the onus of being 'reached' (or not) is on the researched. Another way of considering this is presented by Zea et al. (2003), who contend that being hard to reach is less about particular group characteristics and more about the researchers' detachment from that population. If we consider it from this perspective, then bridging this distance becomes the responsibility of the researcher. Shifting the focus from the individual and/or their 'group' ('hidden', 'vulnerable', 'complex', etc.) to the 'relationship' – the distance between the parties – changes the nature of the interaction and its intent. As researchers we can become less focused on assessing 'are they capable?' and more concerned with what we can do to minimise the power differential and establish relationships that enable participation, including the development of inclusive and non-stigmatising research methods (Flynn and Saunders, 2015).

Consider the issue you started to wonder about in Chapter 1, or a topic/area that you are working on at the moment. What individual and environmental factors might interact to create or exacerbate inequality for potential participants?

For researchers who work within a positivist paradigm (you will recall we discussed this in Chapter 2), and see research as an objective endeavour, this power differential is less important, as they believe that a range of strategies can be drawn upon to *neutralise* the relationship between researchers and participants. You may recall some of these strategies, perhaps from your studies in other disciplines, such as using: standardised or structured data collection techniques, measuring the extent to which participants' responses suggest they are acting in a socially desirable way (and then discarding their data from analysis), using anonymous self-administered questionnaires or perhaps using a *double-blind technique* (where neither the participant nor the researcher collecting the data are aware of what the core focus of the study is). You can see that these strategies are focused only on individuals in a data collection setting: they may also not be appropriate for the research/practice problem you face, or may simply not fit with your interpretation of the problem and what needs to be known.

We have outlined our own position as pragmatic researchers in the Introduction, and would be inclined to argue that we have to find different ways to acknowledge and confront inequality, rather than pretending it doesn't exist. In the conduct of research, this is something you will need to attend to from the beginning planning stages, as it is likely to have an impact at varied times throughout the study. For the purposes of this chapter, we focus in particular on establishing the study and when people are deciding about participation.

Establishing a study: challenging power and inequality through participation and reciprocity

Hugman et al. (2011) talk about 'reciprocal research': that which is based on the idea of exchange – both of ideas and of the benefits of research. We introduced PAR in Chapter 1 and how this challenged thinking about research relationships. Pyett et al. (2013) outline key strategies for using such a collaborative approach to research with disadvantaged communities (and provide some excellent examples of where this approach has been used). The key feature of this approach is the central role played by the participant group/community in the research from the outset: the issue for investigation is identified by the community, and they are involved in all facets of the doing of the study – establishing the methodology, data collection, analysis, reporting and implementation. Community knowledge is respected and utilised. A clear research agreement with the community/group ensures that roles and accountability are clear, while establishing an advisory group provides appropriate oversight and guidance for the research. The authors are clear that this approach requires time to engage in adequate consultation, to build relationships and establish trust, to build research skills and capacity, and to give back to the community by working with them to implement findings.

Participatory approaches, based on strong partnerships, are now almost embedded in research with Indigenous communities, with a significant paradigm shift evident in recent years, away from 'research on' to 'research with and for'. The National Health and Medical Research Council (NHMRC) in Australia now gives specific guidance both to researchers and to Indigenous communities about engaging in research (NHMRC, 2003). Core values include reciprocity, respect, equality, responsibility, survival and protection, and spirit and integrity. Pyett et al. (2009) suggest a similar process to that for collaborative research generally, but also imply that participation, whilst empowering, may also be a burden. They remind us that for many individuals research may not be a high priority, given their many other pressing concerns; it is up to researchers then to act with integrity, to demonstrate their commitment and to work with individuals and communities to enable meaningful and manageable participation.

Similar approaches have been discussed and recommended when researching with children (see Greig et al., 2013). Flynn and Saunders (2015) describe researching with children who have experienced parental incarceration. They describe a reference group as shaping, guiding and scrutinising the research as it progressed. They highlight the additional learning opportunities for participants here – to be empowered with knowledge about research. The value of children's knowledge is emphasised, both in shaping appropriate language and terminology for the research and in the developing of robust and meaningful methods of data collection. They emphasise the importance of allowing time for relationship building. The importance of relationships is also emphasised by Bigby and Frawley (2010) as being fundamental to collaborative research with people with intellectual disabilities. Noting the limited practical accounts of such research, they provide a reflective case study of the processes of implementing such an approach. They conclude that such an approach requires working from a strengths perspective: realistically assessing the collaborator's abilities within a rights framework; using strategies such as on-the-job training and support; as well as having a research mentor who works alongside and in alliance with the collaborator.

The ability to construct and conduct research in a participatory way is shaped by the broader research context. Both Bigby and Frawley (2010) and Pyett et al. (2013) draw attention to the limitations imposed by the political and economic context and funding bodies. Pyett et al. (2013) give an example of where the problem of alcohol use in an Indigenous community was understood very differently by the funding body than it was by the community; they highlight the need to acknowledge these differences, negotiate and compromise. MacLean et al. (2009) provide broader comment on the impact of the political and policy environment on researchers' capacity to work in more collaborative and participatory ways. They describe what they see as the current challenge in Australian universities, where due to time and funding models, the time-consuming nature of participatory approaches is not rewarded or seen as important.

This compares, for example, to Cossar and Neil's (2015) report on their research into post-adoption support in the UK (you may recall we introduced this example in Chapter 1), which appears to be a successful example of how to engage what might be seen as a hard-to-reach group – birth parents whose children have been placed for adoption. The UK, however, has embraced and developed 'consumer participation' as a broad umbrella, whereas, in Australia, apart from mental health, this philosophy is very much in its infancy.

Awareness of power and inequality at recruitment and beyond

As researchers you will also need to be aware of power and inequality when you start to recruit participants into your study and enable individuals to choose whether or not to partake. As discussed above, in our discussion about power and inequality, there are several factors that can act as barriers to people giving free and informed consent. These include age, language differences and dis/ability.

Some strategies that we have found useful include:

Pre-empt likely issues that may exacerbate inequality or vulnerability, and reduce capacity to give informed consent. You can then address these issues in your recruitment. For example, for those with likely low literacy skills, you could provide recruitment information in simple/ plain language (there are excellent online resources that address the use of 'Easy English'), as well as allowing time to read through this with potential participants. For those whose mother tongue is not English, you could provide your recruitment information in relevant community languages, as well as having interpreters or translated documents available for data collection. Whatever strategy you choose, it is important to encourage potential participants to ask questions, and actively remind them that non-participation is a realistic option. If you are still not sure if your potential participant understands what you are asking of them, it is a good practical strategy to ask them to explain to you in their own terms what the research entails.

Your preparation and consideration of possible inequalities may also lead you to choose to include/exclude participants. For example, if you are conducting research in your own organisation, then it is better to exclude participants with whom you have worked directly (as they may feel both obliged to participate and/or to only give glowing reports of service). As an alternative you could have a co-researcher gather data from these participants. If you are researching a potentially emotional issue, you may choose a particular time frame in your inclusion criteria; see our example below.

Case study

Managing risk by thinking about timing

Alexis, the student researcher introduced in Chapter 2, decided that when recruiting participants to her study of women's experiences of hospital treatment after miscarriage, that she would exclude participants who had sought treatment within the previous 6 months. This was to minimise the possibility that participants would be 'discussing very recent, possibly upsetting, issues' (McLean and Flynn, 2013: 787).

Acknowledge and name the inequality and likely impact. The following examples demonstrate the researcher's recognition of likely power differences: 'I know in this environment it may be difficult to see that you can freely choose to participate … but …' or 'I know it might seem like [mum, dad, teacher, worker, etc.] really wants you to participate … but …'

Acknowledge and seek to reduce the power difference. Early feminist researcher advice remains useful: spend time building non-hierarchical relationships; consider how to incorporate reciprocity into the relationship; consider if your research problem allows you to use methods in which the discussion is led by the participants not the researcher; and share results with research participants.

Be aware that it is difficult for people to leave an interview/focus group situation once they are there, so make sure they come of their own volition and want to be there. This has been noted particularly in research with young people, but has wider application.

Be aware of the environment: Is this coercive? What are the power dynamics of the setting (are you sitting behind a desk?)? Can you be flexible with where you gather your data?

So, the research environment is significant – what we can do as well as how we do it. This environment may also have an impact on the researcher. We flagged in Chapter 1 the issue of student researchers often being in less powerful positions, particularly if they are researching 'up' about organisations, policies or programmes provided by professionals. Such inequality may also be evident more broadly; it is important to take into consideration the research environment, the issue being examined and the participant group.

Thinking about researcher vulnerability. One issue that gets little attention in teaching or scholarship about research is researcher vulnerability. See the combined vignette below, which gives reflections from Alannah and Susan, who both conducted research in prisons: Alannah on mothers with a mental illness and Susan on psychological distress in older prisoners. While both feel that procedural ethics processes rightfully protected the autonomy and wellbeing of the research participants, there was limited consideration given to the researcher themselves.

 ## Case study

Researcher vulnerability

Alannah and Susan consider their vulnerability as researchers in relation to the research participants and the research environment:

Research participants: While the topic of ageing prisoners conjures up images of a largely vulnerable and powerless group of participants, in reality the research involved interaction with a wide variety of prisoners in a broad spectrum of correctional environments. Given that interviews were arranged locally by each prison, I found myself habitually entering closed spaces with an unknown prisoner, and required to navigate interview processes with very limited information at hand. Though not a component of the research, participants sometimes disclosed offences for which they had been imprisoned, and perhaps because of the age focus (thereby capturing those doing long sentences), contained an over-representation of those sentenced for sexual offences and homicide. There were also instances of participants assisting me by providing or otherwise explaining institutional information. At times I was almost reliant on the prisoners to help navigate the institution which was their home, but comparatively foreign to the visiting researchers. These power dynamics were once again thrown out when post-release interviews were conducted with participants in the community. Although generally held in public locations, any real or symbolic protection previously offered by the prison institution to me was no longer present. I was confronted by various situations including being asked to get into a participant's car, and being asked out on a date by another participant. These experiences each challenged the perception that power in the researcher-researched interaction inherently lies with the researcher and vulnerability with the participant. (Susan)

In many respects, the participant is truly the expert in prison: knowing the rules, procedures and prison timetable, for example. In these instances the assumption of researcher power is questionable, as the relationship between the participant-researcher is negotiated and shifts in response to the identities and experiences of those involved. It is incorrect to assume that people in prison are automatically vulnerable. (Alannah)

The prison environment: Gaining access to the prison system involved compliance with administration and security regulations, procedures and rules. At a practical level, at every visit I had to have an identification check, an x-ray of all supplies entering the prison (interview schedules, pens, and even my lunch), and to be scanned by a metal detector; in some environments, I also had to have a retina scan. Once successfully completed, I then had to be escorted at all times by a staff member, with wait times dependent on escort availability. Although in the beginning, this environment was novel, I was very clear that I had very little control. (Alannah)

The power dynamics of prison research are wider than just the 'researcher' and the 'researched'. At the most basic level, prisons control access to participants and can constrain what is permissible to ask about in an interview. Funding grants play a role in defining (or constraining) the research agenda, and influencing what we study, as well as how we do research and share the findings. The use of certain research designs such as longitudinal studies and analytical elements which benefit from extended deliberation are often necessarily minimised in many contemporary research environments. Researchers do not control these deliberations. (Susan)

To address and manage researcher vulnerability, self-awareness is vital. We have already discussed this extensively in Chapter 1, particularly discussing strategies such as maintaining a research journal and making use of supervision. We suggest you go back and read this if you need a reminder. Davison (2004) also provides an excellent discussion of these issues, drawing on her own experiences and research with researchers, reminding us of the unanticipated repercussions of research: that research can 'profoundly affect and change a researcher' (Reinharz, 1992, cited in Davison, 2004: 390). Acknowledging and working with our vulnerabilities can only improve our work and the final research outcomes.

Balancing individual rights and protection

In social work and social care balancing rights and protection is an ongoing challenge. In research, this is seen at a number of junctures, including recruitment and seeking informed consent (we discussed strategies for addressing inequality above) but is also evident when making decisions around data presentation and notably about anonymisation.

Anonymising data/results is accepted as standard practice in research, to protect participants. In more recent times, however, researchers, particularly those using visual methods have challenged this, with some suggesting that anonymisation is outdated. Wiles et al. (2010) conducted research with visual researchers in the UK, who indicated that this was the key ethical issue they faced. Findings indicated a split in views, with some respondents seeing it as an issue of rights and that participants wanted their images to be shown, whilst others were more cautious of the longer term impact. The latter group were of the view that there can be significant changes in individuals over time, and 'the type of person they are happy to be identified as or the views they are happy to espouse at one point in time might cause them embarrassment or distress at a later point' (Wiles et al., 2010: 13).

One view put forward to challenge this was that we all do things that we later wish we hadn't, but that this can be pre-empted by researchers being explicit about the use and longevity of data/images and clarifying the decision about anonymity with the person more than once. We would argue that any decisions about anonymity specifically and the presentation of data more generally needs to be shaped by a clear understanding of the participant group, the sensitivity of the topic and the nature of the research environment (including if this is in any way coercive or equally if this has been particularly 'safe' for participants: in both cases, the issue for consideration is, is the participant likely to have shared 'too much'?). Hugman et al. (2011, citing Barnes, 1979) argue similarly that as researchers, we must bring to these situations our knowledge of the likely ways that research may expose those in vulnerable situations to scrutiny. See our case example below, detailing recent research conducted with colleagues in Papua New Guinea about social work practice in that setting, where a documentary was the chosen method of data presentation.

 Case study

Managing anonymity when using documentary methods

Catherine and her colleagues were very aware that in discussions about international social work there are concerns that models of social work developed in the west are imposed on other countries where they might not be appropriate; for some this is seen as a form of professional colonisation and imperialism. There are subsequent concerns that indigenous models of practice are neither seen nor recognised.

They thought that using a visual documentary to describe social work practice in Papua New Guinea enhanced the potential for the voices of local social work academics and practitioners to be heard. By contrast the development of a written report would have primarily reflected the researchers' understanding of the story. Given the non-sensitive nature of the topic (social work practice), it was decided that the use of identifiable images of the participants posed negligible risks; it did not infringe upon human values and/or rights; all participants were able to withdraw prior to finalisation of the report/documentary; they were also given final veto on this product. Anonymising data or presenting these in a more traditional written form would have been more ethically unsound and oppressive. This documentary, directed by Cameron Rose, 'Envisioning tomorrow: social work in PNG' can be viewed at https://vimeo.com/61228676.

Chapter summary

We have covered considerable terrain in this chapter: the why, what and how of ethical research, along with practical application in the social work and social care context. In the next chapter we move onto constructing the literature review, which also requires consideration of ethical practice, both in examining the findings of previous researchers and in establishing the merit of any research you propose to conduct.

Key take-home messages

We bring the skills/knowledge and values of social work and social care to our role as researchers; this ensures that we can hold an ethical framework in mind as we go about developing, implementing and disseminating our research. We incorporate respect, integrity and justice into our research, shaped by an awareness of power and a commitment to balancing rights and protection.

To respond appropriately to the complex context that social research presents us with we need to think critically, ask questions, work out the best response, but be prepared to revisit these decisions.

There is a need for ongoing attention to self-awareness and reflexivity, as outlined in Chapter 1. Making use of a research journal and supervision will ensure that you keep these core issues in mind as you go about your research to ensure that you are an engaged and active participant in this process.

Additional resources

Davison, J. (2004) 'Dilemmas in research: issues of vulnerability and disempowerment for the social worker/researcher', *Journal of Social Work Practice: Psychotherapeutic Approaches in Health, Welfare and the Community*, 18 (3): 379–93. This article is one of the few we have seen that discusses key challenges in research in social work and social care with respect to the likely, and unpredictable issues we will confront and the vulnerability of the researcher.

Tomossy, G. (2006) 'Vulnerability in research', in I. Freckelton and K. Peterson (eds), *Disputes and Dilemmas in Health Law*. Annandale, NSW: Federation Press, pp. 534–59. Although not a social work and social care example, it describes a number of examples of unethical research.

Israel, M. and Hay, I. (2006) *Research Ethics for Social Scientists*. London: Sage. This is an excellent resource, which although it is not specifically about research in social work and social care, gives a clear historical account of human research ethics along with localised practical examples.

Pyett, P., Waples-Crowe, P. and Van Der Sterren, A. (2013) 'Collaborative participatory research with disadvantaged communities', in P. Liamputtong (ed.), *Research Methods in Health. Foundations for Evidence Based Practice* (2nd edn). Oxford: Oxford University Press. This chapter provides a clear framework and guidelines for collaborative participatory approaches, with attention to the limitations and the research context. It provides excellent concrete examples of research in practice to demonstrate key concepts.

Flynn, C. and Saunders, V. (2015) 'Research with children of prisoners – methodological considerations for bringing youth in from the margins', in S. Bastien and H. Holmarsdottir (eds), *Youth at the Margins: Experiences from Engaging Youth in Research Worldwide*. Rotterdam: Sense Publishers. This chapter, although focused on a particular group of children, those who have experienced parental imprisonment, shares both broad and specific strategies to enable children who may be vulnerable to actively participate in research and have their opinions heard.

4

Arriving at a Research Question

Building on Existing Knowledge

In this chapter you will learn

- Why we conduct a literature review
- The key ingredients of a good literature review
- Skills in critically reading the literature
- How to conduct and write a competent and context-responsive literature review
- Some strategies for drawing conclusions from the literature review to develop your research question.

Introduction

You can see from the title of this chapter how important we see the literature review to be in setting up your study. Using your literature review to question and build on existing knowledge will help you to shape a good research question and therefore a good study. It is important at this point to pre-empt an issue that at least some of you will be voicing: 'but I already have my research question!'. This will be mostly true if you are a practitioner researcher faced with an issue in your day-to-day work (e.g. I want to know if this intervention is working or what the needs of a particular client group are). This is all fine. All of us begin our research by wanting to know something – with hunches – and all of us have a question that guides our reading and reviewing of the literature (definitely more of that later in the chapter). These questions we have at the outset can range from quite loose to much more specific. But even if you feel you have a specific research question before conducting your literature review, it is still best to treat this as a guiding rather than final question. This just means that if/when unexpected material turns up when you are reading and reviewing the literature, you can 'fine-tune' your research question.

In the chapters so far we have looked at the contexts in which we 'do' research, the impact of that context, as well as the frameworks underpinning that knowledge. In this chapter we will cover the why, what and how of examining existing knowledge (note, when people talk about a 'literature review', this is simply what they mean – looking at the existing knowledge on your topic). So we will talk *about* the literature review, why do one and what it should contain, as well as explaining ways to approach *doing* your literature review. As with previous chapters, we will use real-world examples to show common sticking points and resolutions, including our 'chorus' of student and practitioner researchers and their experiences of conducting a literature review. You will be encouraged throughout to reflect on your ideas and engage in self-directed learning.

So, to start ... a literature review is both a *process* and a *product* (Bruce, 1994, cited in Bryman, 2012): something that you do – an argument that you build – as well as something that you have produced at the end. However, having taught many research students, and worked with many practitioners, we know that the role of the literature review in research can be a little unclear.

Perhaps you see it as having a minor role: information that is added after you have completed your study, to 'set the scene'. Maybe it is the descriptive background to your study. Or maybe even something which you are required to do (perhaps by your supervisor or lecturer), but you do not see any connection whatsoever with the research question you want answered. We hope that if any of these thoughts resonate with you, by the end of this chapter you will be clear about the role played by the 'lit review' in helping you to formulate a meaningful, and importantly answerable, research question, a responsive methodology, and to locate and contextualise your findings (but more about this in Chapter 12).

Why conduct a literature review?

Short answer: If you don't, you risk 'reinventing the wheel' with your study, and nobody wants to waste their time doing that!

Longer answer: A well-rounded understanding of the existing knowledge in your chosen area ('the topic') is a key, and early, step in any research project. A well-rounded understanding requires balanced attention to two core areas: what knowledge exists and how this has been generated.

What knowledge? As discussed in the preceding chapter on ethics, the literature review will establish the need for and merit of your study. It must demonstrate that you are aware of what has gone before, how it has been constructed and developed and what your contribution will be. This contribution should also be relevant to social work and social care and congruent with the value base, as discussed in Chapter 1. You will need to comment on the extent to which your topic has been canvassed, as well if the research question you pose has been asked/answered before, with a clear justification for asking it in the way you propose.

How has knowledge been generated? It is necessary to pay attention to the manner in which your topic has been considered and investigated before. This allows you to learn from the experiences, including the mistakes and omissions, of those who have gone before. This examination of methods also requires consideration of ethical research practices (as discussed in the preceding chapter) and the implications for the knowledge produced.

Keeping these two issues in mind as you complete your literature review will ensure that the research question you pose and the study you construct is relevant to the profession, is ethical and is methodologically sound. We will revisit and reiterate each of these issues throughout the chapter when we discuss how to conduct the literature review. Here is a simple definition of a literature review, which we will use as both an anchor and a guide over the chapter:

> The literature review shares with the reader the results of other studies that are closely related ... It relates a study to the larger ongoing dialogue in the literature about a topic ... It provides a framework for establishing the importance of the study as well as a benchmark for comparing the results of the study with other findings. (Creswell, 2003: 30)

As will be clear throughout this chapter, our approach to the literature review is a pragmatic one. The literature review process is understood as iterative; it is not predetermined. As the researcher, you are an active agent in this process, making decisions, developing and refining your focus, shaped by what you need to know for your study and what there is to know in the existing research.

The 'ingredients' of a good literature review

A range of writers discussing research in social work, social care and social research have shared their views on the ingredients of a literature review. Aveyard (2010), in what has become a much-used text by beginning researchers in health and social work and social care, identifies research as the key component. Holosko (2006: 8) provides a useful checklist for deciding what constitutes 'research', arguing that it will have all of the following elements: a specified purpose, a rationale, a specified method, analysis of data and a conclusion. He contrasts this with common 'non-research' papers, which tend to describe or evaluate existing literature, policy, theory, law or a particular methodology, etc., and lack a systematic process of investigation. Once you are clear on what is research, Aveyard (2010) argues that when selecting material for inclusion in a literature review, you should use a hierarchy of evidence (see below, from Sackett et al., 1996, cited in Aveyard, 2010: 62). She suggests that those engaged in a literature review should aim for evidence 'at the top' as this is 'more robust and close to objective truth' (2010: 61).

1. Systematic reviews and meta-analyses
2. RCTs
3. Cohort studies, case-controlled studies
4. Surveys
5. Case reports
6. Qualitative studies
7. Expert opinion
8. Anecdotal opinion.

She moderates this position somewhat to argue that this will be shaped by your study/ purpose, and that, dependent on your area of research and purpose, you should formulate your own hierarchy.

D'Cruz and Jones (2004: 22) in fact argue that in the area of social work and social care, 'existing knowledge' is not always accessible or located in 'the [research] literature', hence researchers need to include 'all aspects of knowledge making relevant to the topic and the research question'. Bryman (2012) and Bell (2005) provide more direction about key 'ingredients', suggesting that a literature review should also include the study's theoretical/conceptual framework, which, as opinion-based material, would be seen as much less rigorous on the hierarchy noted above. It is evident here that not only does our context shape what we are concerned with (what we want to know more about or to change) but it also influences what prior knowledge exists or is considered relevant. It is our view that hierarchies of evidence are useful tools. What is important for you as the researcher to know, when you are at this stage of the research process, is *what type of evidence is available on your topic*, then aim to seek out and *include the most rigorous*. We agree with Aveyard's (2010) position that the substantive material in a literature review should be empirical research, but this can be complemented and framed by a discussion of relevant frameworks, specifically theory and policy. The latter may be necessary to provide the context that is required to understand and critique the empirical material.

Research context

As discussed in Chapter 1, your research context (practice based, academic, etc.) will shape the focus of your research as well as how and why you carry it out. So too will it have an influence on your literature review.

Remember that the relative weight of each of these components will vary depending on your context and discipline. The experience of Alannah, a PhD student, provides an illustrative example.

The specific content of your literature review will vary depending on your context and the aim of your study: its scope and parameters. If, for example, you are an undergraduate/

qualifying student, conducting your literature review as part of your course requirements, the scope will be dictated by the subject's learning aims. You will perhaps focus more on demonstrating that you understand how to conduct a literature review and can locate and critique a limited amount of knowledge (perhaps in predefined areas).

If you are a higher degree student, the aim will be more expansive and self-directed. Holbrook et al. (2007) in their study of examiner expectations of PhD literature reviews, found that examiners wanted the literature review to show that the student understood what literature was relevant to include, had a working understanding of that literature and could connect their results back to this material. Obviously with this type of research, the aim is to make an original contribution to knowledge.

As suggested by our discussion in Chapter 1, if you are a practitioner researcher, your focus will likely be much narrower. As practice research is typically short term and seeking practical benefits for service users and/or their organisations (Shaw, 2005; Mitchell et al., 2010), it is necessarily focused on your own practice or that of your peers/team or on a current practice or organisational issue. Research such as this aims to develop knowledge for specific practice. Bell's (2005) guide for first time researchers in education, health and social science, advises that for small studies like these, it may be unnecessary to do an extensive literature review. Your review may focus on a small number of studies or systematic reviews of a specific intervention you are keen to implement, with some attention to local or organisational policy and procedure.

As you can see from this discussion, the external environment in which you do your research has a direct impact on your literature review, largely because it informs the purpose and focus of your research. Gathering and reviewing relevant literature allows you to develop what we call a 'context responsive' study, that is, a study which is well informed and appropriate to meet the needs of a specific practice/research problem in a specific context. Again, pragmatism as the foundation framework is evident here, though the primary focus is on context and our main concern is the practical outcomes of our research.

Take some time to consider the following:

Alannah, PhD student

My study is looking at how mothers with a mental illness facing prison, are able to manage and respond to their children's care. My literature review focuses mostly on the empirical research about imprisoned mothers. But I realised that I also needed to understand the political and policy context, and the influence of feminist criminologists to be able to present a critically informed analysis of the research I was reading; that is:

how knowledge has been developed, and who or what has influenced this.

What is the context in which you would be conducting a literature review? What is the anticipated practical application of the study? What are the subsequent expectations about the role and scope of the literature review?

What type of information would be most appropriate for your literature review? What evidence would be prioritised – placed at the top of your hierarchy?

Examining the literature

In our experience, there are four relatively simple steps to a good literature review (you will see, however, as we discuss these that this is typically not a linear process):

- Situate your topic in context (you will revisit this as you develop your literature review; most of us begin too broadly and need to revise and refocus)
- Identify relevant literature
- Decide which literature to include
- 'Read' and review the literature.

Step 1: Situate your topic

When choosing your topic, as discussed in Chapter 1, this should be relevant to professional practice and congruent with the value base. Paying attention to a broader professional mission and obligations will help you to think beyond yourself and make sure that it is not just your own personal interest that drives the process. The practical application or contribution to social work must be clear.

A level of self-awareness (which we introduced in Chapter 1, and discussed at length in Chapter 2, in relation to epistemology and the implications for how research is carried out) is therefore necessary to you from the beginning stages of the research process.

The helpful impact of this attention when conducting the literature review is highlighted in a reflection from Rebecca.

Actively bringing your expectations and interests (including personal and professional history, as well as your epistemological position) to awareness ensures that you can read the literature more accurately, and less clouded by your own filters. As a consequence, the research question you pose will be more professionally relevant. Self-awareness is ongoing work. As outlined in Chapter 1, Engin (2011) recommends the use of a research diary as a tool for reflecting on or justifying decisions, posing questions and considering alternatives. Tools such as this fit well within a pragmatic framework, as they ensure that research is grounded in experience. Using a tool like a research journal allows the researcher to be fully

Rebecca, Masters qualifying social work student

In developing a research proposal on the topic of the provision of Single Session Work to clients on a waiting list by Family Support Workers, my initial interest was motivated not only by the problem being of daily concern in my work organisation, but by my own values about evidence based practice and a desire to ensure a service user voice. Being aware that I had existing opinions about the topic, I sought to suspend what O'Leary (2010: 33) calls our 'initial judgements'.

I did this by actively seeking to review research from a variety of perspectives.

This enriched my understanding and it became evident that there was already a substantial body of research on client satisfaction; therefore, my focus and direction and hence my research question changed to address the gap in research regarding practice skills required for Single Session Work.

engaged as an active agent in the process, reflecting, adapting, responding and restructuring where appropriate. It is a strategy we highly recommend throughout the research process, even at the stage of the literature review!

If you are a student, your topic is more likely to be identified broadly. For example, you may be concerned about a social issue you have observed in your community, or puzzled by something you have come across in your reading for your studies, or even just curious about an issue you have become aware of via the news or social media.

As a practitioner, it is more likely that this will be something more specific, something you have come across in your day-to-day work: an emerging issue about which you or your organisation knows little, a problem that needs to be solved, or even just working out if a current intervention is having the desired effect.

Alex reflects on an issue observed during placement in a public hospital.

Alex clearly wanted to understand what was going wrong for older people after they were sent home from hospital, and to know if there was anything that could be done during their hospital stay or during discharge planning to prevent this.

You may play a large role in determining your topic, or your organisation may have its own priorities. Either way, the importance of you getting curious about your environment is emphasised by Ballenger (2007: 27); something we would reiterate as a key activity in social work and social care more generally.

If you have a specific project you are working on now, or planning, take a few moments to gather your initial thoughts on that topic (you will have already done some reflecting on your epistemological position when reading the previous chapter).

What are your expectations or hunches about your topic?

Alex, Masters qualifying social work student

In a hospital acute general medical ward, there appeared to be a high rate of re-admissions amongst older adult patients. Seeing familiar faces of previously discharged patients seemed almost like a daily occurrence. This was concerning because many patients were re-admitted to the ward only a short time after they were discharged. It appeared that many patients were re-admitted for reasons related to their initial admission, as well as other possibly preventable causes.

I was also aware of a recent report which reiterated my observations - nearly one in ten admissions to public hospitals are unplanned re-admissions within 30 days of discharge.

As you will remember from the start of the chapter, a key role of the literature review is to frame your study by engaging in dialogue about your topic (Creswell, 2003). To begin this dialogue, you need to get more specific about your area of interest. This will help you to determine the key sources that you will need to review. A useful way to begin is to brainstorm:

- What is your *primary concern*: is it an issue, an intervention, an outcome, a service user group, etc.?
- What is the *connection to professional practice*: do you seek to know more about a new problem or a new service user group, or do you need to evaluate the impact of a current intervention, etc.? What are the practical consequences with which you are concerned? What do you want to change/improve?

- What is the range of possible *perspectives* on or approaches to this problem? See the example of women and depression in Chapter 2. (It may be helpful at the beginning to think specifically about what academic disciplines may have an interest in the issue.)
- What *type of material* is likely to exist about your problem? (Is this research, theory, policy?)
- What are the *key words* or *concepts* associated with the problem? It would be usual to revisit and revise these initial key words, either broadening or reducing, depending on how much material you generate initially. You will need to pay attention as you begin to search and read to see what terms are being used in your topic area.

You will also need to maintain your self-awareness to ensure the 'best possible' interpretation of the literature. Perhaps revisit the self-awareness strategies discussed in Chapter 1: make use of a research journal or talk to others, such as colleagues, peers or your supervisor.

Is the epistemological position of the researcher/s evident in the terms chosen? What is the impact on what they find?

Are there contested terms in your topic area? For example, do researchers use the term 'victim' or 'survivor' of domestic violence? (Recently we have seen the neutral term 'target' used. This shifts the focus of attention from the individual characteristics of the person who has been subject to abuse onto the behaviour of the perpetrator - a subtle but significant difference.)

Engaging in this process will help you to develop an initial guiding question for your search of the literature. As noted above, if you are a practitioner researcher, you may already have a driving research question. An important message here is that the question should be inquisitive and open, acting 'as a compass rather than as an anchor' (Eakin and Mykhalovskiy, 2003: 190). Remember the aim of a literature review is to refine and develop a research question (this will ensure that you do not just reinvent the wheel!).

Depending on how you learn and think, visual tools can be really useful at this point to identify, in a preliminary way, core and more peripheral material/issues. See Figure 4.1 as an example. This is from Catherine's exploration of the impact of maternal incarceration on adolescents. From this diagram you can see that her overall topic was largely embedded in a broader discussion of 'children' and 'imprisoned parents'.

As you can see from this, identifying relevant key words, and associated terms, is an important part of getting started on your literature review.

Step 2: Identifying literature

Now that you know *what* information you need, you are one step closer to knowing *where* you can locate this. If you are a student, you will have access to a wide range of databases from which you can source peer reviewed research. Remember, if you are a student, it is always helpful to form a good working relationship with your university or subject librarian – they will be invaluable in assisting you with developing information literacy skills; these are absolutely necessary in a rapidly changing knowledge environment.

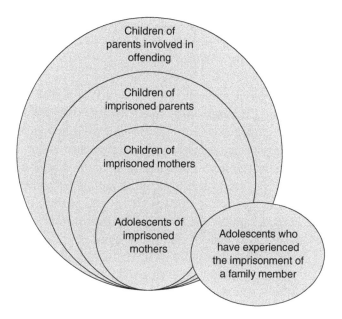

Figure 4.1 Visual mapping of literature

On the topic of identifying literature, our librarian colleagues[1] remind us to think laterally about locating relevant material, by searching: in books (e.g. for theory or a more general overview of the topic), via the web (e.g. for government reports or policy documents – given the amount of research done in our field of social work and social care that is *grey literature* (government papers, organisational research, conference proceedings), this is an important tool) and via databases, including 'Google Scholar' (e.g. for journal articles).

If you do not have access to a university library, then you may make use of tools such as the Directory of Open Access Journals (DOAJ) or other open access repositories such as ResearchGate.net or Academia.edu. How and where you search and your search strategy depend on what material you need to locate.

Some good advice coming from research by McFadden et al. (2012) is that searching for research in the field of social work is a complex task and that for the best results you need to use multiple strategies. Whatever method/s you choose, this should be structured, methodical

Where would you need to search for relevant literature? What resources would you need to implement this?

[1]Acknowledgement here to Cassandra Freeman and Sarah Cahill, from Monash University Library, for their work on literature searching via the internet, from which they created an interactive online tutorial, available at: www.monash.edu/library/skills/resources/tutorials/academic-research-internet.

and documented. This record ensures an explicit (and replicable) process, which is comprehensive and focused. You may do this through your library's online tool, via endnote or via your own organisational system (we will also discuss a systematic approach to documenting the content of what you read a little later in the chapter).

If, when you begin, you generate too much, or irrelevant, material, you will need to draw the boundaries of your search a bit more tightly. You might do this for example by focusing on a specific age range of children rather than children more generally, or by reducing the time frame of your search; this is particularly useful if your topic area is one that has generated a lot of material quickly. Conversely, if you don't generate enough material, you will need to broaden your search (this was the case with the example about adolescents experiencing maternal incarceration above). This may involve thinking about related service user groups, as well as brainstorming other terms that may be used in relation to your topic. A good example is that of 'domestic violence': other terms include 'family violence' and 'intimate partner violence'; we have also seen the use recently of the more inclusive 'family and domestic violence (FDV)'.

Step 3: Deciding what literature to include

Please note, while steps 3 and 4 are presented here as sequential, it is more of a cyclical process: you will find that decisions you make about what literature to include will continue to be shaped by your critique of the individual readings. In deciding what literature to include, this is where clear boundaries around your research focus are vital. If you have engaged in visual mapping of your topic, this can be a useful tool to focus supervision sessions or discussions with colleagues, and make decisions about the inclusion/exclusion of literature.

From a pragmatic perspective, it is helpful to ask yourself the following critical and reflective questions about each piece of material, with regard to both quality and relevance, to ensure that you are drawing from rigorous research that you can see has applicability to your research context:

- How has the *quality* of the work been assured? *Peer review* (blind review of submitted articles by qualified academics) is a commonly applied standard, but you should still approach reading with a critical eye. Jesson et al. (2011) remind us of the potential for publication bias: reviewers are often chosen for their expertise and experience in a specific area. This may also mean they have much vested in their 'position' and may find it difficult to see alternative viewpoints
- Is the material *relevant* ('closely related')? What is the specific connection to your topic? (Does it examine the same intervention, or investigate the needs of the same or a similar service user group, etc.?)
- What is the *relationship between the 'quality' and 'relevance' of the material*? And if the information is deemed relevant, does this outweigh quality? Relying only on 'quality' ingredients – peer reviewed, published material, which is higher on the evidence hierarchy (discussed earlier) – may not always be the most appropriate strategy in our area of work. Much research, particularly in more marginalised areas of practice is done by small not-for-profit organisations or is commissioned by government departments. As a result, as social work and social care researchers, we

have to use our informed professional judgement when conducting a literature review. We would argue that you can include a study/piece of material of lesser quality in a literature review if it has a direct relationship to your topic of interest, if it contributes to meaningful dialogue about the issue and you clearly acknowledge the limitations of the material. This requires individual assessment of literature and more nuanced decision-making

- Is it *recent* – reflecting the most up-to-date knowledge? (In the past decade is the typically accepted standard.)
- Is it *seminal*, ground-breaking work that set the scene for what came after? (In these instances, being recent is then obviously less of an issue.)

Let's take some time now to consider how a hypothetical student, Jane B. Swift, conducts her literature review, searching and selecting material to include.

 ## Case study

Searching for and selecting research literature

Jane B. Swift wanted to look at the role of self-esteem in adolescent delinquency. She went into Psych Info, typed in the key words *self-esteem* and *delinquency*, and crossed them. The search indicated 1,589 articles; she put in adolescent girls to limit the search and got 79 articles. She printed out the abstracts for these articles and found 17 articles in the library that looked most promising. She wrote her review based on the articles and, in some cases, the abstract if she could not find the article. 'It really didn't take that long', Jane said. (Heppner and Heppner, 2004: 52)

What is your assessment of Jane's strategy for identifying relevant material? Did you consider the following?

1. *Reliance on one database*: Remember the advice of McFadden et al. (2012) noted above. In Jane's case, what other disciplines would have an opinion and research on this issue? Criminology? Law? Social work? Others? Or might there be a specific government or educational website that would contain relevant grey literature?
2. *Narrow terminology*: Or perhaps even outdated terminology. Is the word/concept 'delinquent' used in your context? (It has certainly not really been used in Australia for the past 20 or so years.) This is also an issue you need to be particularly mindful of when searching international databases, e.g. while the word 'teen' is not often used in Australia, it is in the USA. In your context, what other terms might you have considered?
3. *Reliance on abstracts to identify relevant articles*: These provide only the author's summary of the study. (Catherine somewhat cynically refers to this as the 'sales pitch'.)
4. *Writing her review based partly on abstracts*: In the abstract the authors tell you what *they* think is important, but it is your responsibility to review more critically and in an in-depth way each study's findings and methodology, to reach your own conclusions about the contribution the study makes to your topic and your research.
5. *Lack of a methodical approach when selecting materials*: How did she identify the 17 articles? What does 'looked promising' mean? Would these papers meet Holosko's (2006) criteria for 'research'?

Step 4: Reading and reviewing the literature

An essential skill in conducting a literature review is your capacity to 'read' well and critically. Jesson et al. (2011: 46–57) provide excellent practical suggestions for managing the reading of material for your literature review. They emphasise that reading journal articles, which you will probably do a lot of when conducting a literature review, requires complex reading skills. They argue that journal articles have a tighter word limit than books and subsequently contain a lot of key information in a short space.

What do you think is the likely impact on Jane's literature review (and her understanding of the existing knowledge) of her approach?

To help you to manage this, Jesson et al. (2011) suggest a structured process, outlined below, to precede writing, to ensure you understand the core concepts of what you are reading:

1. *Skim reading*: They recommend doing this twice - once to scan and include/exclude the paper for your review and then again to garner the main points.
2. *Reading and note taking*: This involves not just summarising, but questioning what you read and making interpretive notes, so that you interact and become familiar with the text. This will allow you to understand and recall the key points and make connections to other readings.
3. *Synthesis* of ideas.

At this stage of reading you are engaging with the ideas of the author/s. Keeping good notes is the beginning of writing and developing your own ideas. See our 'Toolkit' at the end of Part II for a template for summarising the key features of each paper in tabular form. There are a number of easily available critical appraisal tools, such as the Critical Appraisal Skills Program (CASP).

Writing the review

> Writing is thinking … You may think you have a clear idea, but it is only when you write it down that you can be certain that you do. (Rapley, 2007: 73)

'Reviewing the literature' involves not only reviewing individual readings/articles, but synthesising these and bringing the discussion to a logical conclusion in a written format. Thomas (2000: 38) argues that your review must be 'informative, evaluative and integrative'. Hence, a literature review needs to do three things: describe, evaluate and compare material, to form a coherent argument on which to base a research question.

Description

This should indicate *who* conducted the study/ies, along with *when*, *where* and *how*. This does not need to be a slavish description of the entire study, but should provide sufficient detail to frame your account of the findings; if you understand these issues, you are also better able to comment on the applicability of the findings to your own environment. Sufficient attention to methodology also means that anyone reading your review can better understand and evaluate the conclusions you present.

Evaluation

Evaluate how the studies were conducted, methodologically and ethically: what are the strengths and weaknesses of each individual piece?

The sorts of methodological questions you should ask about each include:

- Does the study's methodology allow data to be generated that respond to the research problem and aims of the study – considering:
  - Data collection methods
  - Sampling
  - Ethical practice
  - Data analysis
- Are the author's findings and conclusions justified?
- What is the applicability of the findings to your research?

Evaluation also requires an overall view of the methodological trends in the literature. These may include issues such as:

- A preference for or avoidance of particular methods, approaches or paradigms – what is the possible impact on findings?
- An expansive or limited range of data sources utilised – what perspectives are included or excluded?
- Consistency or inconsistency in defining of key concepts. See Catherine's example below.

 Case study

Managing inconsistencies in the literature

Catherine had to evaluate the literature about the impact of parental imprisonment on children, but found this challenging, given the very different ways that the term 'parent' is used in the research:

- Tudball (2000): a parent who had contact with their child/children in the 12 months prior to imprisonment.
- Sack et al. (1976: 619): a parent who had 'extended contact' with their child during the 12 months prior to imprisonment.

(Continued)

(Continued)

- Hounslow et al. (1982): a parent who had contact with their children prior to imprisonment, but no specification of any time limits or level of contact.
- Tomaino et al. (2005: 4): a parent or anyone else who was the legal guardian of the child – 'even if you're NOT the natural (biological) parent, or if you haven't seen your kids in ages, or if they live interstate' (emphasis in the original) (Tomaino et al., 2005: 53).

With such variation in parenting roles, it was important for her to discuss how useful and accurate these studies were in understanding children's experiences.

Importantly, when faced with observations as in the example above, you need to consider the implications of these trends. What do they mean in terms of the knowledge about your topic?

At this stage in your literature review, you also need to demonstrate that you have an understanding of the ethical principles for good research, as discussed in Chapter 3, and can use these to assess each study's ethical conduct, along with the implications for the findings presented and overall knowledge development.

Drawing from these ethical principles, the sorts of questions you may ask include:

Did the researcher/s demonstrate respect?

- Were participants able to consent to participation freely and without coercion?
- Who invited them, and how, and what information were they provided with?

Was there attention to justice in the study?

- Were participants unduly burdened?
- Are they an 'over-researched' group (by this we mean, easily accessible or convenient for the researchers; some might say university psychology students fit this mould!).
- Does the framing of the research question cast those being researched in a particular way, e.g. as vulnerable, dysfunctional, etc.? Fine et al. (2000) remind us that we have a social responsibility not to contribute to unhelpful stereotypes.
- Are there groups who were (indirectly) excluded from the research? (In the example given above, the literature review found that children of prisoners are often not directly involved in research about the impact of parental incarceration, with researchers commonly describing a desire not to further traumatise them as the rationale. From a justice standpoint, however, is it ethical for researchers not to find a way to hear the voices of children?)

Remember also, evaluating means giving a balanced account, not just finding problems with the research. Once you have a balanced understanding of each piece, you are more able to compare the findings generated.

Comparison

Comparing the studies: this final step in your literature review requires you to draw on your assessment of what you have located and read, to give an informed view of the state of knowledge in your area. This is a vital aspect to a literature review, which moves it beyond the realm of an *annotated bibliography* (a list of research papers, including a brief description and evaluation of each). You need to demonstrate your skills in integrating information, highlighting where studies 'fit', either complementing and supporting each other or contradicting. It is helpful to consult with a supervisor, colleagues or peers at this stage, to get feedback on your work to date.

Here is a hypothetical example that shows one approach to combining evaluative and comparative writing, assuming a topic of 'Undiagnosed mental health problems in secondary school students in Melbourne'. When you're reading the literature look for these kinds of strategies, which researchers use in different ways.

 ## Case study

Combining evaluative and comparative writing in a literature review

Bloggs (2011) investigated undiagnosed mental health problems in secondary school students in Auckland. Two hundred young people participated via an anonymous online questionnaire; this compares favourably with sample sizes of other similar studies (name at least one). The findings indicate (something about the content ...), which reiterates (or perhaps contrasts with?) the earlier work of [who ...]). Because of the anonymous nature of the data collection, Bloggs' (2011) findings are likely to be quite accurate (could reference here some other research which has reported on this), although of course, they do not capture the views of students who do not have easy access to technology (who might have been excluded? and why might this be important to your topic or context?). You could conclude with a comment here about the applicability of the findings to your population – similarity/otherwise of Auckland/your city/area?

One way to start is when you feel you have read sufficient literature, to consider how you might group your literature, to clearly tell the 'story' of the existing knowledge.

You may do this in a number of ways (this is not an exhaustive list):

Practitioner researchers at a health service

Write the skeleton of your argument and circulate it to the group for discussion and feedback ...

Writing up seemed so arduous but it was helpful in identifying how to build on the literature.

I used sub-headings so I was able to introduce different authors and their arguments.

- *Type of literature*: You may want to start simply by grouping your material into theory, policy and research
- *Topic/theme*: For example, in a literature review on women's re-entry into the community after release from prison, the discussion could be grouped and presented in terms of the challenges identified during this period: housing, employment, relapse, family, debt, etc. Perhaps comparing policy aims with the experiences and outcomes identified in the research

(Talbot and Verrinder, 2008, which we include as a resource at the end of this chapter, discuss this well)

- *Location*: For example, international vs. local literature. This can be a useful strategy if there are distinct differences in trends in different countries, and/or if knowledge in your context is just emerging
- *Process*: For example, in some recent research on responding to children when parents are imprisoned, in the literature review, material was presented grouped around key decision-making/action points – arrest, sentencing and imprisonment
- *Contentious issues*: This works well if there are particular issues on which authors disagree; for example, in the literature examining the physical punishment of children ('smacking'), there are clear and contrasting views about any long-term impact
- *Methodology or methods*: For example, in a review of literature into the impact of familial incarceration on adolescents, the material was grouped into qualitative and quantitative methods, as they represented different streams of research and differing approaches. The former were motivated by service delivery, and developing an understanding of young people's needs, and included young people as research participants. Those based on quantitative methods focused on measuring the association between children's experience of parental incarceration and subsequent life events. None of the latter gathered data directly from young people. Findings could then be compared and contrasted
- *Chronologically*: As knowledge has progressed over time. This could almost be seen as the default (simplistic) position for a literature review and you would need to have a clear reason for this approach, and be sure that this did not slip back into being an annotated bibliography. That said, it may be a useful strategy when knowledge in your area has developed in a particularly linear or smooth fashion
- *Research paradigms*: This can be particularly enlightening if these approaches reflect different research 'groups', such as disciplines, consumers/service users, stakeholders, research consortia, etc. For example, PhD student Alannah observed, in her literature review on mothers facing prison with a co-occurring mental illness, that the research on mental health tended to be positivist in orientation (measuring and counting diagnoses or co-morbidities), while that on mothers in prison tended to be interpretivist – seeking women's understandings of motherhood and separation, etc.

How you will group and present the material is a decision you will have to make, shaped by what you see to be the relevant trends in the literature; this is not a set formula. It would, however, be usual for the literature review to move from the more general material, highlighting areas where knowledge is developed or lacking, taking the reader logically to the more specific topic (also known as 'funnelling'), and then to the research question.

An important point to make is that we have been talking about the literature review and the steps to a good review as though this is a linear process. You will probably have already discovered by now that this is not the case. You may find that in your identification stage you generated too much information and perhaps needed to refine your topic and search again before reviewing any of the literature. As noted above, you may also find that the deciding and reviewing processes are simultaneous.

Getting to the research question: drawing conclusions from the literature review

As discussed at the outset of this chapter, the main purpose of the literature review is to inform and shape the research question, by identifying 'gaps, niches, disputes, blank and blind spots' (Thomson, 2013, para. 8).

By this stage of the literature review, you will have developed an educated opinion about the 'landscape' of your topic. You can use these observations and conclusions to help you to formulate your research question.

Remember, this is not a process of trying to find 'the' research question hidden in the literature. In any topic area, there are many gaps and areas needing attention. Where you place your focus will be shaped by your analysis of existing knowledge and gaps, your epistemological position and what interests you, as well as your context – organisational or academic – and the overall purpose of the research (i.e. what we need to know).

Social work practitioner researchers at a health service

Do lit review and then your question comes – hard to know what's there, so begin with the broader area, do the lit review and then the question appears ...

The lit review helped to refine my question ...

Our questions became shorter and clearer as we got going ...

I changed my question after talking with my manager – I wanted something that worked for the team.

Particularly if you are working in a team environment, you may find that your research question develops over time, often in response to issues arising in the work context.

We suggest wording your research question simply and specifically, being clear about whether you are seeking to *explore* a new issue, *describe* in detail a problem or need or to *explain* an outcome. These three types of questions correspond to the three underpinning research designs in social work and social care, which we will discuss in the next chapter.

Your research question will contain a number of key terms, for which you will need to provide relevant definitions (you will recall we discussed the challenges of consistent definitions above).

Definitions both limit the scope of your work and make it comparable to others. To ensure that your research makes a meaningful contribution by being reliable and comparable to others, your definitions should be informed by previous research or theory or current legal/policy definitions.

Once you have drafted your research question/s you can compare it to the FINER (Feasible, Interesting, Novel, Ethical, Relevant) checklist, developed some years ago in the field of epidemiology by Cummings et al. (1988).[2] This requires you to balance thinking back on your literature review and forward to how you could answer the research question.

---

[2]These ideas have been developed subsequently by a range of other authors and applied in social science research: Alston and Bowles (2012), D'Cruz and Jones (2004), Williams et al. (1995).

Feasible (is the question answerable?)

- Are there data available?
- Do you have the necessary resources? What resources were needed by/useful to previous researchers?
- What have been the methodological challenges noted by others to answering similar research questions?

Interesting

- To what extent are you interested in and motivated by this topic and making use of the findings?

Novel

- How does this research question generate new knowledge?
- What does it add? (How does it build from/compare to previous research?)

Ethical

- Has your review of the literature demonstrated a need for this research question and study?
- How can the research question be answered ethically?
- Does your research question impose an undue burden on participants, or does it exclude participants?

Relevant

- Does the research question respond to knowledge needs identified in the literature review?
- Does the research question respond to an issue of concern to the profession, practice or policy?

Chapter summary

This chapter has covered the content and process of a literature review. We have outlined key skills required in both the reading and writing stages to get you to a well-informed research question. And now you are armed with a do-able research question, we will move in the next chapter to describing how you build on this review to develop an appropriate research design.

Key take-home messages

You can't develop an ethically and methodologically responsive research question and study without a solid, well-informed literature review. Conducting the review is an iterative process; you will engage critically with the existing literature, asking questions and assessing quality and applicability.

A good litmus test is to ask yourself at the conclusion of the literature review:

From my reading of the existing research, is there sound and ethically obtained evidence to suggest that this is an important and relevant issue for the profession that warrants investigation in the way I propose?

Additional resources

Aveyard, H. (2010) *Doing a Literature Review in Health and Social Care. A Practical Guide* (2nd edn). Milton Keynes: Open University Press/McGraw-Hill. This is a short, accessible and readily available text book that makes the literature review seem do-able!

Jesson, J.K., Matheson, L. and Lacey, F.M. (2011) *Doing Your Literature Review. Traditional and Systematic Techniques.* Thousand Oaks, CA: Sage. This is an excellent and comprehensive book, which is easy and enjoyable to read. The chapter on reading skills is particularly useful when getting started on your literature review.

Talbot, L. and Verrinder, G. (2008) 'Turn a stack of papers into a literature review: useful tools for beginners'. *Focus on Health Professional Education: A Multi-disciplinary Journal*, 10 (1): 51–8. This article is most helpful for those just starting out writing the literature review. It provides a clear and simple process, using visual strategies, to help you to identify core concepts in what you read and to map these patterns in your review.

You will also find a template for summarising and reviewing research at the end of Part II in our 'Toolkit'.

PART II
Doing Research

5

Research Design

Shaping Your Study

In this chapter you will learn

- How to design a research project
- The key features of the main research designs: exploratory, descriptive and explanatory
- The differences between research designs
- How research design shapes the next steps in your research.

Introduction

In this chapter, research design is presented as the structure that will help you to build your study, so you can respond effectively to the problem with which you are confronted. As we talked about in Chapter 1, research in social work and social care covers a wide spectrum, including: assessing needs/need for services; obtaining feedback from service users; using research to develop and evaluate programmes/services; engaging practitioners in reflection in and on practice and making practice change; as well as engaging with the consumer voice. As you can see from this list, all of these are outcome focused, and arguably pragmatic. They seek 'useful evidence for social workers needing to make informed decisions in practice' (Plath, 2012: 235) and aim to 'produce positive change in the world' (Bishop, 2015: 7), drawing on a range of understandings and experiences of that world.

The focus of this chapter is a very practical one: it aims to make sure that the study you develop generates the knowledge you need to answer the research question you ask, and that you choose the most appropriate approach and tools so that the study aims are met.

As Evans and Hardy (2010: 91) argue, from a pragmatic perspective, '[w]hat matters is that the research design and method adopted are suitable and feasible to answer the question at hand'. Although we will introduce a range of data collection methods in this chapter, we will address these specifically in the following three chapters. We will spend a bit of time on terminology, largely because it is an area of considerable variation and confusion (we will aim to be clear and consistent!). The bulk of the chapter is spent on describing the range of research designs and how these will shape your methodological decisions. We provide a detailed example for each research design to illustrate the most important concepts.

Research design: shaping the next steps in your study

Firstly, be aware, if you aren't already, that you will see many definitions and iterations of this term 'research design'; at its most basic, research design simply means the chosen framework or 'blue-print' for the study you will conduct. As discussed in Chapter 2, all of us bring particular paradigms to our research. We are in agreement with Morgan (2014: 1045) however, that although 'there may be an affinity between paradigms and methods ... there is no deterministic link that forces the use of a particular paradigm with a particular set of methods'. Our pragmatic perspective encourages plurality: matching and 'mixing' methods to the needs of the problem. So, why do you need to care about research design specifically? Quite simply because it is the 'coat-hanger' upon which all of your subsequent decisions must hang. Your 'design' will influence the aims and outcomes of your study, who or where you seek your data, what type of data, and how you collect and analyse them (see Figure 5.1). Being clear about your research design is fundamental to setting up and carrying out a good study.

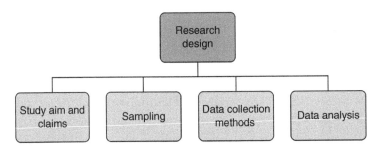

Figure 5.1   Research design: shaping methodological decisions

Firstly, however, to give you some idea of the range of ways of thinking about this concept, Figure 5.2 shows a selection of research design *typologies* (this just means ways of grouping things). As you can see, all of the typologies presented vary in how they cluster the different types of research. We are in agreement with D'Cruz and Jones' (2004: 84) reflection here that:

[a] little confusingly, the term 'research design' is used in slightly different ways ... but that research design can be thought of as providing a bridge between conceptualising and operationalising research. It becomes a means of defining what will be done in order to answer the research question.

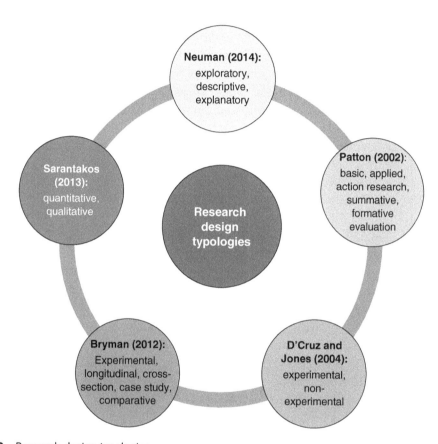

Figure 5.2   Research design typologies

Our chosen approach is that most recently described by Neuman (2014: 38), which suggests that any and all research can be grouped into one of three possible purposes, seeking to either: 'explore a new topic, describe a social phenomenon, or explain why something occurs' (you will recall at the end of Chapter 4 we suggested wording your research question to suit one of these purposes). Hopefully it is clear that in this approach, practical application and consequences of the research are key concerns.

Have you heard of any of these typologies before?

Do any of these 'fit' with your thinking about research? (Why?)

The reason for choosing Neuman's (2014) typology over others is that we believe it fits best with our chosen *pragmatic* approach. This should be a familiar term to you by now. We introduced this concept and discussed its connection to social work and social care research in Chapter 1; where such research is shaped by a specific value base and theoretical understanding of the world (McDermott, 1996) and 'implies action, pursues social justice and collects systematic information in order to make a difference in people's lives' (Alston and Bowles, 2012: 9); you will also remember that we have continued to make reference to this idea in subsequent chapters. Neuman's (2014) typology holds that inquiry and research decisions must be driven by purpose: by the presenting needs of the problem you are investigating. Does the situation need exploration, description or explanation? This indicates an understanding of the context-bound nature of problems, inquiry and findings; we need a range of designs to investigate different problems experienced by diverse groups in varied contexts, at different stages of knowledge development. Feasibility is a core issue. As noted above, this typology brings an assumption of the practical application and consequences of research. It does not divide inquiry into basic (also called theoretical or pure research) and applied (or practical) research. Our chosen typology is not shaped by paradigmatic allegiances (Patton, 2015), or dogmatism (Brewer and Hunter, 2006). Consequently, it does not dichotomise research into being either quantitative or qualitative. This is an important distinction, as it implies, from a pragmatic perspective, that all research can draw from quantitative and/or qualitative methods and data as appropriate to the research question and the study needs. You will see that in this book we do not group research by 'quantitative', 'qualitative' or 'mixed' methods. It is the problem you are seeking to understand through research, and the subsequent research design, which shapes the methods you choose. Please note, not all researchers would agree with this approach, but we find it the most useful and the simplest. Pluralism (using a variety of methods) means that we are better able to respond to presenting problems in the social world that from a pragmatic position are 'continually presenting us with ambiguities and complexities, confusions and contradictions' (James, 1907/1975: 17–18, cited in Borden, 2013: 261).

This approach, therefore, bridges the divide between realism and constructionism (you will recall we discussed in Chapter 1 this position that the world exists, but there will be different ways of experiencing and knowing about this). In this typology, all research is about practical application, with a theoretical and political purpose. As will become clear in our discussion below, this typology is based on an interactive and developmental view of knowledge, that research must build from an exploratory foundation to more sophisticated levels. This typology also covers all possible research, and importantly, each design type is mutually exclusive (this means less confusion for you as the researcher!).

To give this discussion some context, this framework builds on that originally proposed by Finestone and Kahn (1975), during a time when shifts towards empirical practice were beginning to take place. These developments sought to bring a stronger research orientation to practice, and specifically sought simpler research approaches that would fit better with social work practice. What Finestone and Kahn (1975) proposed was that social work research needed to capture a wide range of experiences and hence must encompass many different types of research methods. Although not described as such, this approach, prioritising research that was contextually responsive, grounded in practice and focused on consequences, was clearly influenced by pragmatist philosophy. They therefore proposed a model which involved a hierarchy of research designs. This was a clear challenge to the then-dominant psychological approach, which relied on experiments as the sole design type. Importantly these authors argued that social work research must start from the problem selected and that the design must be shaped by the nature of what we do or do not know about it, and what we need to know. As you can see from Table 5.1, this resulted in a hierarchical framework, reflecting what Finestone and Kahn (1975) saw to be the four different aims of research. This has been developed by later scholars, including Tripodi (1985), who sought to specifically emphasise the consequences of each design, in terms of what knowledge was developed, and most recently by Neuman (2014), who has simplified this to the three 'levels' outlined earlier.

Table 5.1 Research design developments over time

Finestone and Kahn (1975) Research design – aims	Tripodi (1985) Research design – knowledge objectives	Neuman (2014)
Exploratory	Hypothetical–developmental	Exploratory
Descriptive	Quantitative–descriptive	Descriptive
Explanatory	Associational	Explanatory
Experimental	Cause–effect	

As can be seen in Table 5.1 this typology sees knowledge as building from foundational to more sophisticated levels. It is important to remember, however, that this does not imply that any one design is better than another, simply that different problems require diverse responses, and that different designs will be a more appropriate 'fit' with these. As is evident, this typology has both stood the test of time, but not remained static. It provides a broad underpinning framework for the wide range of practice-oriented research we do.

You may well be asking 'what does this mean for me?' How can I use this?

Your design is the framework that provides the study's structure: as indicated in Figure 5.1, each design level will lead to different options (or requirements) with regard to the aims (and later claims) of the study, the sampling strategies, as well as how we collect and analyse our data. It provides us with the 'rules' or boundaries within which we need to work; this is very useful when dealing with the messiness of research in the real world of social work and social care. The key message is that the way you construct your study has to fit with the problem identified, the knowledge needs of that problem and subsequent purpose of the study.

We will now outline the three research designs: exploratory, descriptive and explanatory. For each design we will describe what they entail in relation to the three key areas noted: aim, sampling and methods, as well as outlining when each design is appropriate. We will make brief comments about data analysis, but this is covered in specific detail in Chapters 10 and 11. A detailed case example will accompany each to illustrate the key points of learning.

Exploratory research

Exploratory research, as the name suggests, is used when there is little prior research in the area, and you are starting out on the knowledge journey. Unsurprisingly then, your research question will likely be at the 'loose' end of the research continuum – with the specific study focus emerging as you progress (Punch 1998, cited in D'Cruz and Jones, 2004).

Aim: Research at this level aims to discover knowledge about an issue, to gain initial insights or clarifications, and to test whether or not any propositions or hunches you may have, have any merit. Exploratory research simply seeks to identify factors or variables that are key to the research problem or phenomenon, not test or measure these.

Data source – sample (this concept is covered in detail in Chapter 6, but for a brief explanation, see comments from Susan in our chorus): Data collection in exploratory studies is typically small scale and in-depth, often drawing on 'expert' sources of data (e.g. people who have direct or lived experience of the issue you are concerned about, for example, caring for those with dementia, youth homelessness or the refugee experience, etc.). As the focus in an exploratory study is on gathering initial data to establish the groundwork for future, more sophisticated (or rigorous) research, the sample does *not* need to be *representative* (that is, most like the population in make-up and therefore an accurate reflection of the population from which it is drawn); you are seeking to say the first word, not the last word. Flexibility with regard to sampling is the norm at this level of design. You will see this written about as '*non-probability*' sampling – see our discussion in the next chapter.

Methods: Flexibility is a key component here too – in new and emerging areas of research, expect the unexpected. Punch (1998, cited in D'Cruz and Jones, 2004) describes this as the

Susan, PhD student

'When we sample, we select some cases to examine in detail, and then we use what we learn from them to understand a much larger set of cases' (Neuman, 2014: 246).

My study looks at the experiences of psychological distress in older prisoners (who are a rapidly growing group in prisons). In setting up the study I knew I wouldn't be able to speak to all older prisoners, which would have been thousands! So I chose eight prisons which released the highest number of older prisoners in my catchment area, and made sure that I got participants from both male and female prisons, from a range of security settings and with both public and private prisons. I got 173 participants. Because I wanted to be able to make comments about distress with regard to ageing in prison, I also recruited a smaller sample of 60 younger prisoners. I will then be able to draw some conclusions (with limitations of course) about older prisoners more generally.

research process unfolding. Being able to adapt and amend research strategies (e.g. your data source, sample, approach to sampling or how you collect your data) is important when unanticipated issues arise. Qualitative data and methods are most common with this design given the typically holistic and knowledge development focus.

Common methods used in exploratory designs include: interviews, focus groups, visual images, etc. (we will discuss these methods in Chapters 7 and 9). Data analysis tends to be more basic and flexible. We will discuss approaches for qualitative data in Chapter 10 and quantitative data in Chapter 11.

Case study

Exploratory design: case example

My people: Exploring the experiences of gay, lesbian, bisexual, transgender and intersex seniors in aged care services.

Aim: This was a research area with little formal knowledge, but considerable historical knowledge and context with regard to discrimination more generally. It was considered an important area to examine because of human rights imperatives and to ensure responsiveness in aged care as Australia's population ages. This study was initiated in response to anecdotal reports to community organisations about discrimination being experienced by sexual minority groups in aged care. The study therefore sought to begin to understand and describe the aged care experiences of this group of people.

Data source – sample: Researchers wanted to engage with and gather data directly from LGBTI aged care service users, but were aware that this would be difficult as potential participants were likely to be quite hidden (closeted) because of their past experiences of discrimination. Because of challenges in recruiting, they expanded their data source to also include carers, friends and service providers, succeeding finally in recruiting a total of 25 participants (some of you who are used to more quantitative research might see this as a very small sample, but it is reasonable for an exploratory study). Researchers reflected on the challenges of recruiting in this area, and the impact of fear and the perceived implications of participation; they report no participation from individuals who identified as intersex and a limited number of lesbian women.

Methods: Participants were interviewed three or four times each, using a *semi-structured interview schedule* (we discuss this method in Chapter 7, but for some introductory comments, see comments from Paula in our chorus) with a 'checklist' of general topic areas, including both positive and negative experiences of aged care, and their self-defined needs as a GLBTI senior. This approach allowed the researchers to gather rich, in-depth qualitative data, capturing participants' experiences, feelings, observations and suggestions.

This material pointed to some clear initial findings about the impact of historical discrimination. Participants described continuing to conceal their identities, with their true needs then being invisible. Flow-on effects were noted to be unmet needs, increased stress, and a likely lack of awareness amongst service providers.

(Continued)

(Continued)

These initial findings were framed as the first step in building knowledge in this area, designed to shape later research into service provider knowledge and provisions. This research has contributed to the development of a self-assessment audit tool for aged care services in relation to GLBTI responsive aged care.

Barrett (2008) *My people: Exploring the experiences of gay, lesbian, bisexual, transgender and intersex seniors in aged care services.* Melbourne: Matrix Guild Victoria Inc. and Vintage Men Inc. (available at www.matrixguildvic.org.au/docs/MyPeople_Exploring-Experiences-2008.pdf).

Paula, PhD student

'Semi-structured interviews follow a set outline of topics with some pre-tested questions and prompts in each section. These are the triggers for the main direction of the interview … Thus the interviewer is allowed more initiative and has more ability to respond to the perceptions and priorities of the respondent' (Alston and Bowles, 2012: 142).

I am exploring Australian multiculturalism, by investigating the settlement experiences of African refugees. I interviewed a number of settlement support workers who had also completed an online survey.

I used the semi-structured interviews to further probe specific areas of resettlement identified in the survey, in ways which allowed the respondents to elaborate and explore ideas, in their own terms, describing what was most meaningful to them. This approach was important because these workers are the human face of the settlement system, who 'interpret' and enact policy with and for their clients.

Conducting exploratory research is common for beginning research students (you will recall we discussed Alexis' exploratory study of women's experiences of hospital treatment after miscarriage in Chapter 2). This is also a common approach in practitioner research, which tends to be smaller in nature, focused on particular programmes or service user groups, and focused on an individual's/team's practice (Mitchell et al., 2010; Shaw, 2005). Exploratory research has an important role to play in bringing attention to issues. Remember that you and other exploratory researchers are aiming to generate initial ideas and/or hypotheses for further examination, not to say the last word on your topic. On that note, research at an exploratory level does not need to be totally 'new' (completely unheard of!): it may be that aspects of the problem are unknown, perhaps in relation to a particular client group or in your geographical area or field of practice. See below for two examples.

 Case study

Responding to limitations in methodology or content

When Alexis conducted her study, there had already been considerable research investigating the consequences of miscarriage for women. This was typically quantitative – measuring women's psychological functioning and/or mental health – with some smaller more holistic studies of women's experiences. Little research had focused on women's views and experiences in hospitals, key sites of treatment, and none had been conducted in the local environment, hence her study was framed at an exploratory level.

Similarly, when Catherine conducted her research into the impact of maternal incarceration on adolescent children, there were many existing studies describing children of prisoners, but only a handful about adolescents, and none about adolescents in Australia – her research context (see Figure 3.2). So, her work was also framed as exploratory.

Both of these two studies highlighted issues for ongoing consideration and examination. Catherine's research drew attention to the difficulties which arise in planning children's care; this is an issue which has been the focus of subsequent collaborative research (e.g. see Flynn et al., 2015); while the concerns noted in Alexis' study have been picked up and commented on by other researchers examining miscarriage.

Exploratory design: summary

- Used when knowledge to date is limited, or where it is difficult to access (and knowledge development is slow or 'patchy')
- Because knowledge is limited, flexibility is necessary so as to be able to respond to likely changes in the research environment
- Aims to identify factors or issues and/or to test feasibility
- Sample size can be small and less rigorously generated as you are seeking specific and rich data from 'expert' sources
- Seeks to say the first word, not the last word; therefore, does not seek to generalise.

Descriptive research

Aim: Research at this level seeks to accurately describe the characteristics or qualities of a specific group, or '*population*', such as a study of 'the needs of homeless youth' (see Alannah's comments from the chorus for an example and some of the challenges). This is a relatively simple design, and you do not need to have extensive knowledge on which to base your study. You typically do, however, need to have at least some exploratory findings as your foundation. A descriptive study might attempt to build on and seek more extensive understanding of the issues highlighted in exploratory research, such as the study by Barrett (2008) described above. For example, a descriptive study of aged care service providers may seek to map provider/staff understanding of the issues that were identified in the exploratory study: measuring staff awareness of GLBTI residents and their needs, as well as their knowledge of the consequences of invisibility, etc. Descriptive research can be differentiated from exploratory research in a number of ways, related to sampling particularly, but also the most common methods used.

Data source – sample: As research of a descriptive design seeks to give an accurate account, or a profile, of a particular population or phenomenon, the sampling strategy/ies implemented must be rigorous, obtaining a sample that is representative of your study population. We will discuss the range of possible sampling strategies in the next chapter – but representativeness is most commonly achieved by *probability sampling* (see Chapter 6 for a detailed discussion). You must be rigorous about sampling because this design is about measuring and describing, and if you do not sample carefully your results are unlikely to reflect the population you want to describe. A good understanding of the study population is necessary at this level of design. The ability to do this, however, may be shaped by a number of factors, some beyond your control.

For example, while the population of older people receiving aged care services is known (and can be counted), the willingness of older people of diverse sexual orientations and gender identities to self-identify will affect the researchers' ability to have a firm grasp on this specific population and achieve a representative sample (this was evident in the exploratory study discussed above). You will see that this is also evident in the example about Alannah's study. The boundaries around a population may also be a little unclear because of different understandings of the issue or differing definitions, for example, homelessness – would this include unstable or unsafe housing or only those who had no 'roof'? As researchers we always need to be clear about the definitions we are using, already discussed in Chapter 4, with regard to research questions.

Methods: Given that the aim is to describe accurately, researchers need to be able to gather comparable data from participants or sources. This typically means an emphasis on quantitative methods, including structured interviews, questionnaires, validated scales or checklists, or 'mining' existing data sources (we describe and discuss these methods in detail in Chapter 7), seeking yes/no or scaled answers or short responses. Another outcome of needing to accurately describe is that although this design is relatively easy to develop and implement, and is quite a common research design in social work and social care, it is not flexible. It means that you need to have a 'well-developed idea about a social phenomenon' (Neuman, 2014: 38) as a solid foundation and be clear about your study population, boundaries, sample, definitions and variables at the outset; you will not be able to change these (however, if you find along the way that you have missed something, you may be able to acknowledge this as a limitation of the study – we all have them!). See Chapter 11 for a discussion of working with quantitative data and descriptive statistics (common with descriptive designs) and Chapter 10 for a description of methods to 'map' and quantify qualitative data.

Alannah, PhD student

Because I am investigating the experiences of mothers with mental illness coming into prison, my *population* of interest is imprisoned mothers with a mental illness.

But, this is not a known or set population for a number of reasons: there is no 'list' of such mothers at any given time; people move in and out of the prison system regularly; there may be mothers in prison who have an unacknowledged or undiagnosed mental illness; and women may see themselves as currently 'well' and not subscribe to the label. So, this population is likely quite fluid and changeable. So I had to redefine my population: mothers in prison with a self-reported mental illness.

Case study

Descriptive design: case example

'Study of reported rapes in Victoria: 2000–2003'

Aim: Violence against women, including sexual assault, is a global concern. It is well known that these crimes tend to go under-reported and remain hidden. Exploratory findings have indicated that the experience of reporting to police and the subsequent responses may be largely negative, and many women are thought to withdraw their complaints. The aim of this study was to build on this existing knowledge, to examine and describe the factors which influence the outcome of rape investigations. The researchers were especially interested in the factors present when victims withdraw complaints or where the police do not proceed with the investigation. Researchers were clear at the outset, however, that this was not a study of rape, but of reported rapes.

Data source – sample: To meet this aim the researchers chose 850 cases randomly from the 2902 cases recorded on the Law Enforcement and Assistance Program (LEAP) database held by police in the state of Victoria, Australia, during 2000-2003. This database holds information about all offences brought to police attention in that jurisdiction and was the only statewide source of data on reported rapes. To ensure that the cases selected (the sample) were representative of the state's population across city and country areas, the sample was weighted (or 'stratified') so that each of the 23 police divisions was represented.

Methods: This method of 'mining' of existing incident records and associated case narratives allowed researchers to access details about the victim, the alleged offender, the nature of the offence, actions and outcomes, and sought both quantitative and qualitative data (i.e. numbers and demographics, as well as the observations and interpretations of police officers). These data, collected over an extended period, avoided problems associated with short-term data collection (e.g. technical problems such as the database being 'down', or seasonal fluctuations in patterns of offending such as the rate of assault being higher in the summer months). However, there were limitations: not all cases were recorded on this system, with researchers unable to say which cases were not recorded or why, and those cases that were recorded were also not recorded in a consistent or systematic manner.

Findings indicated some interesting and concerning trends. Police investigations did not proceed in more than 60% of cases, with only 15% of complaints ultimately prosecuted; just 2% were deemed to be false allegations. Those victims who were most likely to see charges laid included men, those who were not substance-affected at the time of the assault, and those who suffered a physical injury. While victims who were younger, had consumed alcohol or drugs and had even a cursory relationship with the alleged offender were most likely to see no further action from the police.

It is important to note that these data are descriptive: while the researchers may have some hypotheses about why these trends occurred, strong claims on the basis of these findings cannot be made. It is also important to note that the study can say nothing about any groups who may not engage with the police at all. What is clear, however, is that the outcomes of reporting sexual assault to the police show considerable variation according to particular demographic characteristics and circumstances. 'These findings provide Victoria Police with a strong evidence base regarding the case characteristics and case outcomes of reported rapes, and will be considered in improvements to its response to victims of sexual assault' (Heenan and Murray, 2006: 2).

The next step in research would seem to be to investigate how victim or offence characteristics and police attitudes intersect, to understand how and why these outcomes vary.

Heenan and Murray (2006) 'Study of reported rapes in Victoria, 2000-2003'. www.ncjrs.gov/app/abstractdb/AbstractDBDetails.aspx?id=243182.

Descriptive design: summary

- Aims at identifying in detail the characteristics of population/phenomenon
- Design is rigorous in terms of population and sample
- Needs some foundational knowledge – evident in the researchers' ability to clearly define the phenomenon and gather specific ('tight') data
- Cannot claim to be able to say 'why' a pattern may occur.

Descriptive designs can be really useful in direct practice settings. As social work and social care practitioners, we often have clear study populations to draw from, and about whom we are concerned. You may want to assess the changing needs of your client group or to survey their experiences of your service. You may simply want to generate a clear picture of who your service user group are by using your existing case records. This sort of knowledge, an accurate 'picture' of client needs, experiences, outcomes, is really useful when you have to demonstrate what you do and who you do this with, and what their needs are, for funders or for the broader organisation.

Explanatory research

At the final, more sophisticated, level of design, we have *explanatory* research, which is used to discover and explain relationships between variables. With this type of research, you will be positioned at the 'tight' end of the research continuum (Punch, 1998, cited in D'Cruz and Jones, 2004) with a greater degree of specificity in your research question and in your overall approach. Explanatory research is made up of two sub-sets: evaluations, and experiments (including quasi-experiments). Whilst both of these approaches focus on uncovering relationships, it is only experimental research that can establish *causation* (when one variable causes changes in another), whilst evaluation shows *correlation* (when variables co-occur). In social work and social care, it is much more common to conduct evaluations, although quasi-experimental research is becoming more popular.

Evaluation

Aim: Research at this level aims to understand the relationship between fixed factors, which are not manipulated by the researcher; for example, the impact on men's violent behaviour as a result of attending a men's behaviour change programme. Bryman (2012) describes the key focus here as being on real life interventions in the social world.

Data source – sample: It is important that the sample you select for your evaluation is representative of the study population, so that your findings about the impact or effectiveness of a particular programme are relevant and accurate (you would not want staff to hand-pick those in a men's behaviour change programme who have been doing really well as the participants (data source) for an evaluation of the effectiveness of the programme – the findings would be clearly skewed!). Evaluation is a design we find is able to be implemented quite easily – it is a feasible design and one which suits human service organisations' purposes of learning more about the effects of the interventions they are offering.

Methods: *Surveys* (also called questionnaires) are common at this level of design, allowing the collection of accurate and comparable data, but they are often used as one of a number of data collection instruments. For example, a researcher might survey the staff and clients who participated in the above-mentioned men's programme, but also use other methods of data collection, such as using *validated scales* (a standardised series of questions that identify and quantify particular characteristics or sets of characteristics, e.g. there are scales to measure such things as psychological distress and depression); document analysis of case records; alongside focus groups and interviews (we will discuss these data collection methods in the upcoming chapters). One area that needs close attention in programme evaluation is clear agreement about how you will define the indicators of programme goal achievement. For example, in an evaluation of a community-based support programme for families with high-risk infants, one of the core indicators of programme success was that the infant would be 'living safely at home'. A number of challenges are evident in this goal. What is 'safe'? What would be defined as 'living at home'? (Shared care, weekend access?) These were issues debated by the research team, the programme staff and the study's advisory committee before the commencement of the study, with agreement that 'living safely at home' would mean that the child was cared for in the family home by his or her primary caregivers the majority of the time; 'safely' did not preclude child protection intervention, if it allowed the child to remain in the family home. Evaluations often involve analysing data for relationships or associations; we discuss this in Chapter 11.

 ## Case study

Explanatory design – evaluation: case example

'Moving from dependence to independence: a study of the experiences of 18 care leavers in a leaving care and after care support service in Victoria'

Aim: There is considerable evidence that describes the circumstances of young people exiting from Out of Home Care (OOHC); unfortunately an extensive range of problems are indicated, including homelessness, mental health, etc. St. Lukes is a non-government organisation in Victoria, Australia, which provides a range of OOHC and child welfare services. In 2003 they introduced the Leaving Care and After Care Support Service (LCACSS), providing housing, family and living skills services to young people, and later introducing employment support and mentoring, to address identified problems in employment, social inclusion and connectedness. The organisation wanted to know if the programmes assisted young people leaving out of home care to transition to independence, to what extent, and how.

Data source – sample: All data were sourced from young people who had accessed either the employment and/or mentoring programmes. All young people approached agreed to participate in the research. It is important to note that in the field of OOHC research, there has been considerable commitment to ensuring that young people are actively engaged in this process and have a considerable 'voice'.

Methods: Eighteen young people were interviewed and provided self-reported data on their functioning in key areas: housing, health, mental illness, legal issues, family relationships, employment, etc. Interviews were conducted at the conclusion of the programme and 12 months later – to assess if the trends described initially had been sustained.

The findings indicate that although the housing, employment and mentoring programmes have a positive impact on the lives of young people, for those with additional needs/challenges, the transition to independent living is more difficult. The need for specialised support services in areas such as parenting was indicated.

(Continued)

(Continued)

While the study clearly provides the young people's perspectives, the findings about programme effectiveness could have been strengthened with additional data, perhaps agency records about the continuation/cessation of mentoring relationships, or the mentor's assessment of the relationship and outcomes; or concrete ('objective') measures such as the obtaining and sustaining of employment, housing, etc.

Mendes (2010) 'Moving from dependence to independence: a study of the experiences of 18 care leavers in a leaving care and after care support service in Victoria', *Children Australia*, 35 (1): 14-21. (NB this article only reports on data from the first of two rounds of interviews.)

Quasi-experimental and experimental

Experimental and quasi-experimental designs aim to test a hypothesis about a specific relationship between variables; they seek to answer 'why' questions.

Aim: To evaluate a specific cause–effect relationship based on a *hypothesis* (a proposed explanation). This design is most appropriate when there is already considerable knowledge on the problem available to the researcher. You need this level of knowledge to construct a suitable and specific hypothesis. For example, building on the findings from Mendes (2010) above, you might develop (hypothetically in this case!) a hypothesis as to why the transition from OOHC to independent living is more difficult for young people with disabilities. Let's say, for example, that the findings indicate that this group of young people, because of their additional needs, struggle to interact effectively with an increased number of service systems. You might hypothesise that offering specific case management support to negotiate and manage these systems would be helpful. You would then implement such a strategy and measure the outcomes for a group of young people who receive this new service compared to those who don't (it is definitely not really that simple, but more on the methods below). You may have also seen this design referred to as a *randomised controlled trial* or *RCT* (where people are randomly assigned to the treatment being studied). Experiments are often referred to as the 'gold standard' (i.e. best, or most rigorous) study design. While they are common in health/clinical settings, they are least common in social work and social care research.

Data source – sample: Rigorous sampling from the study population is needed to ensure strong findings that reflect the wider population. Given that it is usually not possible to include all the relevant or eligible people in the experiment (though it sometimes is achievable when working with small client-based populations, such as all of those eligible for a particular service), the researcher selects a sample from the total population to create the *experimental* group (those who get the specified intervention) and the *control* group (those who do not get the intervention). Neuman (2014) explains the importance of *random assignment* (allocating participants to each group on a mechanical basis, ensuring that each participant has an equal chance of being in either group) as lying in the researchers' confidence that the groups being compared really are comparable, and do not differ on important characteristics, which may influence the outcome. This process controls for both participant and researcher bias (e.g. individuals with specific characteristics may 'sign up' for a particular intervention influencing the outcomes, or workers/researchers may be more inclined to put those most likely to do well into an experimental group, etc.).

Methods: The over-arching 'method' of experiments is the manipulation of specific variables; typically this involves providing some type of intervention or service to a specified group. As indicated above, experiments use an 'experimental' group and a 'control' group. This allows researchers to assess the impact of the intervention and to be able to compare the outcomes with those of a comparative group.

You will recall we mentioned quasi-experimental designs above. Where pure experiments and quasi-experiments differ is in the make-up of these two study groups. Quasi-experimental research does not require random assignment, and therefore typically uses a 'comparison' group rather than a control group. This approach is more common among social work and social care researchers. It allows for some comparative data but avoids the ethical concerns that go along with randomly allocating people to a service or treatment (and hence randomly denying people access to a service). Another approach might be to give the intervention to the control group at the conclusion of data collection, so the people randomly assigned (or just assigned) to the control group are not denied a service. See, for example, Crowe et al. (2015), who looked at the impact of a group education session on knowledge of and attitudes to advanced care. A further strategy could be that the 'comparison' group is not simply offered nothing: they may be offered usual 'best practice'. If we continue with the example above about young people with disabilities leaving OOHC, this may involve offering young people with disabilities in the comparison group the usual LCACSS services.

Researchers typically seek to 'match' this comparison group to the experimental group on key characteristics relevant to the study. Using the same example again, we might want to match our groups on gender, type of disability and age, as well as other features. Or researchers may construct a comparison group, for example, from a waiting list for their service. This matching seeks to minimise the influence of these other characteristics on the study outcomes. However, considerable research at this level allows participants to voluntarily 'sign up' to an intervention or comparison group. There are clearly limitations then on what can be claimed from the findings, as researchers cannot be certain that any differences in the outcomes are the result of the intervention or some other intervening variable. Data analyses most used with this study design are covered in Chapter 11.

 ## Case study

Explanatory design – experimental: case example

'Long-term mother and child mental health effects of a population-based infant sleep intervention: cluster-randomised, controlled trial'

> *Aims*: This study was built on considerable existing research knowledge that (1) maternal depression is a risk factor for adverse child development and (2) infant sleep problems commonly co-occur with maternal post-natal depression. The researchers therefore sought to investigate the long-term impact of an intervention for infant sleep problems on maternal depression and parenting style, as well as on child mental health and sleep.

(Continued)

(Continued)

Data source – sample: Forty-nine Maternal and Child Health (MCH) centres from six socio-economically diverse local government areas were selected. Nine hundred and eighty-two mothers, with babies born during June–July 2003, attended the free 4-month infant 'check-up'; 782 expressed interest in the study. Three months later, 328 mothers reported an infant sleep problem and were recruited into the study. This overall sample was then divided into two groups: a treatment group (174 families), who received a small number of sessions from a MCH nurse trained in a specific behavioural approach to infant sleep problems, and a control group (154 families), who received 'usual care'.

Methods: Researchers compared the control families, who received usual care, with the treatment families, who were provided with the brief behaviour-modification intervention, targeting infant sleep problems. The noted limitations were the exclusion at the 4-month check by MCH nurses of (1) those mothers whose English language skills were seen to be insufficient to complete a questionnaire and (2) babies born at less than 32 weeks' gestation.

At follow up, when children were 2 years of age, a range of measures were taken: maternal depression symptoms; parenting practices; child mental health; and maternal report of a child's sleep problem. Findings indicated that mothers in the treatment group were less likely than those in the control group to report depressive symptoms. Slightly fewer children in the treatment group were reported by their mothers to have a sleep problem than the control group. However, parenting style and child mental health were reported to be similar across both groups. The researchers concluded that the intervention did no harm and may be useful for mothers. They planned a further 5 year follow up to examine the longer-term impact.

Hiscock, H., Bayer, J.K., Hampton, A., Ukoumunne, O.C. and Wake, M. (2008) 'Long-term mother and child mental health effects of a population-based infant sleep intervention: cluster-randomized, controlled trial', *Pediatrics*, 122 (3): 621-7.

Explanatory design: summary

- Existing knowledge must be high
- Aims at testing cause–effect relationships: this is strongest with experimental designs, because of the use of control groups, but quasi-experimental designs also seek to do this using a comparison group
- Rigorous sampling is needed
- Clear definitions are needed for variables and measurement.

To sum this up, choosing an appropriate level of research design is based on your assessment of the relevant context. This includes:

- Your prior knowledge of the issue. You need to consider if knowledge of the problem is basic/emerging or sophisticated. This has a clear impact on how specifically we can frame our research question (i.e. loose vs. tight), define variables and ask questions. As a rule of thumb, the less we know, the less specific we can be, and the more exploratory our study needs to be
- The aims or purpose of the study (do you need to explore, describe or explain?)
- Feasibility, for example, access to data (locating 'hidden' participants, the existence of reliable data), time and/or funding constraints, or funding conditions.

Chapter summary

This chapter has been the first of our methodologically focused chapters. It has emphasised research design as the practical foundation that underpins and shapes your research. Our chosen design typology (exploratory → descriptive → explanatory) was justified and linked to our pragmatic orientation: that all research should be driven by purpose with a view to practical application. We provided detailed case examples to explain key concepts.

What does this mean for you? Think about an area you are interested in researching: are you aiming to establish knowledge in this area, wondering how to describe this problem or situation accurately, or explaining the relationship between this issue and an intervention? What research design would be most appropriate for this area of research?

Key take-home messages

All research requires a rigorous approach.

Keep your research question and your study design at the forefront of your mind to guide your methodological decisions: it will ensure coherence throughout your study.

No research is perfect: be aware of and acknowledge the strengths and limitations of your chosen approach.

As outlined in Chapter 1, making use of a research journal and supervision will ensure that you keep these core issues in mind as you go about your research.

Additional resources

Finestone, S. and Kahn, A.J. (1975) 'The design of research', in N.A. Polansky (ed.), *Social Work Research*. Chicago, IL: University of Chicago Press, pp. 38–67. Although this is now an old chapter, the core message remains relevant and important: that research must be developed to meet the needs of the presenting problem.

Neuman, W.L. (2014) *Social Research Methods: Qualitative and Quantitative Approaches* (7th edn). Harlow: Pearson New International. His discussion of design follows a similar vein to Finestone and Kahn (1975). It is simple and clear.

Alasuutari, P., Bickman, L. and Brannen, J. (2008) *The Sage Handbook of Social Research Methods*. London: Sage. This resource, particularly Part II, provides some more detail about research design.

6

Selecting and Accessing Data

Ensuring Rigour

In this chapter you will learn

- Strategies for selecting and accessing data for your study: probability and non-probability sampling strategies
- How to develop a study which is methodologically rigorous
- A reflective exercise for reviewing progress on your study.

Introduction

This chapter builds closely on the previous one, which addresses research design – the practical framework for your study. We now give you some more specific information about accessing data and making sure your study is rigorous, before moving on to how to gather your data in the next three chapters. Again, our focus is a practical one.

We describe the basic division in sampling types: between probability and non-probability strategies, showing how and when each approach may be appropriate. Clear links are made to research design; we discuss sample size and make-up, as well as the implications for findings. Case examples are used to illustrate the various sampling methods, their strengths and weaknesses.

We then move onto strategies for ensuring methodological rigour in your study. In this chapter we compare 'conventional' strategies (reliability and validity – we discuss these in the chapter) with strategies that are more appropriate for what has been called *naturalistic research*

(research that takes place in the real world, not an artificially created setting; Patton, 2015). We end the chapter with a reflective exercise that encourages you to consider the ideas we have presented in the book so far and apply these if you are currently working on or planning a study.

Selecting and accessing data for your study

Once you are clear on both the aim and the real-world context of your proposed study, with a clear research design, a source/s of data needs to be identified. It may be self-evident, but as indicated above, in most studies, you will need to gather data from a selection of people (your *sample*) rather than from all people who have experienced the issue you are concerned with (your *population*), be that homelessness, family violence or a specific disability. Sampling, therefore, involves 'choosing who or what we wish to study in order to answer our research question' (Alston and Bowles, 2012: 87).

In this next section, we deal with both the logic and the logistics of accessing relevant data. A good place to start is by being clear about the differences between sampling and recruitment, two related, but different concepts. Sampling is a theoretical activity, selecting who/what you need to collect data from in order to meet the aims of your study; it must be informed by your study design. Recruitment is the practical activity of accessing potential participants, informing them about your study and inviting them to participate – sampling must shape your recruitment strategy.

O'Leary (2005: 78) says of sampling that 'you can't ask just anyone, and you certainly can't ask everyone'. This quote sums up sampling simply. It is about balancing *feasibility* (asking 'everyone' is unrealistic) and *rigour* (simply asking 'anyone' will be unlikely to generate the data you need). This quote also implies that sampling decisions involve more than deciding on the size of your sample. Hardwick and Worsley (2011) point out that we have to consider 'who' as well as 'how many' in our deliberations about 'who to ask'. We would also argue that in addition, there are ethical considerations when deciding on 'who'. As discussed in Chapter 3, this includes an awareness of power and inequality, as well as an understanding of the possible risk and unpredictability of the research environment and the possible burden to participants. Re-read this chapter if you need to remind yourself about some of the issues that need to be managed during this process.

Sampling

It is important that you understand that there are two main types of sampling, which we flagged in our discussion of research design in the previous chapter.

1. *Probability*: This strategy requires each and every one in the study population to have a known chance of being selected. You need this type of sampling with sophisticated research designs when you want to be able to claim that the results generated from your study's sample are reflective of

the broader population. It is generally accepted that this is the best strategy to employ if you need to obtain a representative sample.

2. *Non-probability*: This type of sample does not rely on all in the population having a known chance of being chosen; it is about creating a sample that is 'fit for purpose', seeking specific people or data. Understandably then, it is most commonly used in exploratory research.

You may have seen probability and non-probability sampling described in other text books as quantitative and qualitative sampling (e.g. see Alston and Bowles, 2012; Neuman, 2014). Our view however, shaped by a pragmatic approach, is that the sampling strategy you choose is more closely linked to your study design, that is, what you are aiming to achieve, as well as what is feasible.

These two broad sampling categories can then be broken down further, as you can see in Figure 6.1. This list is not exhaustive (and there are other texts that focus on this in more detail, for example, both Bryman (2012) and Neuman (2014) have excellent detailed discussions, as does Patton (2015: 266–72) – with a comprehensive comparative table). We focus here on what we have seen to be the most commonly used strategies in social work and social care research. We provide a brief description of each, with some comments about when each strategy may be most useful, as well as pointing out potential problems to look out for.

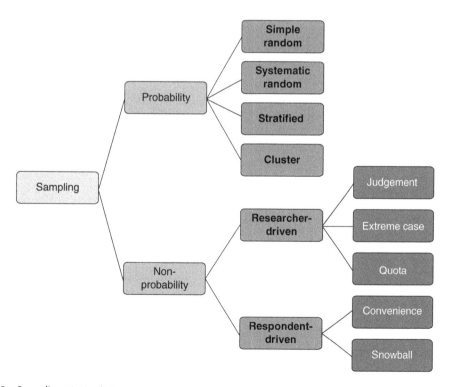

Figure 6.1 Sampling strategies

Probability sampling

As noted above, this is most often used when you need your sample to closely represent your population; hence it is used in more sophisticated study designs, typically explanatory, and descriptive. It is a powerful strategy to use in research when you want to make strong and definitive claims based on your findings.

Before we talk about some of the common approaches to probability sampling, here are some concepts and ideas that you will need to grasp when you are using this method. Firstly, it is important to understand that probability sampling is based on a mathematical concept called probability theory (Rubin and Babbie, 2013). Secondly, there will always be some error when you rely on data from a sample rather than a whole population. This is called *sampling error* and is the difference between the estimated population measure obtained via your sample and the actual population measure. The amount of sampling error is influenced by three factors:

1. *Confidence intervals* (CI) provide you with a margin of error for your quantitative results. For example, let's say you ask a random sample of adults from a population about their attitudes to violence against women, and you use a confidence interval of 5. If your survey results show that 60% of respondents are 'very concerned', you can be confident that somewhere between 55 and 65% (i.e. the finding from your sample of 60% +/– your confidence interval) of the entire population would have given that response.
2. *Confidence levels* (CL) indicate how certain you can be about the findings, for example, from your community survey. This figure simply shows *how often* the percentage of the population you identify will give a response within the confidence interval. Most studies use a 95% confidence level (it should be clear here that even with robust sampling methods, no research is perfect or absolutely precise).
3. *Sample size*: the *absolute size of the sample*, rather than the size of the sample in relation to its population, increases the precision of your findings with a random sample. For example, for a population of 4,000, where you want a CI of 5 and CL of 95%, you need a sample size of 351; but, to achieve the same CI and CL with a population of 4,000,000 you only need a sample size of 384 (there are useful online tools that can assist you in calculating the best (and most achievable) sample size for your study, see for example: www.surveysystem.com/sscalc.htm).

Any more detail about such statistical formulae and calculations is beyond the scope of this text, but is covered well in Rubin and Babbie (2011).

Now onto some of the more common types of probability sampling, which will be relevant to you in your travels as a social work and social care practitioner researcher.

Simple random sampling

This requires that all in your study population have an equal chance of being selected (please note, the word 'random' here does not mean in an unplanned way as it does in the general vernacular). Random sampling strategies include such things as where names are drawn out of a hat or are randomly generated by a computer program (here is a great online tool to help you to do this: www.psychicscience.org/random.aspx). To be able to obtain a simple random sample, you will first need to know and be able to put a clear boundary around your study population; this usually involves having some type of population 'list', this might be an electoral roll, a phone book, a class list or client database (this is also called the *sampling frame*). Simple random sampling is most useful when your study is seeking to access typical, rather than specialised knowledge, such as a survey of *community* attitudes to violence against women. However, this approach assumes that your study population has characteristics that are evenly spread and that a random selection of individuals will capture a representative range of views.

If we go back to the example just presented about a community survey on violence against women. Do you think that community views on this area are evenly spread? Might individual views on this be influenced by other characteristics or population sub-groups to which they belong? For example, is it possible that the level of education people have completed may have an influence on these views? And would a simple random sample necessarily capture participants from across the differing levels of educational achievement? (In situations like this, a better approach here would be stratified random sampling, which we discuss below.)

With simple random sampling you need to be rigorous about how you access your population. In recent years, telephone interviews have been common in large community surveys (you may have even participated in some – we certainly have!), with the sample typically obtained by randomly generated landline numbers. However, there are clearly changing patterns in telecommunication use; it is now thought that around 25% of the Australian adult population have no landline, and use only a mobile phone; there are unsurprising age variations with these trends. So, if you were to seek to complete your community survey about attitudes to violence against women and only rely on landlines, it is possible your results will not represent the actual views of the community, as you will likely miss one quarter of the population, who are likely to be younger (perhaps with some different views on the issue).

Systematic random sampling

This is based on the same basic principles as simple random sampling, but takes a systematic approach, for example, selecting every *n*th person from your population list, e.g. from a class list or a telephone directory. This approach is useful because it ensures that you sample from the entire breadth of your population. However, if there are patterns in the population list that are not easily seen, or if your list is ordered in some way, this can lead to bias and problems with your sample. Here are some examples to illustrate. If you use a phone book, there will be some names that occur far more frequently and that would therefore be selected more often. Or if your population list is ordered specifically as male/female/male … and you choose every 10th person, you would always choose a woman. Or if you were conducting a household survey, you would need to be mindful of the fact that odd and even numbered houses are on opposite sides of the street. You might be thinking 'so what?', but imagine it was a community satisfaction survey ('How happy are you in your community?'). See Catherine's example about the impact of something as simple as street numbering.

I live in a very hilly environment, where all even numbered houses are located on the 'low side' of the road. This also means that all even numbered houses have similar problems with water run-off into properties when it is very rainy, with subsequent flooding, etc. If I wanted to find out about living in my community and used an approach which systematically chose odd numbered houses, I am sure that this would not reflect the concerns of the breadth of the community.

Understanding how your population list is constructed and ordered is very important in deciding if you want to use this approach.

Stratified random sampling

This strategy, whilst again seeking a typical range of views, assumes that your study population is not homogenous and that researchers need to ensure that specific segments of the population are not missed. Dudley (2011: 147) specifically reminds us that as social work and social care researchers we need to be aware of diversity and social justice issues when sampling, particularly asking us to consider 'Which … characteristics could be easily overlooked?'. One way of addressing this is to use a stratified approach. The population is divided into separate (mutually exclusive) subgroups (also called *strata*); this may be by gender, cultural grouping, age or any factor deemed to be relevant to the study and the research question under investigation. A random selection is then drawn from each sub-group independently. Stratified samples can be *proportionate* (where the size of each subgroup reflects their proportion in the study population) or *disproportionate* (where the size of the sub-groups is not set in relation to the population). Your choice will be determined by the aims of your study. If you need your findings to accurately reflect the views of the population, then a proportionate approach would be best, whereas if your study is more concerned with comparing the views of the sub-groups, then disproportionate would be appropriate. See the case example below.

Bryman (2012) reminds us that you need to be practical when using this general approach: he suggests using this only if it is easy to identify and allocate units to each stratum. For example, you want to know about the outcomes of a housing support programme by reviewing a random sample of case files, but you have also been wondering if service user experiences and outcomes might vary based on cultural group. If you have gathered information about cultural identity from clients and recorded this in files, then you will be readily able to identify each group, and then draw a random sample from each separately. Without this information, a stratified sample would be extremely difficult.

The relevance and impact of stratified sampling can be illustrated by an example.

Case study

Uncovering sub-group trends

Disproportionate stratified sampling – uncovering trends in population sub-groups: Early studies of parents in prison in the 1960s suggested that the lives of their children were little affected, as the vast majority remained at home with their other parent. Whilst this was numerically accurate, it was based on a view of 'imprisoned parents' as a homogenous group, when in fact, what became evident was a clear gender difference that had been overlooked, largely because women are such a small group in the overall prison population (about 7%). When studies were done using disproportionate stratified sampling, with men and women sampled separately but equally, and compared, very clear differences in children's care arrangements became evident; indeed almost opposite patterns of care emerged, with children of mothers in prison being much more likely to move from the family home and to be cared for by people other than their parent.

Cluster random sampling

This approach draws on naturally occurring 'clusters' (such as cities, towns, social work courses, hospitals, etc.) and considers each cluster as the *sampling unit* (this just means what is considered the 'individual' in the sample). It also assumes that each cluster is reasonably similar. This approach is appropriate when you do not have knowledge/list of your population of interest, for example, all students enrolled in social work courses in Australia. In this instance, you would consider the schools of social work as your population and then draw a sample from this. You would need to be sure that these schools were homogenous (have similar student groups). Sampling could be done in a range of ways, depending on your knowledge of that population; it may be that you place schools into a strata based on geographic location, or perhaps by teaching mode, such as on or off campus. A separate random sample would then be drawn from each of the selected schools.

Non-probability sampling

Non-probability sampling really means everything other than probability sampling! It involves a range of possible approaches, which are all more flexible, but less rigorous than probability sampling (which has obvious implications for how representative the sample is and how confidently you can infer your findings to the wider population). Despite being seen as less rigorous, non-probability sampling has an important role in much research conducted in the fields of social work and social care, and we would argue that these approaches are nuanced and sophisticated. They are definitely not inferior! They need to be considered carefully and used purposefully and appropriately to the needs of the study, with a clear justification, and a link to your research design. Non-probability sampling is most appropriately used for studies of an exploratory design, as such research is not seeking generalisable findings. You could argue for using one of the more robust non-probability strategies, such as maximum variation/quota (we discuss this below) for a descriptive design, but you would need to be very clear about the process followed and the likely limitations with regard to the wider application of your findings.

Whilst Patton (2015: 264) describes all non-probability sampling as 'purposeful', that is '[s]trategically selecting information-rich cases to study, cases that by their nature and substance will illuminate the inquiry question being investigated', we would argue that non-probability approaches can be further split into 'researcher-driven' and 'respondent-driven' strategies. Researcher-driven strategies include: 'judgement' (sometimes called purposive), 'maximum variation' and 'extreme case'; these approaches seek and select specific information-rich cases. While what we call respondent-driven strategies include: 'availability/convenience' and 'snowball sampling'. These latter strategies do not allow for the selection of information-rich cases; in both instances, the researcher is far more reliant on what is presented to him or her by respondents and the research environment. Whilst both of these strategies are frequently and sensibly used in exploratory studies, there are considerable limitations, as we will discuss below.

Judgement/purposive

This approach works well when you have prior knowledge of both the population and the issue being examined, as this approach relies on you, the researcher, selecting those cases you think are most useful to enabling your study aims to be met.

 ## Case study

Drawing on relevant knowledge and using your judgement

Alannah (the PhD student you have already been introduced to), in an earlier piece of research, was examining the longer term outcomes of prison-based mother–child support programmes. She knew two key things about the issue before developing her sampling strategy: (1) that there was little existing research on the long-term impact of these programmes once women leave prison, and (2) that these women are very difficult to locate once they move back into the community. Adding in the practical constraints of completing the study in her Honours year, she decided that an appropriate starting point would be to seek the observations of professional staff about this issue. So she identified key welfare support staff from a small number of organisations in the community who were providing specialist services to women exiting prison and invited them to participate. This is a good example of 'hand-picking' expert participants (if you are interested you can read the published background-rationale to the study: Burgess and Flynn, 2013).

Maximum variation

Whilst definitely not a probability sampling technique, this approach seeks to ensure that where there is diversity and heterogeneity in the population, this is represented in the sample.

 ## Case study

Maximising variation in a small exploratory study

It was Catherine's view that uncovering core experiences was essential for this study of adolescent experiences of maternal imprisonment, given the limited existing data about this group of children (labelled frequently as 'invisible'). Given the exploratory design and the nature of the study population (difficult to define, let alone access), probability sampling was neither appropriate nor do-able; therefore, maximum variation sampling was chosen.

The very simple aim of this strategy was to maximise the range of data gathered. Given the negligible existing knowledge in this area, the sampling strategy focused on relevant and definable demographic variations, so as to obtain a sample that represented the broadest group of participants possible (to ensure the best possible broader application of the findings). To secure a sufficient range of participant experiences, a sampling matrix was developed, incorporating five demographic variables: security classification of the mothers' prison setting, pre-prison care arrangements, urban vs. rural location, and the age and gender of the children. This matrix was used to ensure that all domains were actively covered when recruiting participants.

This approach is sometimes called *quota* sampling (though quota sampling is more typically used to describe a strategy that seeks proportionate representation of specific characteristics). Rubin and Babbie (2013) describe a number of limitations that result from this approach, including the need for up-to-date, accurate information about the population and the subsequent quota. This is particularly challenging in areas in which the population is subject to change. For example, you want to investigate the experiences of refugees entering a country, and have decided against a stratified random sample (even if your immigration department has a list of all such entrants, locating and engaging with them is likely to be difficult for a range of reasons). You do, however, still want to be able to ensure that your findings represent the diverse views of the different refugee groups. Deciding on what quota groups to use would remain very challenging, however, certainly in Australia, as what countries/groups are targeted or prioritised for entry varies regularly.

Extreme case

This rests on researcher knowledge of both the issue and the population, as it relies on you identifying an exceptional case (sometimes called a *deviant* case); this can either be a really good or bad example. Neuman (2014: 273) says that the focus here is on identifying cases that differ substantially from the 'dominant pattern'. This allows us to learn from unusual manifestations of our phenomenon of interest. Patton (2015) describes these as exemplar cases. The basic principle of this approach is that we can learn much from looking outside of what is expected. This can fit well with the value base of social work and social care; it can draw from both strengths and solution-focused perspectives to ask 'despite the odds, when and how is this working?'. Catherine's doctoral research into adolescent experiences of maternal imprisonment is a good example.

 ## Case study

What can be learned from 'unusual' cases?

Catherine found that it was very uncommon for the care of adolescent children whose mothers were imprisoned to be well planned and secure. However, in one case, despite considerable challenges – including both parents being imprisoned and having six children – care at the points of imprisonment and release was carefully planned with good outcomes.

(Continued)

(Continued)

This case was specifically sampled for additional exploration. This case was not intended to represent a typical family in these circumstances, nor typical of responses. Choosing this case demonstrates the importance of selecting exemplars of good practice (Flynn and Lawlor, 2008: 25), to highlight 'what works'. This close examination clearly highlighted specific, effective practices (for those of you who are interested, these included an underpinning collaborative approach with all key players' active participation encouraged and enabled, which supported the mother in her parenting role, facilitated parent-child contact and provided a staged re-establishment of the family post-prison).

As noted above, respondent-driven strategies include: convenience/availability and snowball sampling. By respondent-driven we mean that you as the researcher have a less active role in constructing the sample, less control of the data and less robust findings.

Snowball sampling

This is a strategy commonly used to gain entry into what may be seen as a less accessible population, and/or where the boundaries of the population are unknown. It involves identifying an initial 'case' (ideally a typical case) and then asking this person to identify and seek further participants. (Some researchers talk about this initial participant providing you with the contact details of other possible participants, but we would be very cautious about using this strategy for ethical reasons. Giving someone's personal contact details without their consent could be seen as a breach of privacy. How might you feel if, unbeknownst to you, a researcher was given your personal details, and then contacted you specifically to ask if you wanted to participate in a study about what will presumably be a personal issue?) While Neuman (2014) argues that snowball sampling is most appropriate when we actively want to study networks, such as friendships, sexual partners or crime connections, it is a strategy more often used in social work and social care to access hidden or stigmatised populations or problems (rather than their networks per se). One of the key limitations of this approach is that the resultant sample and data can be quite homogenous, as all participants are somehow connected, even if we follow Alston and Bowles' (2012) advice to continue until your sample is *saturated* (generates no new information). For example, let's assume we are interested in the experiences of street violence for homeless young people. If we begin our data collection with a young woman who had previously been in the state care system, it is likely that the subsequent participant group will be quite skewed, perhaps by gender, or by pre-homelessness housing arrangements. How might these factors impact on their experiences of street violence (e.g. specific types of violence? perpetrated by particular groups of people?)? Using snowball sampling requires you to select your initial participant carefully and to be aware of the limitations of this approach.

This is really the least robust sampling strategy available to us as it uses those participants/ cases which are convenient to the researcher (this may simply be people you know, colleagues, service users, people you come across whilst in a particular environment); there is a limited relationship to the broader population. Patton (2015) consequently argues that this approach should be our last possible option when developing a sampling strategy as it provides 'information-poor' (2015: 309) data, which has 'low credibility [and is] easy to attack' (2015: 310). While Neuman (2014: 248) describes the key attraction of this type of sample to be that it is 'easy, cheap, and quick to obtain', and is critical of its use, it remains a strategy that can help establish the grounding for further research. It may be particularly useful for practitioner researchers who draw a sample from their own caseload to begin examining an issue of concern. Though this is clearly not generalisable, it is a reasonable 'first word'.

In summary, there are two main types of sampling: probability and non-probability. While probability sampling is seen to provide a more rigorous and representative sample (needed for explanatory and often descriptive designs), non-probability sampling strategies can assist you to locate and generate rich data, most relevant to exploratory studies.

Making sure that your study is rigorous

Conventionally, *reliability* (getting the same result consistently) and *validity* (getting an accurate measure) are the tools for evaluating methodological rigour (you can see the clear positivist framework here). An alternative framework for considering rigour in *naturalistic* research – common in social work and social care) was developed by Lincoln and Guba (1985). They argued that researchers in this area needed to have ways of addressing concerns about reliability and validity (such as subjectivity, bias, etc.), ensuring that research findings are seen to have truth value and wider applicability (which seems like a very reasonable requirement for all research!).

They proposed the following concepts: credibility, transferability, dependability and confirmability, which parallel the conventional notions of internal validity, external validity, reliability and objectivity respectively, as outlined in Table 6.1. We have also tried here to give you some examples of techniques that will help you to build a robust study. We discuss some of these below.

Internal validity (measuring what you think you are measuring) and *credibility*: controlling for other variables (making sure they do not have an impact) is the conventional method of achieving internal validity; however, where research is exploratory in nature, this is

Table 6.1 Comparing conventional and naturalistic strategies for ensuring methodological rigour

Criterion	Conventional term	Naturalistic term	Examples of conventional techniques	Examples of naturalistic techniques
Truth value	Internal validity	Credibility	• Controlling for other variables	• Prolonged engagement • Persistent observation • Triangulation • Referential adequacy • Peer debriefing • Member checks • Reflexive journal
Applicability	External validity	Transferability	• Random sampling	• Thick description • Purposive sampling • Reflexive journal
Consistency	Reliability	Dependability	• Test–retest • Clearly defined variables • Consistent research environment • Use of current, not retrospective data	• Dependability audit • Reflexive journal
Neutrality	Objectivity	Confirmability	• Standardised data collection	• Confirmability audit • Reflexive journal

Adapted from: Lincoln and Guba (1985), Erlandson et al. (1993) and D'Cruz and Jones (2004)

typically not possible or desirable (we want to be open to all possible factors at play). Alternative strategies can build credibility:

- *Prolonged engagement*: this involves the researcher gathering data over a longer time period, via multiple data collection sessions, seeking to mitigate distortions due to social desirability (when participants act in ways to 'impress' the researcher) or 'newness' from both the researcher and the researched
- *Triangulation*: the combining of approaches: data sources, collection strategies, etc., in one piece of research. This provides a more rounded or holistic view of an issue. Whilst some researchers see this simply as a way of validating or confirming findings (these researchers would be influenced by positivism – see Chapter 1 if you need a reminder), Fine et al. (2000) argue that triangulation allows us to actively engage in the range of and the likely contradictions within the data. Rubin and Babbie (2013: 263) reiterate the importance of diversity in findings, arguing that it can 'reveal different perspectives about a phenomenon'
- *Peer debriefing*: where researchers meet to 'exchange alternative perspectives and new ideas about how they are collecting data, about problems, and about meanings in the data already collected ... the peer debriefing process increases the likelihood of spotting and correcting for biases and other problems in data collection and interpretation' (Rubin and Babbie, 2013: 263). This process ensures testing and challenging of ideas. In reality, peer debriefing could be done with your research supervisor, other expert consultants or even a peer research group (you will recall we

discussed this in Chapter 1, with regard to ensuring your research benefits from researcher self-reflection and self-awareness)

- *Member checking*: this means 'checking' the accuracy of your data with your participants. This is typically described as being done after data collection: providing participants with transcripts for reviewing, or with a summary of your findings for comment. If you were using a more participatory approach, participants may be engaged as co-researchers who would be having input into the analysis of data. This process can also be addressed during data collection, by using paraphrasing, clarification and summarising skills (this is most useful where you are unlikely to be able to access your participants again after data collection)
- A *reflective journal* ensures management of subjectivities and the establishment of an audit trail.

External validity (generalisability) – *transferability*: whilst random sampling is traditionally used to ensure generalisability, it is not always possible, necessary or ethical. Other strategies can be drawn from to strengthen the transferability of your study's findings:

- *Thick description* of the research process and environment allows other researchers to assess the applicability to other settings and/or to replicate the study themselves
- Use of a more *robust non-probability sampling strategy*: seeks to maximise the range of data collected, while providing explicit discussion of and comparison to relevant data sources, which enables the researcher to comment with greater confidence on the similarity of the sample to the population.

Reliability (the replicability of the research process and outcomes) – *dependability*: typically reliability is addressed by engaging in a test–rest process, in a consistent research environment and gathering current data, which therefore does not rely on memory. Whilst these strategies are sometimes useful, a wider range of strategies can be considered to ensure dependability of your findings.

- Maintaining a research journal and clear project documentation allows for auditing of dependability; this allows the examination and explanation of methodological choices, for example, explaining how and why the particular strategies are inappropriate. For example, whilst current data are recommended to enhance reliability, sometimes retrospective data are gathered for methodological reasons (e.g. having access to an existing study population who can provide data – this is particularly appropriate where the study population is described as hidden and difficult to access); or for ethical reasons (e.g. for sensitive topics, it may provide a less distressing research environment to allow participants to reflect on a past experience, with a degree of emotional distance).

Objectivity (unbiased) – *confirmability*: that the results are truthful and reflect the data presented, rather than the views of the researcher. It is common for this to be achieved in research through the use of standardised data collection tools (e.g. structured interviews, questionnaires or validated scales: tools that are highly structured and work to remove interviewer influence; all questions are asked of participants in the same order and in the same way).

- *Member checking,* as discussed above, also allows the researcher to confirm that it is participant views, not researcher views that are being represented
- Maintaining a *research journal* enables ongoing researcher self-awareness and management of subjectivities.

Individual reflection: considering the elements of your proposed study to date

Bryman (2012) describes a research proposal as a good way to get prepared for your research as it provides you with a concise summary, as well as highlights any gaps. At the end of Part II in our 'Toolkit' we provide a template that you might find useful and practical. For now,

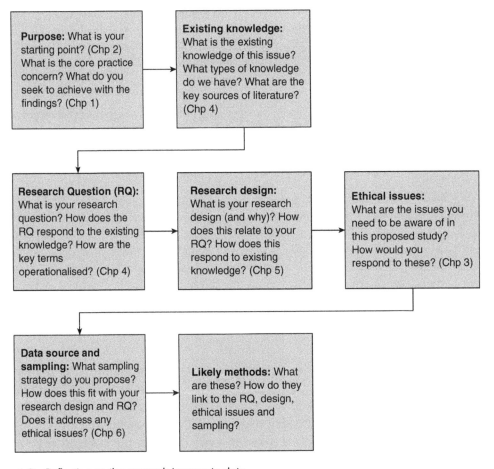

Figure 6.2 Reflecting on the research journey to date

whilst we have not covered all aspects of your methodology yet, it seems a good time to draw on these ideas and 'touch base' with where you are up to.

Make sure you take the time here to consider how the components of your proposed study fit together. Figure 6.2 walks you through the stages of the research we have covered so far by asking you questions about each stage. We begin by getting you to reflect on your ideas/decisions, remind you where to find the relevant information in the previous chapters and encourage you to note both your progress and any outstanding issues. We also ask you to think about possible data collection methods, which we will cover in the next three chapters.

Chapter summary

This, the second of our 'doing research' chapters built on our discussion of research design in Chapter 5. The impact of research design on selecting your sampling strategy and your sample was highlighted, and we discussed a range of common approaches to sampling. We rounded out the chapter with a focus on methodological rigour, comparing conventional and naturalistic techniques, and concluded by asking you to 'touch base' with your research through the use of a research proposal. In the next three chapters we discuss the range of methods you can employ in your study.

Key take-home messages

Research is like putting together a puzzle: you need to be very sure that the pieces fit together in a coherent manner. When constructing a study, this means that you need to pay attention to how the existing research shapes your research question and subsequent design; your sampling strategy then needs to be consistent with these.

No matter if your study gathers qualitative and/or quantitative data, is of a foundational or more sophisticated design, or what your epistemological position is, all research must be methodologically rigorous. Your job as a researcher is to decide if it is most appropriate for you to use conventional or naturalistic strategies.

Additional resources

There are plenty of methodology texts out there, which discuss sampling comprehensively, including:

Neuman, W.L. (2014) *Social Research Methods: Qualitative and Quantitative Approaches* (7th edn). Harlow: Pearson New International. This text provides plenty of detail about the range of sampling strategies.

Bryman, A. (2012) *Social Research Methods* (4th edn). South Melbourne: Oxford University Press. Useful examples make the chapter on sampling an easy and helpful read.

Patton, M.Q. (2015) *Qualitative Research and Evaluation Methods. Integrating Theory and Practice* (4th edn). Thousand Oaks, CA: Sage. The discussion of sampling in this text is more concise than the previous resources, but its particular strength is its focus on the range of non-probability strategies.

You will find a template for writing a research proposal at the end of Part II in our 'Toolkit'.

7

Speaking and Listening

Interviews, Focus Groups and Community Forums

In this chapter you will learn

- How research methods take on particular relevance, character and structure depending on your

  - Theoretical position
  - Epistemological position
  - Ethical considerations
- How to use the skills of speaking and listening in the various research methods

  - Interviewing
  - Focus groups
  - Community forums.

Introduction

This chapter begins our exploration of research methods by grouping those that require the active engagement of the researcher in two primary activities: speaking and listening.

In all courses preparing social work and social care workers for practice, emphasis is placed on the interpersonal capacities and skills required for engaging and working with service users. As practitioners in these fields you will rely on these capacities and skills every day as you build a relationship and work with those using your services, with colleagues, managers and associates. Relationships are shaped and developed through speaking and listening. Through this means, we learn about the experiences of others, we form connections with them, we make and refine our assessments of priorities and decide on any actions to be taken.

In doing research our interests are often similar although not identical. Importantly, however, the skills that we use in practice are the same skills of speaking and listening that we are likely to hold already and have the ability to draw on in doing research. The extent to which speaking and listening skills are drawn upon does depend on the kind of research we are doing, and that in turn depends on our theoretical and epistemological position (you will remember that we introduced these concepts in Chapter 2). And this brings us to a very important point: from a pragmatic position, methods themselves are 'epistemologically free'; that is, they are 'merely' the way in which we gather data, which will be driven by what you need to know – the problem and its context. What these methods 'look like', what they are designed to do, how we use them, where we use them and what we do with the data we gather through using them, depends entirely on the epistemological perspective from within which we are researching.

Epistemology and methodology

These two terms belong together. We have already defined and described a range of epistemological positions: positivist, critical, interpretivist and pragmatic. As we noted in that chapter, clarifying our epistemological position, deciding what constitutes knowledge, and hence how we might go about acquiring more or different knowledge about phenomena has required us to clarify which paradigm best captures our view of the world, of what constitutes reality, of what it means to be a human being. Embedded in that is our view of methodology – how we go about finding out what we believe can be known. Methodology, as the word implies, refers to the *logic* underpinning our choice of methods. So, for example, if we see ourselves as working from an interpretivist or social constructionist paradigm, we are likely to see human beings as meaning-making. This suggests that *logically* we are likely to choose a data gathering method which seeks human subjects' interpretation of the meaning that is relevant to the phenomenon we are interested in understanding better.

Theory, epistemology and methodology

As we have noted (also in Chapter 2) theory has a vital role to play in formulating our research questions, ensuring that we consider specific aspects of the phenomena in which we are interested. Again, when we come to make sense of the data gathered, theory guides us in attending to aspects which can be significant. Theory gives us a 'home base' and a 'common language' amongst other scholars and researchers with similar interests, perhaps assisting in strengthening the theory's compass or suggesting flaws or inadequacies in it. As we shall see a little later, our theoretical perspective will be reflected in the way we 'speak' and 'listen'.

As we have noted, data gathering methods relying on 'speaking' and 'listening' – as is the case with all methods – do not necessarily belong solely within one paradigm. Methods themselves are essentially 'epistemologically free'; that is, it is the way they are used that matters. For example, let us imagine that you are a researcher with a strong commitment to psychodynamic theory. Psychodynamic theory proposes that much of what we know is outside our awareness, it is unconscious. You may interview research participants about the meaning that they give to being a 'good parent', for example, but psychodynamic theory, most accounts of which would relate to positivist or post-positivist perspectives, alerts you to the likelihood that the answers participants give will refer to their 'surface' thinking and you, as researcher, might use psychodynamic theory in order to explore these responses on a 'deeper' level, revealing what may not have been said but accords with your interpretation of their unconscious thoughts and reactions. This is a very different approach to interviewing arising from an interpretivist or narrative perspective where your interest might be in posing questions that enable a narrative or discursive account of participants' own understanding of 'good parenting' to emerge, and what is said rather than not said becomes the basis for your thematic analysis.

Speaking and listening

These activities include both active and passive approaches to data gathering. 'Speaking' in the form of a verbal exchange between people is one amongst a range of different ways of communicating. Non-verbal 'speaking', for example, through such utterances as 'hmmm', or laughter, or so-called body language, such as crossing arms or finger-tapping, are other ways of 'speaking'. Researchers also 'speak' through the written word, and participants might additionally 'speak' through writing or poetry or drawing or photographs (more about this later in Chapter 9 'Looking and Seeing').

'Listening' because of its centrality to interpersonal communication, has been much theorised and analysed within the literature: see, for example, Bodie (2011) in a special edition of *The International Journal of Listening*, 25 (1–2). The act of 'listening' is what happens when the researcher receives the communication from the respondent. It may be the spoken word or the written word or the non-verbal utterances or the body language that is 'listened to'. The researcher may respond or not respond: this will depend on the type of method that is being used. Through the act of 'listening' the researcher is also interpreting the meaning of what is being said, and again, depending on the method being used, may or may not seek clarification from the researched that they have heard what was intended.

In this chapter we will describe and discuss the various methods associated with 'speaking and listening'. Although surveys and questionnaires may also involve 'speaking and listening', because they more often make use of quantitative measures, we have discussed them in the next chapter as methods involving 'counting and measuring'.

So in the following pages we will explore:

- Interviewing and the interviewer
  - Face-to-face interviewing
  - Telephone and video interviews
  - Advantages and disadvantages
- Focus groups
  - Advantages and disadvantages
- Ethical considerations
- Community forums
  - Where they may work best
  - What is involved in establishing and facilitating them.

Asking questions: what do you really want to know?

This question is at the heart of the design and construction of all data collection tools. And 'What do you really want to know?' is the question that we need to return to frequently in order to be sure that the questions we are asking are the ones which can answer our research question.

It is through forming and framing questions that we operationalise the variables or delineate the phenomena we want to study. Importantly, arriving at these questions requires reading, talking to people and reflection in order to be sure that, indeed, it is through asking questions of particular people in particular ways (interviews, focus groups, etc.) that is the best way to answer our research question.

When to use what method?

As a rather rough rule of thumb, these guidelines might be helpful for determining which method to use when:

- If we want to ask a large heterogenous sample of people about their self-reported beliefs or behaviours, a survey may work best (Neuman, 2014). Mailed out interviews or surveys, which were valued for their cheapness and geographic span, have perhaps been superseded by the use of internet surveys using tools such as SurveyMonkey. They are useful for accessing large samples and where potential respondents are connected to the internet, and are literate. We will discuss surveys in the next chapter
- If we want to ask a small homogenous sample, say 7-10 people, about their experiences of a personal, perhaps sensitive, issue, then a face-to-face interview may be best
- If we want to ask a small sample, say 7-10 people, about their views on a 'topic', then a focus group might be best

- Telephone or video interviews may be best where participants are more easily reached by this means, perhaps due to distance or convenience or with reference to their particular situation, for example, a physical disability
- Whichever method you use, keep it as short and focused as possible, bearing in mind that respondents may become tired, bored or frustrated and either abandon the task or answer with less concentration
- Consider the characteristics of the people from whom you are seeking to gather data, for example, their age, literacy, abilities and disabilities, and use this understanding to avoid asking questions that they might struggle to answer for any of these (or other) reasons
- Think about how you'll analyse and measure the responses to whichever 'speaking and listening' method you use: more structured instruments are generally easier to analyse, while the less structured require analytic strategies, such as coding answers (but more about analysing qualitative data in Chapter 10)
- Pilot test your questions (see below).

Pilot testing

This means doing a 'dry run' with your questions, checking to see whether others respond in the way you intended, whether your questions are easily understood and whether other or different questions need to be added, or if existing questions should be removed. You can also test to see how long the interview or survey takes. You might invite volunteers such as fellow students or friends to do this.

Bell (2005: 147 and 148) suggests these questions on the right for pilot testers.

- How long did it take you to complete?
- Were the instructions clear?
- Were any of the questions unclear or ambiguous? If so, will you say which and why?
- Did you object to answering any of the questions?
- In your opinion has any major topic been omitted?
- Was the layout clear/attractive?
- Any comments?

Ethical considerations

While we have discussed these in detail in Chapter 3, now we can explore them with reference to your specific research project. Entering the field and beginning to engage people as research participants signals a need to consider two important ethical issues relating to methods using 'speaking and listening' designs.

The first relates to privacy. Talking to people about issues of concern to them in the social work and social care fields usually relate to matters of social policy, social programmes and social problems or experiences. These are often matters more likely to be considered within the private rather than public domains. For that reason, your application for ethics approval will most likely have required that you ensure that potential participants are aware of the kinds of issues they will be responding to in person or on paper, and will have had the chance to reflect on whether these issues require some form of disclosure from them about, for example, their health or mental health status. Dodds and Epstein (2012: 88) have noted that, where issues are sensitive, it may be better practice to ask these on a survey rather than in a face-to-face interview: on a survey, anonymity can be preserved and anxieties about self-disclosure avoided. In order to avoid the possibility that the research will invade their privacy and/or expose them to a situation of discomfort, the information for participants and the consent documentation must explain and address such issues.

When Kerry and Catherine were planning to gather data from their research students, their final choice for data collection was influenced by ethical and methodological considerations.

Kerry and Catherine

We were both involved in teaching and supervising research students and wanted to ask recently grad-uated students about their experiences of super-vision, to improve our understanding and teaching.

Both [of us] were of the view that to develop knowledge in this area a qualitative exploratory approach was ideal. We were very aware, how-ever, that although all ... graduates were likely to be in professional practice and able to form their own views regarding the appropriateness of any involvement in research, some unequal relation-ship may remain. To ensure that no potential par-ticipants felt coerced to participate, [we] adopted an anonymous online survey. (Brydon and Flynn, 2014: 371)

If a focus group or community forum is to be a data source, then obviously, anonymity is not possible. However, particularly in focus groups, confidentiality can be sought from participants in so far as they are in agreement that the specific details of focus group attendees will not be shared outside the group. Often, it is helpful to provide participants whom you are inviting for face-to-face, phone or Skype interviews or a focus group with the questions you are asking before the meeting. This gives them clarity and certainty, as well as an opportunity to consider their responses in advance.

The second ethical matter addresses issues of relative power in relation to any data gathering method. When considering such issues in relation to methods of 'speaking and listening' you need to think about the nature and scope of the research question, who your participants are likely to be and where they 'sit' in relation to yourself as researcher. For example, how sensitive is the question you are asking of participants? This will of course depend on whether par-ticipants could be considered 'vulnerable'; that is, somehow put at risk by the research. These risks might be emotional or psychological or political. For example, if your question is about 'people with psychiatric disability', then using this terminology may already identify partici-pants in what is often considered a stigmatised social position. If you want to speak with them, how can they best be protected from any possible negative effects? Will a survey rather than a face-to-face interview be more appropriate? If you want to ask people about their experiences of an emotionally demanding situation, for example, the death of a child, will it be better to interview them face to face so that you can monitor the impact of the interview process?

Given what we have said about issues of privacy, how likely are participants to disclose difficult situations or experiences to you if you are, for example, a research student? A social work practitioner in an agency dealing with the issues your question refers to? An academic requesting participation from students in your course? As outlined in Chapter 3, each of these different situations needs to be carefully examined in order to minimise any negative impact on participants, for example, a sense of pressure on them to participate because of who you are, or the likelihood that no one will respond to your invitation to participate because of anxieties about who you are. As Dodds and Epstein (2012: 88) note '(at) the back of a participant's mind (or perhaps at the front) as they respond to interview questions or allow themselves to be videotaped is the question "what will you do with what I say?"'. This is an important question and it is vital that you as the researcher address it. Your information and consent processes should include discussion of this, noting why potential participants have been invited to take part, what questions will be asked, whether you will seek identifying information, how the data (their answers) will be collected (the methods used), how these data will be analysed, and whether and how participants will be informed of the research findings. In short, this document identifies the degree of power and control the research participants have over the research process and its outcomes.

Interviewing

Conducting an interview generally means that the researcher and the participant speak directly to one another, either in person or via telephone or video. Interviews where the researcher and participant can see one another add a non-verbal dimension to the conversation, which may or may not be part of what is included in the analysis but which will, undoubtedly, affect the way both interpret the other. It is worth bearing in mind that a great deal of our 'listening' includes cues and signs that are given and received on a level which is outside our awareness, but nonetheless influential in the interpretations we form of who is saying what to whom and what they mean. Our epistemological position (more on this in the paragraphs below) may direct us towards including these data and using various means, for example, psychodynamic theoretical constructs, to interpret them. Others, for example, people working within the social constructivist or interpretivist paradigm, may feed back their interpretations of so-called non-verbal cues in order for the other party to confirm or correct such interpretations.

The interviewer

If we return to Chapter 2 briefly, we can see that there are pointers there about how the interviewer will approach the task of interviewing.

For example, those working within the interpretivist paradigm are focused on the way in which knowledge is constructed. This suggests that their interest is in accessing depth and detail in their respondents' understanding of the nature of social reality and how this is reflected in their understanding of the particular issue being researched. They are thus likely to work to establish rapport and create a reasonably safe working relationship in order to facilitate the respondents' involvement in the process. They may see the interview as closer to a conversation than a question and answer session and so interweave different questions as the discussion unfolds. See Ann's example.

Feminist researchers who include interviews amongst their methods have written extensively on the nature of feminist interviewing (Reinharz, 1992; Oakley, 2005; Ackerly and True 2010).

Ann: I was studying the impact of 'failed adoptions' on adoptive parents. I developed a list of questions to help focus the primary research question but began the interview with a simple question: 'Tell me about your experience of the adoption of (this child)' It turned out that no further questions were needed as this one 'opener' proved sufficient for the participant to cover all the aspects that I wanted to ask about.

Given their epistemological and political position, they are likely to see the interview as a conversation between women who have a shared structural location; this might influence the extent to which they will talk about their own experiences with participants and be comfortable with expressing their emotions in the interview. They may recognise that women's voices may remain unheard unless a variety of ways of sharing their personal experiences are possible: for this reason they may prefer their participants to tell stories indicative of

what they are experiencing, or share their thoughts through the use of diaries and journals. Feminist researchers also have a commitment to action and social change through demonstrating the political significance of the personal experience. From this perspective they may view the interview itself as a form of consciousness-raising.

You will also recall that in Chapter 3 we talked about the personal and sometimes unpredictable nature of gathering data from participants, and how interviewing can create such a safe place for participants that they may disclose information that they later regret. We discussed a range of strategies to pre-empt or respond to this (revisit that chapter if you need a reminder). Alston and Bowles (2012) also provide some useful advice about ethical interviewing. They suggest that there may be times in interviews when we have to move out of our researcher role, perhaps to respond to participant distress. They do not see this as problematic, as long as participants understand which role we are in; participants need to be very clear when we are acting as researchers and hence, which of their communications will be used as data.

Interview 'types' occur on a continuum from structured to unstructured. We discuss these now, with a focus on what these are, when these are most appropriate and some of the pitfalls to watch out for.

Structured interviews

These are interviews that provide a limited range of possible responses to questions, for example:

Which of the following best describes the multidisciplinary team you work with?

- It is a team where everyone contributes.
- It is a team dominated by the team leader.
- It is a team where good decisions are made on a consensus basis.

Advantages with this approach are that responses are easy to record and analyse, using either qualitative or quantitative methods (which we will cover in Chapters 10 and 11, respectively). The interview can be completed quickly. In general, a structured approach to interviewing requires the researcher to have some pre-existing knowledge on the topic; this allows you to develop comprehensive questions which do not miss out on key issues. This approach, which gathers the same data from all participants, is particularly useful with descriptive research designs, which seek to 'map' and describe social phenomena (see Chapter 5). There are some 'down-sides' to this method that need to be addressed if you are considering conducting structured interviews. Firstly, if you have not based your interview schedule (questions) on a solid literature review, you may end up with responses that are not reflective of the participants' actual views, and which do not add anything significant to the knowledge base. Your literature review will ensure that you know what research has been done previously – what they found and by what methods they found this – you can then use this to shape a good structured interview. Secondly, participants can feel that it is the researcher's agenda, rather than their own ideas/thoughts/feelings that are driving the study. Some structured interviews include an unstructured section, such as 'Any further comments', which requires individual analysis and hence extends the time taken to administer and summarise the interview, but allows participants some space to add in issues that are of concern to them.

Case study

A 'structured, semi-structured approach'

Alannah's topic – how mothers with a mental illness entering the prison system respond to their children's care needs – needed to develop knowledge in an area in which little is known. She needed to be open to unanticipated issues and to ask open questions; this was also supported by her knowledge that in previous prison-based research participants had expressed feeling that their primary concerns were not heard. But, she also needed to be able to compare data against a group of mothers who were not experiencing mental health problems, so also needed a degree of structure and some closed questions. Interviewing in a prison setting also precluded the use of recording equipment, so, practically, she needed a tool that allowed her to take good notes and record responses accurately. To respond to all of these competing needs she developed a structured, semi-structured tool, with 50/50 open and closed questions such as: 'Did you know where your child or children were when you were taken into prison this time? Yes or No; if yes, how did you get this information?'

Semi-structured interviews

Semi-structured interviews occupy the middle ground between structured and unstructured approaches. It is a loose term, which covers a wide range of possible interviewing styles. This method typically uses a small number of interview topics, although these are not necessarily worded the same or presented in the same order for all participants. This approach is useful with exploratory and descriptive studies. All participants are asked to provide data on the same issues, so you can compare easily across participants/groups and 'map' or measure the extent of particular responses. But this strategy also brings some flexibility, and allows the direction of the interview to be led more by the participant, within the set boundaries. This is particularly important with exploratory research, as it allows the participant to present issues that you as the interviewer may not have considered (a common occurrence with research at an exploratory level of design).

Unstructured interviews

These interviews are more like conversations where questions may occur in any order depending on the way the interview progresses. For this reason, to conduct an unstructured interview demands significant skill and expertise, in addition to the kinds of skills and expertise social work and social care workers already possess. We discuss this in more detail in the next section.

Unstructured interviews, because of their 'free-range' character, can enable very rich and idiosyncratic material to emerge as the interviewee is encouraged to 'speak in their own voice' and to focus on what is important to them. As such, they are most useful with exploratory studies. Given the quality of such data, analysis can be complicated and time-consuming, even when the number of participants is (by necessity) quite low. In Chapter 10 we will discuss the various data analysis methods that researchers use in working with qualitative data but suffice to say here, this work can be slow, painstaking but often highly rewarding as the researcher arrives at a position of understanding the meaning that the researched wished to convey. However, as unstructured interviews do involve the researcher more closely with the researched than do, for instance, structured interviews, efforts to identify, name and examine possible sources of bias are important in approaching the research task rigorously. The challenge with unstructured interviewing is finding a balance between asking the 'right' opening question, being open and able to listen to unanticipated issues, and providing some boundaries so that you gather data which enable you to respond to your research question (or, with exploratory research, to amend your focus if your early data collection indicates that your study would benefit from refocusing).

If you are planning a study (or have begun a study) and you are thinking about gathering data via interview, what kind of interview do you plan to have? Why? How will this structure influence the way you do your interview?

Preparing for the interview

Most researchers in the social work and social care fields are already skilled interviewers but doing research interviews, whilst exercising similar skills, has some differences. For example, social work researchers sometimes comment that, unlike their work with clients, which often has a clear focus in which they are making assessments, or developing an intervention strategy or plan of action with their clients, the research interview does not have such distinct objectives. Rather, the researcher's focus is on eliciting answers to their research questions rather than on building a relationship or developing plans. This is a more passive role in which the researcher's chief purpose is to listen and *not* be a therapist or counsellor. Holding back on responding to participants with 'social work' responses can sometimes be difficult, and listening and recording requires restraint; some researchers comment on how hard it is to 'just absorb' the participant's words rather than acting on them.

Given this difference in role, it is a good idea to practise the research interview with colleagues and fellow students. Not only does this allow you to 'road test' or pilot your questions, but it also helps to develop your capacity to use your interviewing and listening skills in a different way, keeping in mind the different purpose the research interview fulfils.

Conducting unstructured interviews

In unstructured interviews the researcher's capacities to speak and to listen are particularly important. This is in order to maintain the conversation-like context at the same time as ensuring that the research question is addressed.

Issues relating to the relative power of each participant in the interview (interviewee and interviewer) will be important to consider because of their likely impact on both speaking and listening. Often it is the interviewer who occupies a more powerful position (though see the discussion regarding interviewing elites in Chapter 1) *vis a vis* the interviewee. Generally, it is the interviewer who has raised the question, named the focus and invited the interviewee to participate. Bearing this in mind, the researcher/interviewer might want to ask the interviewee to select the place of interview, or might provide the interviewee with a copy of the interview schedule before they meet. As discussed in Chapter 3, another strategy could be to begin the interview by acknowledging the existence of a power differential and open this topic for discussion with a view to minimising the negative impact of any power differential. For example, the interviewer might say something like, 'How are you feeling about doing this interview?' Other ways of limiting the negative influence of power might include providing for more than one interview, offering feedback with a written summary or transcript. This might mean that the researcher will, with empathy and sensitivity, use probes and reflections to explore and expand the interviewee's responses to issues or considerations raised by the researcher. Within the conversation, the researcher will listen and be attuned to hearing the figures of speech, metaphors and analogies that the participant uses to describe or account for their experiences. Such ways of using language point to the deeper meanings that experiences may hold for participants. For example, if a participant tells us that managing family life with a disabled child is 'like walking a tightrope', we have an insight into the stress and potential catastrophe that the participant sees as present in his or her life, graphically and economically communicated by the use of this analogy.

Focus group

A focus group is often the method of choice when an issue or problem is known to be shared by a number of people. Rather than interview each person individually, a focus group can enable data to be gathered from a number of people at the same time. But it does more than this. When people gather together in a group, the conversations and interactions that take place can offer very rich and multi-layered accounts of how the issue or problem is understood, experienced and dealt with. When people talk together in a group, they build on one another's accounts, sometimes challenging and sometimes taking the conversation about the topic to further and unanticipated areas. See the example from Michael and Jodie below to illustrate.

 Case study

A cascade of responses

In recent research on the psychosocial needs of people in residential aged care facilities, Michael and Jodie convened a focus group of carers. They wanted to know what they considered to be the gaps in meeting such needs for their family member or friend who was in the facility. Their purpose in this research was to discover what role a social worker might play in residential aged care facilities. They began with one opening question – 'What is it like to be a carer?' – intending to explore a number of topics following some general discussion. As it turned out, this first question generated all the information needed – and more! It proved to be the catalyst for participants to express very strong emotions about loss, anxiety and guilt, and powerful feelings that they had been left to navigate emotionally demanding situations once their family member or friend was placed without the support that a social worker might provide. At the end of the focus group, participants who had previously not known one another, decided to meet again and form their own support group.

This example highlights several important points to bear in mind if you plan to collect data using a focus group, chief amongst them, the need to have skills in working with groups (McDermott, 2002). As we saw in this example, a group may 'take off' in unexpected directions and it may be important if you are the convenor to be able to contain the group, ensuring that it works constructively towards exploring the question it has been established to answer. This means that you as convener might have to achieve a balance between enabling a free flow of conversation and keeping the group focused. When a group of people get together it might also happen that participants feel pressure to conform with more socially acceptable commentary and you may have to be alert to allowing opportunities for dissenting voices to be heard safely.

Selecting, inviting and recruiting participants requires that you have identified who may be able to contribute to the group conversation through having information or experiences that relate to the research question. You may therefore consider whether there are particular age groups or places of residence or degrees of homogeneity and heterogeneity that you want represented in the group. For example, depending on your question, will you want both men and women? People in the paid workforce? Students?

It is unlikely, however, that you will be familiar enough with participants to know in advance what kinds of personalities members have and how – or if – these will gel together. Again, having confidence in your skills in working with groups is an advantage in so far as you might wish to make sure that no one voice dominates the group and that more reticent participants have a space to talk.

Preparing to run a focus group

It is important to list the questions you would like the focus group to address. Providing these to participants before the group is often helpful as it gives them a chance to think about how they will answer them and the points they wish to make. It might also ensure that you, as convener, can check that all members feel they have had an opportunity to have their say, knowing that they will have come to the meeting with some ideas in mind.

Most focus group conveners record meetings. This is so they do not need to take notes and be distracted from what is happening in the group: so that they can listen with maximum attention. It is also a record of what was said. If you have the resources available, enlisting a co-convener who takes notes while you conduct the group is very helpful, and a combination of written notes and recorded discussion will ensure that the contribution of the focus group is captured.

The ideal size for a focus group is seven to nine members: this allows for the possibility of some heterogeneity as well as commonalities amongst group members, which will be important to the dynamics of the group. We would suggest having a small number of topics (a bit like a semi-structured interview) – around five to seven. Time for a focus group is ideally 1 hour, at most 1.5 hours. Longer than this will exhaust both you and the participants. This relatively short time frame ensures that there is sufficient pressure on people to 'have their say' within a pre-arranged time. Breaking for refreshments in the middle of a focus group can be distracting and the thread of discussion may be lost. Paula gives a real world example from her PhD on settlement issues for African refugees.

Case study

Preparing for a focus group

One of the main things I did was draw on my previous experience of working with refugees. I know not everyone has this but I did, so I used the things I had learnt working in the field to shape my general approach. I think this also reduced my anxiety and minimised my feelings of inadequacy when interviewing people, particularly in a group.

For my first focus group I took food with me, which turned out to be unnecessary as my participants did not want to eat it and then it was rather awkward trying to decide what happened with the food when we were done. This probably had to do with the fact that we had limited time for the focus group. I think the fact

(Continued)

(Continued)

that we did not have enough time to just talk and get to know one another made the food irrelevant. Time is a precious thing and participants often want to get to know you and talk to you, so if I were to do this again I would make sure that we had more time to socialise and not just answer my questions.

The language barrier is something that I thought a lot about. I did not have the resources to pay an interpreter. I also knew from working in the field that bringing in interpreters can cause issues as people know one another in a personal way and cannot always make the distinction between personal and professional. So, I just allowed time for people to talk in their preferred language; to confer with one another and then respond in English.

Analysing focus group data

While we will discuss data analysis in greater detail in Chapter 10, suffice to note here that it will be important to identify whether you decided on using a focus group in order to gather answers to specific questions, for example, whether a school should establish a bus service for students, or whether your interests were more in hearing about participants' experiences of an event, or situation or phenomenon, for example, their experiences of placing a family member in an aged care facility.

In the first example, you might wish to record the range of ideas from participants regarding the bus service. In the second example, you may be interested in listening to how participants talk about their experiences as much as to the content, for example, practical issues they raise. So, in the first example, you will note these suggestions down from the taped record of the meeting. In the second example, you might want to transcribe the entire group meeting and subject the data to analysis by coding responses and thematic analysis (see Chapter 10 for a full discussion of this method).

Community forums

These refer to gatherings a researcher might organise if she wished to gauge the nature of a larger, possibly representative, group of people's thoughts, beliefs, ideas or concerns about an issue of relevance to them. For example, the research question may concern residents' views about the building of a freeway through their suburb, or parents' attitudes to the introduction of drug education classes in their children's school, or sex workers' ideas about the best ways of providing sexual health services. It might also be the method of choice if the researcher was working within a participatory action research paradigm and was working towards encouraging action to be taken by the community towards addressing the issues raised in her research. There are similarities here to focus groups, but the decision to hold a community forum may relate to the researcher's recognition that a larger group of people – more than 10 – would in itself be recognition of the saliency (or not) of the issue to the larger community. In fact, the number of people required for a community forum would most likely be open-ended: how many attend and who they are (or who they represent), would in itself be an important finding.

Depending on the research question, the community forum might be convened in order to canvass a variety of views and opinions to ensure that the answers to the research question addressed this diversity. Alternatively, a more homogenous community forum might be appropriate where a group, known to be large, had the opportunity to get together when this was rarely the case, for example, the sex workers, and their views were of importance to the wider community.

Organising a community forum is challenging. A researcher will need to call on various resources, including assistance with programming, managing and recording the meeting. Such things as advertising, selecting and financing a venue need to be thought about. These logistical issues suggest that it is not the method of choice for a lone researcher but rather a method that might work best where the researcher already works in a community and can access such resources. In addition, particular skills and expertise are required if the researcher is to work comfortably and effectively with a large group and a very uncertain process: community forums are not for the neophyte or the inexperienced!

Chapter summary

In this chapter we have discussed a number of different methods that rely on 'speaking and listening'. The way you use these research methods – interviews, focus groups, community forums – will reflect your epistemological and theoretical position and the nature of the research question you are asking. We have discussed the kinds of research projects where these methods might be used, particular ethical issues which arise in relation to them and the skills that a researcher needs in order to use them effectively.

Key take-home messages

There are many things to consider in using these methods. In particular, it is important to consider:

- Ethical issues regarding privacy and confidentiality
- The suitability of methods for the particular participants in the research
- The importance of framing questions appropriately
- The value of piloting questions
- The researcher's skills - in engaging with individuals, facilitating focus groups or managing community forums.

Additional resources

This link to YouTube provides an interesting and lively description of how to do research interviews, including examples of 'good' and 'bad' interviews: https://www.youtube.com/watch?v=9t-_hYjAKww.

For more ideas about setting up, facilitating and analysing data from focus groups, check this link to the Community Tool Box developed by the University of Kansas, a World Health Organization Collaborating Centre for Community Health and Development: http://ctb.ku.edu/en/table-of-contents/assessment/assessing-community-needs-and-resources/conduct-focus-groups/main.

Some useful advice and guidance in managing a community forum is offered by Our Community, an information platform for Australian community and not-for-profit groups: https://www.ourcommunity.com.au/advocacy/advocacy_article.jsp?articleId=2412.

8

Counting and Measuring[1]

Questionnaires, Scales and Secondary Analyses

In this chapter you will learn

- About key features of some of the common quantitative data collection methods used in social work and social care research
- When and how to apply specific quantitative data collection measures in your research
- What data mining is and how to do it.

Introduction

This is the second of three chapters focused on understanding why, when and how to use particular data collection methods in social work and social care research. In the previous chapter, we outlined some common data gathering techniques involving speaking and listening, such as the use of interviews, focus groups and forums. In this chapter, we will examine some of the quantitative data collection methods often used in research in our professional fields.

Let's begin by noting the differences in the kinds of data that may be collected in social work and social care research. *Qualitative data* are non-numerical in nature (words), and describe a quality or a type, while *quantitative data* are numerical and measure a quantity or an amount.

---

[1]Co-authored with Susan Baidawi

The choice of which type of data to collect is directly determined by the research question(s) posed (as discussed in Chapter 4). Even though methods are epistemologically free, choices are inevitably influenced by the researcher's epistemological position as outlined in Chapter 2.

Getting started with quantitative data

Quantitative data are more often associated with addressing research questions originating in a positivist paradigm. These questions often aim to discover the nature of an objective reality through the use of the *scientific method*; that is, a way of asking and answering questions which require the use of empirical observations and experiments, the development of hypotheses, and the use of quantitative measures which rely on deductive reasoning. This could include information that quantifies participants' perceptions, experiences or attributes. While the use of quantitative data might not necessarily reflect the philosophical position of the researcher, there are many instances where such data are pragmatically useful in social work research. Here are some examples:

Measuring the extent of a particular social issue or outcome within a population: What is the prevalence of experiences of domestic violence in same-sex relationships?

Examining patterns of service utilisation: What proportion of young people transitioning from out-of-home care access homelessness services in the 12 months after leaving care?

Measuring the impact or effect of a programme/intervention: What is the difference in men's use of violence following successful participation in a men's behaviour change programme?

Having access to such data enables social researchers to 'make a case' in the current political and economic context for further political attention, or resources (including for research or services) to be devoted to a particular social issue. Social workers and social care workers also need to understand how to interpret quantitative data as part of professional practice. For instance, information drawn from quantitative data may enhance social workers' understanding of particular social issues or client groups, and may be helpful in making decisions or offering information to clients about referral pathways, programmes or interventions. For example, a family service agency may want current data on the demographic profile of a suburb in order to plan programmes for families newly arrived from particular countries. These newly arrived families may contribute to an increase in the population of children under 5 years.

Some common methods for collecting quantitative data in social work and social care research include the use of structured questionnaires, which may incorporate validated scales, and mining data from secondary sources. Each of these data collection methods is now discussed in more detail.

Developing and using questionnaires

What is a questionnaire?

A number of terms are used to refer to questionnaires, including structured interviews, standardised interviews, surveys or structured surveys. For our purposes, the term questionnaire refers to a structured list of items administered by an interviewer (either in person or via telephone), or self-administered by the participant (including mail and online questionnaires) to a sample of respondents to collect a set of data.

Questionnaires aim to expose participants to a standardised set of items in a consistent manner, so that responses can then be aggregated. They differ from the unstructured/semi-structured interview described in the previous chapter in that interviewers will generally minimise interaction with participants when administering questionnaires, so as to reduce interviewer-related variation or error. Additionally, items administered by questionnaire are usually short and specific, and may offer respondents a choice of fixed answers. Conversely, unstructured/semi-structured interviews tend to pose more open-ended questions.

Questionnaires are commonly administered in many large-scale surveys that are relevant for social workers, including your national census or health, youth and employment surveys.

When should questionnaires be used?

Questionnaires can be used pragmatically, as a data collection tool at any level of research (exploratory, descriptive or explanatory), as long as the instrument created is capable of addressing the research question(s) posed. They are among the most commonly used data collection tools in social work and social care research and the social sciences more broadly. According to Engel and Schutt (2014), the popularity of questionnaire research is due to the versatility and efficiency of this data collection method, and the capacity to generalise findings from surveys of large-scale, representative samples.

However, like all research methods, there are various limitations to the use of data derived from questionnaire research. This includes some of the problems described below, such as that of generalisability, the introduction of interviewer effects and other bias.

Generalisability: Problems with sampling error (where a random sample happens to over-represent certain subgroups by chance) or the sampling frame (e.g. certain portions of the study population are excluded or under-represented due to the sampling strategy) can result in a sample that is skewed or otherwise not representative of the general population under study. This may be unavoidable due to some sub-groups of the population being more accessible or available to researchers; however, these issues need to be acknowledged as a limitation in any reported findings. See Susan's example.

Case study

Acknowledging over-representation in your sample

Susan recently conducted a study involving survey research with older prisoners in two Australian states. Given that it was impractical to sample inmates from every prison across the two states, the prisons selected were those containing the highest numbers of older inmates, in order to recruit the required sample size. Many of the male prisons chosen tended to accommodate people charged with sexual offences, who were grouped together for protection purposes. As a result, older people charged with these offences were ultimately over-represented in the study sample.

Interviewer effects and other bias: Davis and colleagues (2010: 15) describe interviewer effects as 'the measurement error attributable to a specific interviewer characteristic such as race or gender'; these effects are distinguished from interviewer error or variance, which denote 'the proportion of the total response variance which can be attributed to differences among interviewers' (Dijktstra, 1983: 179). Interviewer effects are not consistent, but rather arise as a function of the interaction between the interviewer and the respondent in the context of the particular research being conducted (Cleary et al., 1981). It is easy to understand that an interviewer's gender may impact upon interview responses from men who use violence regarding their perpetration of violence, for example. Interviewer effects are more likely to occur when interview items query attitudes in relation to socio-demographic characteristics. The direction of these effects is generally 'in deference' to the interviewer's characteristics, for example, race, gender, age or ethnicity (Davis et al., 2010). In order to check for interviewer effects, an analysis of participant responses by interviewers can be performed. Davis and colleagues (2010) recommend that if between-interviewer variance is mild, it can be ignored. However, it is worthwhile when planning a research study to consider which interviewer characteristics may impact the validity of data you are aiming to collect through interviews or questionnaires.

Other forms of bias that may impact the validity of questionnaire responses include *social desirability bias*, which refers to the tendency of some individuals to give responses making them appear in the best light to the interviewer (Engel and Schutt, 2014: 426). These effects might be more apparent when collecting data concerning socially controversial or stigmatising phenomena, such as drug use, criminal behaviour or the presence of mental health symptoms. Of course respondents will vary in the extent to which they exhibit social desirability tendencies, and some questionnaires incorporate scales measuring these participant characteristics to control for these effects (e.g. the Marlowe–Crowne Social Desirability Scale; Crowne and Marlowe, 1960). Similarly, *acquiescence* describes the inclination of respondents to agree with most statements, particularly those that are neutral or do not have a normatively correct answer. Studies indicate this tendency is more pronounced among certain groups, for example, in individuals from cultural backgrounds valuing deference and politeness over individualism (Johnson et al., 2005), and in individuals with limited cognitive capacity (Heal and Sigelman, 1995). Again, there are various techniques for reducing the propensity of acquiescence to bias survey findings, including rephrasing questions that ask about a respondent's level of agreement with a statement. For example, instead of asking respondents 'To what extent do you agree with the following statement: Same-sex marriage should be legal'? and providing answers ranging from 'strongly disagree' to 'strongly agree' it is preferable to ask participants to indicate to what extent they support or oppose same-sex marriage on a continuum ranging from 'strongly oppose' to 'strongly support'.

'How to' develop questionnaires

So far we have discussed the purpose of questionnaires, when they might be useful and some of the limitations associated with this data collection technique. This section provides some additional principles to be considered when developing questionnaires for research purposes.

Address the research question(s)

The foremost consideration when designing questionnaires is to ensure that the data which will be collected are capable of addressing any research questions you have posed. This may seem logical; however, when designing questionnaires it is easy to become side-tracked by including interesting items that may not directly relate to your research question(s). This brings us to the next principle.

Keep the questionnaire length to a minimum

Respondents will inevitably lose concentration and motivation to complete long and arduous questionnaires, compromising the data collected. This is another reason to avoid including unnecessary items, and is particularly important when designing self-administered question-naires (such as online or mailed questionnaires), which need to sustain participant interest in order to collect all data required.

Experiment with the type(s) of items included

Questionnaires can include a variety of item types, including closed questions, which require participants to choose a response from a range of options (yes/no or other forced-choice responses), open questions, which allow respondents to provide their own responses, scaled questions (e.g. those incorporating Likert-scale responses) and validated scales, which are each discussed later in this chapter.

Pilot your questionnaire

It is wise to pilot a data collection instrument before proceeding to collect your data. As we saw in the previous chapter, this can involve testing the instrument with a colleague or small sample of respondents from your target population. Piloting provides an opportunity to identify any issues with the instrument prior to administering it to a larger group of respondents. See our example below.

Case study

The importance of pilot testing

In a recent project, Susan and her colleagues designed an instrument intended to gather data from prisoner health files. Before commencing a large-scale audit of prisoner health files across two Australian states, the instrument was provided to a justice health agency, who piloted it with a sample of five prisoner health files. The service was able to provide feedback which resulted in removal of some items and reframing of others. For example, the instrument initially requested the auditors to tick prisoners' health conditions from a provided list, while the new instrument allowed the auditors to write a freehand list of medical conditions as recorded on the prisoner's health file. This subsequently saved time (and money) when completing the health file audits.

Ensure items are clear and unambiguous

Many research texts (see, for example, Neuman 2014; Bell, 2005) highlight the importance of constructing questions that are precise and focused. Good surveys avoid questions that are:

- Ambiguous, for example, 'How important is it to you to work with colleagues who have many years of experience?'
- Leading, for example, 'As a social work teacher, do you think students will learn the best examples of practice from the text book you have prescribed?'
- Jargon, for example, 'What are the KPIs for your position?'
- Imprecise, vague, for example, 'How likely are clients to provide feedback to their caseworker?'
- Double-barrelled, for example, 'What is your age and the country where you were born?'
- Emotive, biased, for example, 'Do you think people should feel annoyed to be asked for feedback?'
- Leading, for example, 'Many parents of disabled children feel extremely angry and frustrated about their lack of access to services: as the parent of a child with autism, how do you feel?'
- Issues beyond capabilities, for example, 'Do you recall who was the inaugural professor appointed to this department?'
- Future oriented, hypothetical, for example, 'If you were elected president of the Residents' Association, what would be your first act?'
- Double negatives, for example, 'Not to feel welcomed in the community may not be the experience of every refugee: what is your experience?'

When constructing questions, it is also important to take into account the literacy levels of the intended respondent population. This can be of particular importance with certain study populations in social/care research, for example, research with children or adolescents and other groups having potentially lower English language proficiency, such as people from non-English speaking backgrounds or adult prisoners. Lana's research example highlights this.

Consider the order of questions

A generally accepted rule of thumb is to place the less complex questions (e.g. age, qualifica-

I was researching the kinds of legal issues that homeless people require assistance with. I got permission to do a survey with homeless men in a refuge. However, I didn't realise how many homeless men were functionally illiterate. Once I learned this, I reformulated my method and substituted the survey for a face-to-face interview.

tions) at the start of the survey, with more sensitive ones in the middle (e.g. 'On this scale of 1–3, identify which scenario is most likely to make you angry'). Avoid placing any questions that might be perceived as anxiety-provoking or threatening at the end of the survey.

The order of questions within a questionnaire can be influential to the data collected under some circumstances. For example, in a lengthy online survey some respondents may not sustain interest to complete the entire questionnaire, so it may be wise to put any questions of particular importance to your study earlier on in the survey. In questionnaires that are administered face to face with participants, it is sensible to place more sensitive items a little further into the questionnaire, when respondents may have had an opportunity to become more comfortable with the interviewer. Specific 'question order effects' also exist, in which the responses to a previous question may influence respondents' answers to subsequent items. For instance, one study found that participants who were asked to rate their current health status *before* being asked about the specifics of their current health and diseases gave more optimal ratings than those who were asked to rate their health status *after* being asked these questions (Bowling and Windsor, 2008).

And don't forget to conclude by thanking participants for their contribution!

See our example from Priscilla and Nicole, who used a survey to successfully gather data from a staff group, being mindful of the strategies noted above.

Case study

Surveys – an appropriate method to gather data from busy staff

Priscilla and Nicole work in the youth justice service system. It had come to their attention that many of the young people they were working with had some type of intellectual disability, but that there were no specific services or supports for these service users. They wanted to start by finding out the views of other staff about their understanding of the issues – the challenges and the good practices – as well as the perceived gaps in services and any suggestions for improvements. Working together, they designed a questionnaire for staff. This approach was seen to be the best suited method of data collection for this

(Continued)

(Continued)

problem. They had a known study population and wanted to 'map' views and experiences. A questionnaire allowed them to reach a large number of direct practice staff, in both community and custodial settings, across a wide geographical area, and for staff who tend to be 'time poor' to participate in a short survey (15 questions), in their own time. Because these researchers were seeking answers to specific questions (self-assessed knowledge about intellectual disability and available supports; brief views about gaps in service delivery and suggestions for what would assist these young people to curb their offending behaviour) a structured tool like a survey was ideal (and effective!). They had an excellent response rate and clear messages from staff about experiences, views and suggestions, which they used to guide data collection from other key stakeholders.

What questions work best in a survey?

Neuman (2014: 317) identifies six kinds of questions that are used on surveys. We have summarised these in Table 8.1 (and added in a final 'not applicable'/'skip logic' question).

Table 8.1 Questions used on surveys

Kind of question	Example
Behaviour	'Do you regularly use public transport?'
Attitude/belief/opinion	'Do you believe that the death penalty is a deterrent to serious crime?'
Characteristics	'Are you a qualified social worker?'
Expectations	'Do you expect to be a self-funded retiree?'
Self-classification	'Which political party do you consider closest to your political views?'
Knowledge	'Who funds the Department of Social Security?'
Skip or contingency	'If you answered yes to Q2, go to Q4 ...'

How to ask questions on a survey

Open and closed questions

Survey questions may be framed as *open* (allowing respondents freedom in answering), or *closed* (providing respondents with a limited number of (usually) mutually exclusive responses). If closed questions are asked, there are several different ways of so doing. Bell (2005: 138) offers guidance here and this is summarised in Table 8.2.

Open questions provide respondents with maximum flexibility in answering. For example, many surveys include, as well as closed questions, a section inviting 'any further comments', or 'While completing this survey, has anything further come to mind that you would like to add?' Other examples of open questions are those that ask respondents to comment on their experiences of the issue under consideration, for example, 'What was your experience of arriving at the agency on the first day of your placement?' or, 'Why did you want to take part in this survey?'.

Table 8.2   Types of closed questions

Types of questions	Examples
Select answer from a list	What are your qualifications? Bachelor's degree; Master's degree; Postgraduate degree
Select answer from category	What is your age? 18–25; 26–35; 36–45
Rank these options in order of the priority you would assign them: 1 = top priority; 5 = lowest priority	When I finish this course my priorities are: getting a job; travelling; buying a house; having children; enrolling in further study
Quantity: a numerical response in relation to a characteristic	How many home visits to service users do you make each week?
Grid: a table is provided so that respondents can answer two or more questions at the same time	Place a cross in the space on the table below indicating the number of years you have been in your current position and the number of social work students you have supervised
Scale: respondents rank themselves to indicate the strength of their feelings or attitudes about a statement	On this scale, place a mark at the point indicating how well you believe you understand evidence based practice: poorly; to some extent; neither well nor poorly; well; very well

Neuman (2014: 333) has usefully identified many of the advantages and disadvantages of both open and closed questions on surveys. These are summarised in Table 8.3.

Table 8.3   Advantages and disadvantages of using open and closed questions on surveys

Open questions	
Advantages	**Disadvantages**
Unlimited number of possible answers	Different respondents give different degrees of detail
Respondents can answer in detail and clarify	Responses may be irrelevant
Unanticipated findings can be discovered	Comparisons and statistical analysis difficult
Enables adequate answers to be given to complex questions	Questions may be too general for respondents, who lose direction
Encourages creativity, self-expression, richness in detail	Coding difficult
	Articulate respondents have an advantage
Reveals respondent's logic, thinking process, frame of reference	When written verbatim may be difficult to understand
	Takes more time, thought and energy for respondent
	Respondents may feel intimidated
	Answers take too much space

(Continued)

Table 8.3 (Continued)

Closed questions	
Advantages	**Disadvantages**
Easy and quick for respondents	Can suggest ideas that respondents would not otherwise have thought of
Easier to compare respondents' responses	
Answers easier to code and analyse	Respondents with no opinion can answer anyway
Respondents' choices can clarify question's meaning for them	Respondents can be frustrated because desired answer is not amongst choices
Respondents more likely to answer questions on sensitive topics	Confusing if many response choices offered
	Misinterpretation of question can go unnoticed
Fewer irrelevant or confused answers	Clerical mistakes possible
Less articulate respondents not at a disadvantage	Forces respondents to give simplistic responses to complex issues
Replication easier	Forces people to make choices they would not make in the real world

Using validated scales

Much social work and social care research involves the investigation of constructs that may be complex and not easily observable or definable, including such concepts as empowerment, independence, psychological distress or policy activism. The use of scales and indices is one way in which these constructs can be measured or quantified in social work research. Unlike single items, scales and indices provide a means of including the many dimensions relevant to a particular concept and enable the ranking of individuals along a continuum where a phenomenon may be present to various degrees.

What are scales and indices?

Scales and indices are two types of composite measures in which multiple items are joined together to measure a single construct (variable). The use of validated scales may be advantageous in that they have been shown to accurately measure the concept of interest in a certain population, generating greater trustworthiness in the data gathered. We cannot presume this is the case if we are to generate our own question or scale attempting to quantify a particular phenomenon. Where validated scales are available in the public domain without charge, and do not require any kind of specialisation or training to administer, they can be a useful addition to a questionnaire if they assist in addressing the research question(s).

Furthermore, administration of a validated scale may enable the comparison of findings between research studies. See our examples from Susan, and Fiona and Rachel, in different fields of social work practice.

 Case study

Using validated scales

Susan and her colleagues used the 10-item Kessler Psychological Distress Scale (Kessler et al., 2002) to measure the levels of distress experienced by older people in prison. Population data for this validated scale were available from the general community as the measure was included in the latest version of the Australian Health Survey (Australian Bureau of Statistics, 2012). This enabled them to compare the levels of psychological distress experienced by older people in prison with those experienced by older people in the general community.

Fiona and Rachel have been working with social work students doing their placement in a hospital setting to advance their understanding of evidence based practice. Before getting students to do an exercise requiring the collection and critique of systematic reviews focused on health social work interventions, they administered a validated scale – the Evidence Based Practice Process Assessment Scale (Parrish and Rubin 2011) – which measures the degree of knowledge about evidence based practice in social work. Three months later, at the conclusion of the student exercise, the same scale was again administered to students. The results were analysed using a paired sample *t*-test to measure any changes arising from the students' training in evidence based practice.

Data mining: secondary analysis

Data mining is the use of pre-existing data to respond to one or more research questions, bearing in mind that the original data were usually collected by other researchers for a different purpose, for example, census data or records of service use.

Why use it? Collecting data is time consuming and expensive, so where data are already available and accessible, then they form a useful resource for research purposes. Data mining can also be used to compare findings from a specific research project to a larger population to discover differences between groups or samples.

How to use it? There are many examples of pre-existing data sets that can be used for the purpose of secondary analysis. Some data sets are publicly available (e.g. online), others require researchers or practitioners to go through processes to access the data (e.g. corrections data or hospital patients' data).

Some data sets that may be useful for social work and social care practitioners and researchers include those produced by:

- The Australian Bureau of Statistics (www.abs.gov.au) (e.g. Australian Census, Prisoners in Australia series, Australian Health Survey, Australian Aboriginal and Torres Strait Islander Health Survey, Crime and Safety Australia, Continuous Survey of Australia's Migrants)

- The Australian Institute of Health and Welfare (www.aihw.gov.au) (Child Protection Australia, Youth Justice Australia, Australia's Welfare series, Australia's Health series)
- UK government (https://data.gov.uk). This source provides access to non-sensitive, non-personal government data)
- Australian government (https://data.gov.au); providing access to a wide range of government data sets
- US Census Bureau (www.census.gov/data.html); providing information on issues ranging from employment, housing, families, income/poverty and the American Community Survey
- US Centers for Disease Control and Prevention (www.cdc.gov/nchs/data_access/ftp_data.htm): with surveys and data on ageing, healthcare, families, etc.

Clinical data mining (CDM)

For practitioners in the social work and social care fields, clinical data mining (CDM) may be of great value. It is a practice-based, retrospective research strategy whereby practitioner researchers systematically retrieve, codify, analyse and interpret available qualitative and/or quantitative data from their own and other agency records in order to reflect on the practice, programme and/or policy implications of their findings (Epstein, 2010: 71). CDM is non-intrusive and naturalistic as the data gathering does not encroach upon the practice context as the practice being studied has already been completed. For this reason CDM is best understood as being relevant in relation to improving what is known about practice rather than demonstrating its effectiveness.

What data sets are available in your context?

The kinds of research questions for which CDM may be useful are those which are derived inductively, that is, from practice itself (in contrast to deductively derived questions, such as those posed by a researcher wanting to understand an example of practice who poses the questions with little knowledge or experience of the practice context itself). For example, a hospital social worker working with older patients may have noticed that many of them present with complex health and social problems. She decides that she wants to know in more detail whether her observations are correct, what the medical and social characteristics of such patients in fact are, and the frequency with which they are referred to social workers for assistance. With this type of inquiry, she may decide to analyse the files of patients who meet certain criteria, in order to gather data to answer her question.

As we can see with this hypothetical example, CDM would be used in order to convert available data, through the mining process, into retrospective, quantitative and qualitative databases. For instance, the social worker might learn the number and characteristics of patients in this category who present over a set period. These quantitative data might then serve as a basis for delving more deeply into the issue of social work assistance through organising face-to-face interviews with social workers in order to understand what service they provided. Here is an example.

Case study

Clinical data mining of patient files

Laura an honours student (who we introduced in Chapter 1), wanted to study the characteristics of patients who were identified as 'social admissions' in a large metropolitan hospital. She conducted a literature review and from that identified the characteristics usually ascribed to 'social admission' patients. She then devised a template that noted these characteristics, such as their age, gender, medical diagnosis, marital status, living arrangements, length of stay. She reviewed the files of all patients over a 12-month period who had received that label, and analysed the files through the lens of her template. She had included space to record any other factors she noted in the files in addition to those captured by the template in order to build a comprehensive picture of the particular characteristics of those patients so-labelled in that hospital.

Of course, there may not always be adequate or available data on the patient files, for example, poor record keeping may result in incomplete data on many files. While CDM is considered to have a high degree of tolerance for missing data (Epstein, 2010), it will be important for the researcher to recognise the limitations of data availability and quality, and when analysing available data, to consider the meaning of absent or unavailable data. In addition, issues of validity and reliability may arise with reference to whether or not data are 'what they seem to be', for example, are they in fact a record of the services the patient received, or are there gaps on the file due to the social worker's respect for confidentiality?

How to do CDM

Epstein (2010) provides a useful 10-step strategy (2010: 69–122) for undertaking CDM:

10 steps in the clinical data mining process

First, the researcher needs to begin with questions: What are you interested in knowing? What data are currently available in your agency that are in any way related to your interest? How much of this is currently accessible to you?

Step 1: Identify all potential data sources and assess their accessibility, relevance, usefulness.

Step 2: Conceptualise, inventory and sort all available variable dimensions about which there are useable data, for example:

i   Client characteristics – demographics, psychosocial factors, etc.

ii Practice interventions – type, frequency, intensity of social work interventions

iii Treatment or service outcomes, for example, short- and long-term indicators of quality of life, psychosocial factors, morbidity, mortality, etc.

(Continued)

(Continued)

Step 3: Decide on a unit of analysis, for example, aggregate the data for individual clients, single pro-grammes, a total agency, etc.

Step 4: Select a time frame or window within which to collect data. The researcher will need to decide how far back to go in data gathering, or how far forward in order to see programme impact, etc.

Step 5: If needed, decide on a sampling strategy: this could be, for example, a power analysis, or stratified random sampling, etc.

Step 6: Data extraction: Read the qualitative data, then develop a form through which to read the data subsequently. This form is like a forced-choice questionnaire with mutually exclusive catego-ries, such as age, marital status, intervention applied, etc. Many researchers develop a template from both their reading of the relevant literature and their preliminary reading of the file data. This they then use a bit like a lens through which data are read, the template alerting them to relevant information.

If a practitioner is intending to mine their own records, for example, to answer questions about the amount of time they allocate to particular activities in working with their clients, the data extraction form might reflect their own conceptual and theoretical framework, or establish the face validity of key concepts they routinely use. In this case they might be best to test the reliability of their own ratings through inviting a colleague to check the similarities or differences in how they might rate such aspects. This may prove valu-able in assisting the practitioner researcher to reflect on their practice interventions and theories in ways that may be new.

Step 7: Most research requires approval from a human research ethics committee. Even if no contact will be made with patients (as in the case of CDM), ethics approval of such factors as who may have access to patient records may need to be sought.

Step 8 (and this also applies to Step 6): The researcher will need to consider issues of validity and reliabil-ity, or, how much confidence can be place in the accuracy of the data, for example (a) whether it is ade-quately represented (external validity), (b) that it measures what we claim it measures (internal validity) and (c) that it does so consistently (reliability).

Step 9: Establishing plan for analysis:

o   Measure frequencies, percentages, measure of central tendency
o   This reveals existence of missing data, incorrect entries, ambiguous data.

CDM has 'high tolerance' for missing data but may need to reflect on the meaning of missing data.

- Re-inventory variables
- Plan for cross-tabulations or other bivariate analysis: this is based on which variables are considered independent, intervening and dependent: rather than developing hypotheses, practitioners might identify what they would expect to find
- Identify which relationships will be looked at.

Step 10: Data analysis and interpretation:

o   Make sense of relationships found.
o   Analyse both positive, negative and contradictory findings.
o   Consult prior literature – do this last rather than first in order to discover other questions, locate study in broader context, etc.

Chapter summary

In this chapter we have described those methods which rely on 'counting and measuring' – questionnaires, surveys, validated scales, data mining and clinical data mining. We have noted where they might be used in research and the kinds of research questions which they can be used to answer, their advantages and disadvantages.

Key take-home messages

In using 'counting and measuring' methods, remember:

- To consider why these methods – questionnaires, surveys, validated scales, data mining – will generate the data to answer your research question
- That each of these methods requires some preliminary skills in measurement
- That all of them require careful development, construction and piloting before use with research participants
- Often a mix of methods will assist in overcoming the limitations of one method, for example, using both a survey and an interview.

Have a go at data mining in order to answer this research question: *why do people post death notices in newspapers?*

- Read and consider obituaries in your local newspaper.
- Develop a data extraction form, for example: who posts notices? Who is likely to be the subject of an obituary? Mother? Child? Friend? On what days do people post them? What forms of words are used?
- Pilot your data extraction form by collecting all the obituary notices during one typical week and applying it.
- Identify findings; organise findings in relation to criteria identified on extraction template; note missing data; note what data are not collected by the template; identify the next research questions.

Additional resources

All of the sources cited in this chapter are particularly useful in offering advice and guidance for 'counting and measuring' methods.

For useful step-by-step guidance in constructing scales and other ways of measuring behaviour, see the US National Institute of Health e-source for behavioural and social science research: www.esource research.org/tabid/693/default.aspx.

Another site to access for advice on developing surveys, which includes links to other relevant sites such as SurveyMonkey, is: www.wikihow.com/Develop-a-Questionnaire-for-Research.

With regard to Clinical Data Mining and its application in social work and social care, see the paper by Pockett et al. (2010) '"Last orders": dying in a hospital setting', *Australian Social Work*, 63 (3): 250–65, who analysed the medical files of patients who had died in order to discover the extent to which discussions of end-of-life care had occurred.

9

Looking and Seeing[1]
Visual Methods

In this chapter you will learn

- The epistemological positions or paradigms where visual methods are appropriate
- When and with whom these methods may be most useful
- Basic introductory material about several mainstream 'looking and seeing' methods
- The skills needed by researchers for using these methods.

Introduction

In this chapter we have grouped together a number of research methods that rely on 'looking and seeing'; that is, methods which are mostly visual. This includes interpreting found visual materials, creating visual materials, as well as disseminating research findings.

As a diverse group of methods they reach across disciplines and are often used in multi- and interdisciplinary settings. The diversity is evident in both the sorts of images used (photographs, diagrams, relational maps, timelines, self-portraits, film and video, video diaries, collages, maps, memory books, drawings, cartoons and photo-diaries) and the different image sources. Diversity is also evident in the ways researchers use and attribute meaning to images used in the dissemination of their findings. Visual methods are often associated with/employed in ethnographic work, which is why we have grouped 'looking' and 'seeing' methods together in this chapter.

The use of images for social science purposes has a long history but in the past decade there has been a renewed interest coinciding in part with the arrival of the digital age, making images

---

[1]Co-authored with Alex Haynes

cheaper to make, easier to adjust, store and share (Banks, 1995, 2001; Rose, 2001). We live in a world where much of our lives and visual culture is mediated by software and social media platforms (such as YouTube, Vimeo, Pinterest, Facebook, Snapchat, Twitter, Flickr, Instagram). In some ways this interest also emerged from the theoretical (see Grant and Fine, 1992; Banks, 2001; Harper, 2002) and methodological debates (see Schwartz, 1989; Rose, 2001; Pink, 2006) that questioned conventional data collection methods, the nature of the researcher–participant relationship and the knowledge that this interaction is supposed to produce (Lapenta, 2011).

Using 'looking' and 'seeing' methods in your research can help you bring together theoretical, methodological and technological aspects of your study. They 'fit' with a view of research as ethical, participatory, collaborative and shared, and research that harnesses the advances we are experiencing with mobile and digital technologies and social media. The potential of research to contribute to social change continues to develop, and visual methods provide new ways of thinking about applied and activist research (Pink, 2011).

Rose (2015) suggests that several visual research methods have now become relatively mainstream, particularly visual ethnographies, image elicitation interviews and visual participatory research, and this chapter focuses on these.

Epistemological considerations

As we have discussed in Chapter 2, epistemology refers to the theory of knowledge itself. How we go about knowing suggests that we hold a particular perspective on what knowledge is, and how we might go about acquiring more or different knowledge about our world. This perspective reflects a paradigm, a shared set of beliefs and/or world view.

We believe people's experiences are intrinsically difficult to grasp; they are richly textured and complex. No one else can know how experience or sensation 'works' from one moment to the next, how the different aspects of the experience come together or what they mean for this particular moment in their life (Goodrich and Cornwell, 2008). The way people experience their reality goes well beyond the material and the textual. The methods we describe in this chapter are closely focused on evoking, observing and describing the meanings research participants ascribe to their lives and experiences. These experiences may be captured and interpreted through such visual modalities as photos and videos, methods favoured by researchers who locate themselves within the interpretivist paradigm. As we shall also discuss, collaboration between researcher and participant is central to many of these methods. Depending on the research question, however, the participatory aspects of these methods may suggest that they are of particular value when research is motivated by a wish to effect social and/or political change; this suggests that they also have resonance for researchers and participants working within the critical paradigm (revisit Chapter 2 if you need a refresher on these ideas).

If you want to work with participants and attempt to understand and represent their views and experiences, rather than doing research about or on people, Pink (2011) suggests that a collaborative approach demonstrates how many aspects of experience and knowledge are not visible; and even those that are visible will have different meanings to different people. Visual methods can provide a route into, or a practical entry point, for exploring some of the less visible dimensions of everyday life including the complex, multi-dimensional, relational, sensory, embodied and intangible aspects of experience.

Application of visual research methods: when and with whom

Visual methods can be particularly powerful tools for the researcher and participants. In their various forms they can be used at any stage of the research, be used together and as part of multi-method approaches to improve rigour, bridge psychological and physical realities and allow the combination of visual and verbal language.

Methods discussed in this chapter might be appropriate when your interests are in answering research questions, which rely on:

Capturing direct experience: Visual methods draw from sensory experience and enable that experience to be described, explicated and interpreted. For example, the researcher and participant might walk around places defined by the participant. This movement through, sensing of and direct experience can enable the participant and/or researcher to capture images, sounds, memories and descriptions of the place.

Understanding the ordinary and everyday: Sweetman (2009) argues that visual materials can 'reveal what is hidden in the inner mechanisms of the ordinary and the taken for granted' so interviews with participant-generated visual materials can be helpful in exploring the taken-for-granted things in participants' lives. Observational, visual and sensorial methods can create new spaces in which to broker everyday knowledge about people and their lives.

Accommodating different knowledge systems: For example, western and indigenous knowledge systems work within different frameworks and are based on different ways of viewing the world. Mutual understanding will only come via an acknowledgement of and respect for the differing world views in all their complexity. This involves a close reading of the subtexts of meanings and the subtleties of expression, which may be facilitated by 'looking and seeing' methods.

Creating a process of change in thoughts, meanings, interpretations and actions: Visual research methods are often used in reflexive, participatory or action research projects – photovoice, participatory video and digital storytelling are particular kinds of participatory research explicitly aiming to empower research participants by creating visual materials.

Youth worker/researcher, school–community hub

For me it was the photographs and drawings that the teacher asked children to take, rather than my talk with those children that revealed the importance of pets to their lives and the influence that had on the physical activities they did outside school time.

The growing popularity of visual methods is linked to a range of claims about accessibility, inclusivity and the potential for visual materials to prompt different interactions, in some cases discussion that is more emotional, more affective, more 'ineffable' (Bagnoli, 2009). It is also argued that images are powerful conduits for the sensory experience, feel and texture of environments (Latham, 2003).

It is also claimed that visual methods enable researchers to work alongside participants, offering richer understandings of the lives of those who may be unwilling or unable to engage with traditional social science methods (Catalani and Minkler, 2010; Haaken and O'Neill, 2014). This may include:

- People who may not respond to an invitation to complete a survey or participate in an interview because of isolation, lack of confidence, limited language or comprehension
- People who speak a language other than that of the researcher and expressed in the communication material related to the research
- People who have a disability, or may have difficulty with certain ways or methods of communicating
- Those interested in making change happen, or using research to benefit themselves, their communities and campaigns
- Children and young people who may be more easily engaged/interested in using visual methods and technologies than more traditional methods (see Luttrell, 2010; Lomax et al., 2011; Lomax, 2012)
- groups of mixed ages and abilities (such as parents/grandparents with children) (see Mannay, 2010, 2013).

The digital format of video and photography facilitates collaborative work since researchers can share and scrutinise data together (Wiles et al., 2010). It reduces participants' and researchers' reliance on memory and offers strong ecological validity (Baranek et al., 2005). As Pierce (2005) notes, video data are often more emotionally engaging than text data, more closely reproducing the feelings, lived experiences and sensations of the participants, and assisting in the capture of details of everyday behaviour and practice (Hernandez-Albujar, 2007: 284).

Method choices

There is a large and growing array of different methods that involve 'looking and seeing'. In the following pages we describe and provide examples from three mainstream groups of methods: ethnographies, image elicitation and participatory visual methods, as well as discussing relevant methodological considerations. While we have selected some of the most common methods to expand on in the next section, Pink (2011) reminds us that methods are sometimes developed for/with particular projects in mind. Indeed it is not unusual for researchers to 'make up' methods as they go along. Given the collaborative and participatory nature of such methods, their specific use may have to emerge in the field based on the relationships secured and not predetermined. This emphasises the key role that context plays as a primary determinate for the appropriateness and role of visual technologies in research.

Ethnographies

This method uses graphic and written records of observed behaviour and symbol-meaning relations to provide a detailed in-depth description of the social life of people, practice and cultures, which can generate understandings of culture and stories about what it means to be human. Visual ethnographies are not purely visual but rather pay particular attention to the visual aspects of culture (Berg, 2014). We discuss two particular approaches here: participant observation and video reflexive ethnography.

Participant observation

While participant observation is a long-standing method of ethnographic, anthropological and sociological research and not necessarily visual, it is included here as it fits the chapter theme of 'looking and seeing' and it is the platform for visual and sensory ethnographies. As Lofland et al. (2006) point out, participant observation gets you 'closer' to everyday routine than any other method, enabling you to share what people do, listen to what they talk about in action (rather than in interviews) and note what they take for granted, capturing those nuanced understandings they have of what is going on.

Marshall and Rossman (1989: 79) define participant observation as 'the systematic description of events, behaviors, and artifacts in the social setting chosen for study'. Researchers need to develop rapport and establish trust with those being observed; it may be time consuming, and it always demands a high level of patience and a non-judgemental attitude in the researcher.

Participant observation is a method you can use when you are setting out on a study and want to get a 'feel for' the culture under investigation, which might be a community, or an ethnic group, or social workers doing a particular job such as child protection work, or social care workers in an aged care residential facility. See the example below from Alex, which shows how she achieved this.

 ## Case study

Getting to know your setting

Working with a large group of women who were refugees or people seeking asylum, with diverse ethnic and cultural backgrounds, was new to Alex so she started with participant observation. This meant that the group could continue their own activities, get to know her, develop an appreciation of what the research was about and share enough information so she could determine any sensitivities or interests of the group that might influence further method choice or process. The group members, activities and dynamics changed every week, so attending for a few weeks and participating in their activities gave Alex a much better understanding of what might be possible and appropriate. She came to understand the extent to which communication might be a challenge. Alex's initial observation phase enabled her to focus on the group and what was happening, to attempt to understand a little without intervening directly with particular activities or processes designed with limited appreciation of the context.

Spradley (1980) identifies three principles for recording observations:

- Use the speakers' language and accounts
- Make a verbatim record which is concrete and detailed
- As far as possible, make sure that you separate hunches, feelings, notes and memos in order to make sure that field observations and interpretations are not blurred or merged, the goal being to get detailed written descriptive accounts – ideally recorded on the day of the observation.

In addition to note taking you can use video to record detailed observations, which can help you develop insight into the nature of complex, multilayered transactional relationships amongst people and their environments. Video data may be viewed repeatedly, enhancing the capacity to capture gestures, behaviour, body postures, facial expressions and reactions to the environment. For example, in relation to occupational therapy, Bailliard's (2015) video based project with migrants demonstrates the potential which video data contribute to understandings of identity, the physical environment, the stream of occupations and collective occupations.

Alex, PhD student during participant observation and group work

I used a Tumblr blog (closed) to record my observations. This enabled me to enter notes directly on my iPad during or immediately after observation and add labels I could search for later. I had three main types of posts – the first was descriptions about the physical space, who was there, what happened; the second type of post captured thoughts, questions, concerns this raised for me; and the third type included what ideas and links I was generating through the observation.

Visual and sensory ethnographies involve rethinking the core components of ethnography, principally participant observation, and exploring the numerous ways that smell, taste, touch and vision can be interconnected within research and in response to our increasingly digital world. In relation to sensory ethnographies, Lee and Ingold's (2006) analysis of how routes and mobilities are represented in local visual culture through locally produced experiential, audiovisual and photographic narratives offers new understandings of how place is made. Sunderland et al. (2012) suggest that sensory ethnography encourages both researchers and participants to draw on all their senses to help focus on things that are less readily observable to create a deeper understanding of the relationships between place and participants' health and wellbeing.

Video reflexive ethnography

This method involves the video recording of the activity of participants in their natural setting to enable insight into their practices. It involves observation and filming, participants viewing the material and reflexively discussing their practice. Participants might identify opportunities, develop a rationale for change and put these into practice. In this way, the process and the findings offer participants opportunities to build capacity for ongoing critical appraisal of practice.

Video reflexive research has been used in order to assist teams in evaluating themselves. Using a visual medium enables 'clinicians to recognise the distributed, unspoken, and risk-prone dimensions of their taken-as-given sayings, knowings, and doings' (Carroll et al., 2008). As Carroll et al. note (2008: 389), watching a video of ourselves 'at work' in a team influences how we experience our own practices, generating 'new information relations and feedback intensities …' enabling viewers to reshape existing practices.

Mary, medical consultant

As a leader of a multidisciplinary team in a hospital I wanted to research how our team makes decisions. With their consent, I used videos of our team meetings in order for team members to have a look at what happens in our team, for example, who talks, who doesn't, who initiates decisions, etc. Watching the video together, we learned a great deal and made some adjustments to team meetings, including making sure we made time to hear from everyone. We think our decision-making will be a better process, leading to better outcomes for patients, because of this.

Methodological considerations in using ethnographies

It is important to communicate clearly and transparently who you are as a researcher, what your purpose is in observing, what you propose to observe and what you will do with those observations. You should also try to understand the effect of your relationship with the people being observed.

An important consideration to mention here is bias: over and above the effect of observation generally the presence of a camera and the knowledge of being filmed can result in participants modifying or enhancing their performance. However, Iedema et al. (2013) argue that participants are not skilful in acting differently from how they would normally. If they do know how to enhance what they do, they are never able to maintain this for very long and soon lapse back into their normal behaviours (see Dewey, 1922 as cited in Iedema et al., 2013).

If you plan to use ethnographic methods, questions may include:

- How will you gain entry to, and present yourself in the setting?
- Who should you observe or talk to?
- What and how should you observe?
- How should you capture or record what you are observing?
- Will you share your records with participants? If so, how and why?

Ethnography is a relatively involved process over a significant period of time so it is important to recognise the transformative potential of fieldwork where, as you search for answers to questions about people, you may find yourself in the stories of others (Hoey, 2008).

Image elicitation

This approach uses still and moving images as part of the group discussion or interview process, usually with the intention of supporting a richer understanding of participants' experiences (Harper, 2002). The images may be 'found' images generated by people other than the researcher and research participants as a means of evoking memories, feelings and experiences, or they may be images generated by the researcher or participants. These elicitation methods tend to centre on photographs, film or video and drawing, but they may also encompass collage, painting and other visual forms of representation, as well as digital media (Harper, 2002).

Pink (2011), Harper (2002) and Heisley and Levy (1991) all describe an ethically informed research practice that interprets the use of images as an opportunity to empower participants to voice their interpretations thereby giving back to the research participants. Image elicitation based interaction enables the researcher to observe and participate in the discussion and may provide a collective image based representation drawn from participant's consensus regarding how they view their own lives and communities. We outline two key methods here: photo elicitation interviews and video diaries.

Photo elicitation interviews

Photo elicitation is based on the simple idea of inserting a photograph into a research interview. Interviews face the challenge of establishing communication between two people who rarely share social, ethnic or cultural backgrounds. Photo elicitation can help bridge the gap: Schwartz (1989) found that participants responded to photographs without hesitation, and the strangeness of the interview situation was averted.

Images can be:

- Taken by the researcher (e.g. photos of the participant's world or of a particular subject)
- Existing images selected by the researcher (e.g. aerial photos of the local area assumed to have meaning for the participant)
- Taken by the researcher while accompanied by one or more participants who might suggest what and how to photograph (e.g. photos or video from a walk around the town together)
- Taken or chosen by the participant (e.g. existing family photos).

Where images are those that participants have taken or selected themselves, sometimes referred to as reflexive photography or auto driven photo elicitation (see Heisley and Levy, 1991; Clark, 1999), this can provide a means to give 'the informant increased voice and authority in interpreting such events while … provid[ing] a perspective … that makes systems meaningful to an outsider. It also manufactures distance for the participant so they see familiar data in unfamiliar ways' (Heisley and Levy, 1991: 257). For example, Fritz and Lysach (2014) explored how patients understood their self-management of their chronic illness. In their view, photo elicitation interviews led to a detailed understanding of the intricacies of self-management and promoted reflective awareness of beliefs, perceptions and social-contextual influences on self-management practices that participants were, at times, unaware of.

Video diaries

Video diaries are a method that not only captures the narratives of experience and lived cultural practices, but also the visual nature of how people both construct and perform their identity (see Holliday, 2001). Sunderland and Denny (2007) suggest that participant-produced video diaries can arouse anxiety about the 'performed' nature of the recorded activities and this highlights the need to define video productions as cultural documents in need of interpretation. The tapes cannot speak for themselves and the process of analysis is crucial (Chalfen and Rich, 2007).

Methodological considerations in using image elicitation

Epstein et al. (2006) suggest that it is methodologically significant who makes or selects certain images or scenes over others to be used in the interview process. The advantage of researcher-selected photographs is that they can function as a consistent, yet flexibly organised, set of images. These can be used to explore participants' differing understanding or perceptions given the same pictures enabling hypotheses to be tested across a large sample or the comparison of results across studies using the same images. Schwartz (1989) adds that researcher-produced sets of photographs can generate descriptions and meanings that may illuminate subjects initially invisible to the researcher but visible to participants, enabling the researcher to develop new interpretations. The quandary of this researcher-generated image approach arises from questions about whose knowledge the selected pictures actually represented. A range of alternative approaches

Consider your own bias – perhaps take your own photos of the social world you are examining; consider how text and images could be assembled into a photoessay (story). Discuss it with others.

have been developed that involve the participants taking the images themselves or collaboratively producing images, or a mix of both. These alternative approaches enable participants to show researchers their worlds from their point of view.

If you plan to use image elicitation methods, questions may include:

- Who will produce or select the images?
- How will you honour participants' desires for anonymity or representation (such as obscuring identity in photographs; you will recall we discussed this in Chapter 3 as an ethical concern)?
- How will you manage consent of participants and others captured in images?
- How can you structure the interview (see Clark-Ibanez, 2004; Nutbrown, 2011; Phelan and Kinsella, 2013)?

Participatory visual methods

These include different creative forms of communication and expression, such as drama, photography, film, drawing, design, creative writing and music (see, for example, the use of therapeutic song writing in palliative care; O'Callaghan, 2015). Using collaborative processes, participants and facilitators work together to produce powerful stories or representations. Methods like digital storytelling and participatory video are participatory visual methods. We discuss these below.

The diversity of methods and the way methods evolve in relation to context and environment make clear distinction between method types difficult. Methods are used in different ways with different emphasis. For example, a project may involve participants taking their own photos, discussing them and exhibiting them, but the researcher determines the focus and/or process and the research data are drawn from what participants say about their images, so would be akin to image elicitation. Another project may have similar steps (taking photos, discussing and exhibiting) but be working with an existing community group campaigning for change and focus on the participatory and transformational potential of the research, more akin to participatory visual methods, particularly Photovoice. Methods from the three method groups described above are often combined – for example, a project might use participant observation and then image elicitation interviews or digital storytelling methods depending on the research question and the participants.

Methods are also influenced by the medium or tool and the technology used. Each research tool (video, mobile phone, etc.) and technology (social media platform, software) can be deployed alongside different methodologies, philosophical orientations and foci of inquiry. As a result, the specific limitations and challenges of each method will vary according to the particularities of each project. It might be tempting to get carried away with different mediums and technologies but you need to keep connected to your research question and the rationale for your method choice. It is important to remember that not all of these methods will be suitable for every individual or group you choose to work with, so they should be tailored to suit the needs of those involved. If people do not have experience of using the chosen medium or tool, they should be given guidance and support. We focus here on three approaches: digital storytelling, participatory video and participatory photography.

Digital storytelling

Using storytelling, group work, modern technology and different mediums (e.g. film, animation, photos and audio recordings) participants create their own 2–3-minute multi-media clips to convey personal or community stories. Digital stories can facilitate the dissemination of research findings in accessible and engaging ways, for example, to promote health behaviour change (see Cummings et al., 2010: 54) or raise awareness of social justice issues (Jernigan et al., 2012).

Digital stories are typically created through group based workshops, designated for the public or customised for a specific organisation or group (e.g. healthcare providers or patient population). As an example a standard workshop might take place over 3 days and involve 8–12 participants. The first day is used for introductions, an overview of digital storytelling, sharing of personal stories, script review and development. The second day comprises teaching of the technical skills necessary to put the story into digital form, and the third day is used for finishing the digital story and showing the stories made in the group (see Lal et al., 2015 and the Story Center (www.storycenter.org) for examples).

Digital stories are powerful vehicles through which to create and share knowledge. By adhering to the short format, the storyteller is required to get to the heart of the matter so it's effective in capturing life's defining moments or turning points (Lambert, 2013). The format is easily uploaded to the internet (Meadows, 2003), opening up possibilities for file sharing, repeat viewings and audience distribution. While using multi-media increases the potential for an emotional and sensorial experience for the viewer, it is important to remember that multi-media (e.g. photos, music) serve mainly as tools for the storyteller.

Participatory video

This involves participants learning basic filming skills and working together to agree narratives, and shoot and produce their films. It is an empowering process, enabling people to take action for solving their own problems and communicating this to decision-makers, their communities and the wider public.

Participatory video can be used with other methods. For example, a smaller group of participants might use participatory video to collectively analyse and synthesise the stories created through an earlier digital storytelling process.

Participatory photography

Wang et al. (2000) found that using participatory photography methods (in this case Photovoice) enabled participants to define the research agenda through the discussion of the photographs. Rather than asking direct, narrow predefined questions geared around examining an existing academic question, the points of the inquiry were generated by the issues brought up in the photos and the open-ended interviews that followed. Photovoice can encourage the development of a shared interpretation to enable participants to 'voice' their collective view to a 'public' audience of, for example, policy-makers, politicians, etc. Boddy et al. (2014) used Photovoice with primary school aged children to understand their views about, and hopes for, their community. The children were asked to take photographs of their community and the photos were then used in one-on-one interviews in which the children were asked about the content of the photos, why they took particular images and how the photos depict their likes and dislikes and their hopes for the community.

Sonia, researcher working with a community based youth group

The young people really responded to the 'short' and 'digital' format of the digital stories. They loved the opportunity to create a sort of collage with snippets from photos, images and artefacts. Drawing together things that were important to their story helped them organise and prioritise what they wanted to say. The group work involved in introduction, skill building and script development really built momentum and trust that facilitated an environment for sharing of personal stories.

Alex, PhD student working with a community based women's group

Making the video with the Arabic speaking women has been amazing as it is all in Arabic to enable everyone to have a say and feel comfortable expressing complex ideas or detailed stories which they wouldn't attempt in English or with an interpreter. Not understanding what they are saying enables me to focus on their body language, process and in making the video I am not able to influence content, direction much at all. Almost forced into the background, which even though I would like to put myself there, often it is still quite hard to do but this process really forces that handing over.

Methodological considerations in using participatory methods

Participatory methods demand a very considered approach. This type of research requires a significant social commitment and a democratic social and political context. You can draw on the extensive body of literature describing their intent, methodological and ethical issues and processes. If you plan to use participatory methods, questions may include:

- How will you recognise and respond to the context knowing that the depth and type of democracy has implications for the extent of participation, who participates and the framing of the research aims, and therefore the results?
- How will you create a safe space for participants to disclose their ideas, opinions and experiences?
- When and how will you consider the appropriateness of the method(s) to the participants and the previous experiences of research partners and participants?

This research necessarily involves participants having power and control over the form, processes and products of the research. This is a significant shift for most researchers unfamiliar with participatory research.

Ethical considerations when using visual methods

As we discussed in Chapter 3, ethical questions arise at all stages of research projects – from planning to completion and beyond. The multi-faceted process of visual or media production, exhibition and distribution has many variables and risks. Representational characteristics and features of images generate unique ethical issues beyond those of the written word. Researchers need to consider the potential implications for individuals and the institutions or communities of which they are a part, and how the research, and indeed the images, may be used during and after the project, but also into the future.

Alex, PhD student

As I began engaging with some existing community groups I started to ask myself – how will I really inform them of the research, risks, impacts, outcomes, consequences? What happens if some members don't consent? What existing rules and norms does the group operate within? The women haven't been involved in anything like this so they can't imagine what they are consenting to. From the outset we made it okay not to consent, we included everyone in activities even if some didn't consent to their data/images being used they could still participate but their images/data were not included in the project.

Each technique or medium will have specific ethical challenges. Researchers must justify the collection of data and explicate procedures for protecting participant confidentiality and obtaining informed consent. Strict measures for protecting data may be necessary (e.g. storing data on external hard drives in locked cabinets, deleting files from cameras, de-identifying data). Researchers must address the possibility that unanticipated actors will be captured during data collection, which may position them as participants requiring informed consent.

As mentioned earlier in this chapter visual methods enable researchers to work alongside participants, supporting people who might not otherwise participate in research. However, alongside this potential benefit there remain a number of challenges, including how to protect individuals and communities from the possibility of harm that might arise from participating or being recognised in research outputs and, conversely, how to mitigate the potential harm that anonymising and not attributing images may cause (Prosser et al., 2008; Wiles et al., 2010).

Fatima, PhD student

I submitted a high risk ethics application as part of my PhD study and stated that I would not use/distribute images produced during the research. The university ethics committee responded and asked me to consider allowing people to show/exhibit their work (images) if they chose to. They considered it was important for people to have choice and control over their productions.

A quick word about data analysis

We discuss data analysis in Chapters 10 and 11, but it is important to understand that visual methods are likely to generate several different forms of data. At the outset of the project you should consider what data are likely to be generated, and in what form they will be available for analysis (such as photographs, transcripts of interviews discussing images, notes from observation, video from group walk around). The process and staging of analysis and who is involved are also important considerations, particularly if you are using participatory methods. See Michelle's example of how she approached this.

Pick one or more of the following research activities and, depending on what would be most useful at the stage you are at, consider how you will address the ethical challenges they present:

- Recruiting participants
- Generating visual data
- Analysing visual material
- Communicating your research.

 Case study

Managing multiple types of data

In Michelle's project, the methods chosen by the group of young refugees included interviews and focus groups with other young people, but also incorporated a questionnaire, photography projects by the group members, blogs, diaries and mapping processes with groups of young people as ways of generating data. She developed a matrix for all the different sources of data and the types of data generated by each source. Given the multiple sources Michelle and the group decided to analyse each sub-set of data with the people who generated the data (e.g. the young people who wrote a blog came together and discussed all the blogs and developed some key themes). Then the group looked at all the material together through a series of workshops looking firstly at the themes emerging from each source (e.g. what did the focus groups tell us?) and then looking at each theme across the different sources. Throughout the project Michelle kept focusing the group's attention back to the research question about how young people from refugee backgrounds experienced local places to make sure the data would help answer the question.

Throughout your project it is important to explore claims about 'voice'. Eliciting participants' voices is not straightforward. Researchers' and participants' own agendas may mean that participants' voices may be unequally heard in the process of production and intentions may get lost in the process. By paying close attention to the processes involved in the production, analysis and dissemination of images, you are more likely to avoid de facto assumptions about inclusivity and authenticity that are the basis of much criticism of image based research. You need to work hard to provide a transparent evidence base for the data obtained through elicitation and participatory methods (again, maintaining a research journal and making good use of your supervisor and colleagues will allow you to work in a self-aware way).

Have you provided evidence of the choices you made and considered their political and ethical dimensions, and have you provided an assessment of the biases inherent in your work over the project's lifespan? What are the alternative explanations for what you 'see'?

Researcher skills

In this chapter we have discussed a number of visual research methods. Some of the skills that researchers need, or need to develop, to use these methods include the following:

- Technical skills, for example, in operating cameras, or in editing footage
- People skills, such as the capacity to establish rapport with participants, to know how best to present oneself in settings with which one may be unfamiliar
- Personal characteristics such as patience, non-judgemental attitudes, trustworthiness, transparency and openness to collaborate with participants in order to share the data interpretation process
- Skills in time management, which include the capacity to anticipate the amount of time, which might be needed to gain entry to a setting or community, and the time required to arrive at an understanding of the phenomena being viewed or recorded; visual methods, particularly participatory ones, promote longer, more detailed interaction in comparison with other methods
- Ability to respond to dynamic situations and deal effectively with the unanticipated and unpredicted.

In broad terms any researcher wanting to use visual research methods should develop a critical understanding of local and academic visual cultures, the visual media and technologies being used and the ethical issues they raise (Pink, 2006).

Chapter summary

In this chapter we have discussed a range of methods that rely primarily on 'looking and seeing', emphasising that this 'looking and seeing' or data collection and interpretation, is very likely a shared activity between researcher and participant. We discussed the epistemological positioning and ethical issues these methods raise, encouraging the reader to return to Part I of the book for more detailed information. While acknowledging that different 'looking and seeing' methods comprise a fast developing area, given the advances in technology and social media platforms, we chose a number of different methods to describe – observation, visual methods including the use of photos, videos and digital storytelling. The ethical and data analysis challenges were briefly raised as both these facets of research are explored in greater detail in Chapters 3 and 9.

Key take-home messages

Keep your research question firmly at the forefront of your mind as it's easy to get 'carried away' with exciting methods that might produce unexpected outcomes and may threaten to take you in unexpected directions.

Remember that not all of these methods will be suitable for every individual or group you work with. They should be tailored to suit the needs of those involved and people should be given the guidance and support they need to engage in the processes and use the chosen tools.

Each research tool (video, mobile phone, etc.) and technology (social media platform, software) can be used alongside different methodologies and research questions. This means that the limitations and challenges of each method will vary with each project.

Be responsive to participants, balancing their expectations with the possibilities for harm, informed by the wider contexts in which images are viewed and the ways in which these may in turn shape and silence participants' voices or produce unintended consequences for participants.

Additional resources

These two texts provide fuller accounts of practical visual methods:

Rose, G. (2012) *Visual Methodologies: Introduction to Researching with Visual Materials* (3rd edn). London: Sage.
Banks, M. and Zeitlyn, D. (2015) *Visual Methods in Social Research*. London: Sage.

This book and the online resource below are both helpful in exploring ethical issues in visual research approaches:

Cox, S., Drew, S., Guilleman, M., Howell, C., Warr, D. and Waycott, J. (2014) *Guidelines for Ethical Visual Research Methods*. Melbourne: The University of Melbourne.
Wiles, R., Prosser, J., Bagnoli, A., Clark, A., Davies, K., Holland, S. and Renold, E. (2008) *Visual Ethics: Ethical Issues in Visual Research*. ESRC National Centre for Research Methods Review Paper. Southampton: National Centre for Research Methods, available at http://eprints.ncrm.ac.uk/421 (accessed 25 April 2016).

For detailed accounts of the processes of doing participant observation, see:

Fine, G. (2003) 'Towards a peopled ethnography developing theory from group life', *Ethnography*, 4 (1): 41–60.
Bernard, H.R. (ed.) (1998) *Handbook of Methods in Cultural Anthropology*. Walnut Creek, CA: Alta Mira Press.

For a comprehensive account of participant observation, see:

Kawulich, B.B. (2005) 'Participant observation as a data collection method', *Forum Qualitative SozialFORSCHUNG/Forum Qualitative Social Research*, 6 (2), Art. 43.

For further resources on digital storytelling, see:

Story Center (formerly The Center for Digital Storytelling): http://storycenter.org. This centre provides an avenue for those engaged in research using digital methods to partner with others and share stories.

A useful online site – Transformative storytelling for social change: www.transformativestory.org offers supporting resources and case studies as well as a regular blog.

For further resources with regard to participatory video, see:

'Insights into participatory video: a handbook for the field', http://insightshare.org/resources/pv-handbook. This is a practical guide to setting up and running participatory video projects. Another Insightshare publication, 'A rights-based approach to participatory video: toolkit', contains exercises and tools for participatory video facilitators who are keen to adopt a rights based approach to their work.

Template for organising your literature review

We like the suggestion from Timmins and McCabe (2005: 44) for developing a master document that summarises the key features of each paper in tabular form. We have borrowed from this and added some additional ideas which we have organised as a template.

Article: reference; author, title, publication, date	
Purpose of study: study design	
Type of study: methods	
Sample	
Data collection	
Ethical issues	
Findings	
Critical comments	
Implication for application and for your study	

Guidelines for preparing a research proposal

Your proposal can be short and concise, ideally no more than four pages. It might include some or all of the following information:

1. Researcher's name
2. Preliminary title of proposed research, for example, 'An exploratory study of factors which may lead to homelessness for women'
3. The research problem (see Chapters 1 and 3)

   - State briefly what stimulated the study and why it is important; for example, jot down how or in what way the research will advance knowledge in a particular field of social work and social care

4. The research question(s) (see Chapter 4)

   - What is/are the major questions to which you want answers, for example, 'Why do women in inner city Melbourne become homeless?' What hypotheses are to be tested? For example, that there is a causal relationship between depression and women becoming homeless
   - What subsidiary questions, if any, are you asking which you think will shed light on the primary problem or issue you are researching? For example, (1) what are the characteristics of home-less women in Melbourne? (ii) What factors do women who are homeless tell us prompted their move into homelessness?

5. Related literature and theoretical considerations (see Chapters 2 and 4)

   Include:

   - A brief initial review of the literature for similar studies, and/or prior work on the subject, for example, systematic reviews, other literature reviews, similar studies (no more than 500 words).
   - A brief explanation of your epistemological and/or theoretical position, for example, positivism, pragmatism, theories of homelessness, theories of the meaning of home, feminist perspectives on homelessness, etc.
   - Define key terms, for example, 'home', 'homelessness', 'homeless women', 'pathways into homelessness'

6. Logic of approach (see Chapter 5)

   - State how you plan to approach the problem, that is, the research design you have devel-oped for the study. Use this to demonstrate how your approach will provide the information needed. This might include a discussion of your epistemological and methodological position, for example, an exploratory interpretivist study designed to gather and analyse the narratives homeless women tell about how they became homeless

7. Method (see Chapters 6, 7, 8, 9)

   - If the study is essentially experimental, what procedures will be used to extract and organise the data? What are the tentative notions about sampling, controls, reliability tests or other aspects of method pertinent to the study?

- If the study is essentially qualitative or interpretive, include a discussion of the methods to be used, for example, coding, thematic analysis, computer-assisted analysis, etc.
- How will trustworthiness of your interpretations be achieved?
- What role, if any, will the researched play in the data analysis?

8. Ethical issues (see Chapter 3)

   Note the nature of any ethical problems or dilemmas that you anticipate.

   - What plans do you have for exploring and resolving these?
   - What are the requirements regarding getting ethical approval for the study from the organisation or university where you work or study?

9. Outline of the data to be collected and methods of analysis

   - Present an outline of the data to be sought, indicating the kinds of methods to be utilised, for example, collection and analysis of statistical data on number of women using homeless shelters; interviews with homeless women; feminist analysis of policy documents relating to women's homelessness, etc. See Chapters 10 and 11 for suggestions for analysing your data

10. Availability of resources

    - Identify the sources for data you will gather; note the accessibility of these data and how/if your or another organisation will be able to provide this
    - Consider the appropriateness and/or possibility of client participation
    - Note what resources of time, technology, non-material support and funding will be available, for example, designated study leave days, access to library, payment to participants (if appropriate) and where this will come from; postage; booking/hiring rooms for meetings; payment for parking, etc.

11. Relation to a larger project (if appropriate)

    - If the project is part of a larger piece of research, or done under the employment of others, specify the extent to which the design methodology, collection of data and interpretation of findings will be your own responsibility
    - Indicate your obligations to the larger project to make data available, and restrictions, if any, on publication. What agreements have been made about manuscript or material review?

12. Summary of pilot efforts

    - Describe any plans for a pilot study

13. Tentative table of contents for the completed research report or thesis
14. Tentative timetable for your work, for example, date of commencement and completion; when you expect to complete ethics approval processes; when you will begin and end data gathering; time proposed for data analysis; time proposed for write-up; time proposed for publications to be written and submitted. A chart is a useful way of presenting the time line.

PART III
Making Use of Research

10

Making Meaning from Data

Qualitative Analysis

In this chapter you will learn

- When and why you analyse qualitative data
- To distinguish between the range of strategies for analysing qualitative data
- A general structured approach to analysing your qualitative data
- Some core skills in coding and beginning to work with qualitative data.

Introduction

This chapter is the first in the final section of this book, which focuses on generating and using knowledge from our research. We focus here on analysing qualitative data. Some of you will be feeling excited at this point, while others may be feeling confused. Any of us who have worked with qualitative data know that feeling … what to do when confronted with so much material – so many pages. Never fear, our aim in this chapter is to give you some practical tools that you can use to make this process more manageable. We also agree with the position expressed by Miles et al. (2014: 277) that 'People are meaning finders and meaning makers; they can usually make sense of the most chaotic events'.

We start by talking generally about qualitative data and some general principles of analysis; we will also outline the range of ways qualitative data can be analysed. Definitions will be provided for all methods, along with clear descriptions. The need to link the intended purpose of the research with the chosen analytic technique is emphasised, with examples given. The option of using computer-assisted analysis is discussed. Case examples will continue to be used to highlight decision-making about analytic techniques, methods used and examples of analysis. Links to further readings and online materials will be given.

Working with qualitative data: awareness of the personal and environmental context

Patton (2015: 14) describes qualitative data as consisting of '(1) in-depth, open-ended interviews; (2) direct observations; and (3) written communications'. What does this tell us about this type of data? That it includes what you are told directly by a primary source (research participant), what you can see or what can be gleaned from existing documents, such as case files or even images, as we have discussed in the preceding chapter. There are those who see working with qualitative data as the 'soft' or easier option when doing research. From this perspective these data are simply anecdotes ('just' a story, biased and inconsistent), and not 'real' evidence (D'Cruz and Jones, 2004: 66). Miles and Huberman (1994: 56) on the other hand, remind us of the complexity of this material: 'qualitative research is … done chiefly with words, not with numbers. Words are fatter than numbers and usually have multiple meanings … Worse still, most words are meaningless unless you look backward and forward to *other* words'. Clearly, working with qualitative data is not the easy option!

If you have ever gathered data via interviews, focus groups or visual methods, you will know that this generates a lot of data (and plenty of paper if you are like us and still like to 'see' a hard copy!). The key task is to make sense of this in a systematic and replicable way. To do this you need to understand firstly that qualitative data analysis has no agreed upon rules or procedures (Lincoln and Guba, 1985; Erlandson et al., 1993; Kellehear, 1993; Grbich, 1999). Selecting analytic methods depends on the epistemological and theoretical underpinnings of a project and its specific research questions (Derry et al., 2010). General processes have been explicated, however, to ensure that analysis can be systematic, rigorous, defensible, replicable and the results trustworthy. Your job as a researcher is to locate the most appropriate approach for your research problem and your data and to use this systematically; we would also suggest keeping an

What things might make some patterns in your data easier to see than others?

- Issues with which you are most familiar (maybe raised in the literature)?
- High volume repetition of words?
- Data are simple (perhaps a dichotomous variable such as gender)?
- Data 'fits' with what you expect to see?
- Other possibilities?

audit trail of your analytic processes (as indicated in Chapter 5, this will support the trustworthiness of your data). You also need to harness your own skills and attitude. A key skill you will need to bring or develop is being able to see patterns in 'seemingly random information' (Boyatzis, 1998: 7). At this point it is important to recognise that it is easier for us to see some patterns rather than others.

An ongoing commitment to self-awareness is vital to this process. As ever, we can rely on an Einstein quote for guidance. He says that 'A man [sic] should look for what is, and not for what he [sic] thinks should be'; so, keeping an open and enquiring mind when doing data analysis is important.

As you will have heard us say throughout this book already, using a research journal (as discussed well by Engin, 2011 – see Chapter 1 if you need a reminder) will help you to question your own assumptions and expectations. Actively ask yourself, what else could this mean? And examine your data more than just once!

Keeping your research question firmly in mind will also keep you focused (we know you have heard us say this a lot!). As an example, when she began her data analysis, one student wrote her research question in large black print and stuck it above her desk so it was always in front of her – a 'true north' for her explorations.

Catherine

Before I began my PhD, I was working as a research assistant on a study looking at women's access to welfare services after prison. I spent 2 years interviewing women; the first year was all pre-release, so many hours in a prison setting, hearing many stories – with chaos a typical theme.

I later interviewed some of these women and their children for my doctoral study, asking them one question about their pre-prison lifestyle.

When I first read mothers' responses to this question, I coded a range of evident ideas, all mostly negative: drug use, offending, family violence, etc. But when I went back to review these data some time later, I 'noticed' some data I had not seen the first time around; this was all about the women describing parenting duties in their daily lives.

On reflection, it was clear that both my general experience in the prison (seeing chaos) and my expectations of these women specifically influenced my ability to see the data accurately. Revisiting your data and/or having independent peer review (see Chapter 6) are both useful strategies to minimise this.

The journey begins early: engaging with qualitative data during data collection

Unlike with quantitative data, qualitative data analysis typically begins in the data collection phase (Sarantakos, 2013). You may see this early iterative process referred to in research texts as *preliminary data analysis*, or as *beginning analysis*. The aim at this stage is to ask questions of the data; with the assumption being that you are engaging in an inductive process (inducing and developing *broad* concepts from raw data). This fulfils two important roles. It enables you as the researcher:

1. *To revise and shape your subsequent data collection.* New questions in areas of inquiry not previously considered may be added in to subsequent data collection if they emerge as 'of interest' in your beginning analysis. This is most appropriate and useful with exploratory research, which requires a more flexible, enquiring and adaptive approach.
2. *To track and inform your emerging analysis.* For example, in Catherine's PhD study, to understand what care arrangements were made with children when their mothers were going to prison, it emerged in her beginning analysis that she would need to consider 'Under what circumstances are women able to engage in a meaningful and appropriate discussion with children about their care?'

The degree to which you will engage in this early interaction with the data will vary by study; this will be influenced by what is known of the problem already, and what you need to know, as well as the theoretical and ideological orientation of the researcher/s. If, for example, you were conducting a descriptive study (refer to Chapter 5 if you need to remind yourself what this means) it would typically not be appropriate to amend your data collection once you had commenced, as research of this design requires you to be able to accurately map and compare your data across participants. Whereas some approaches, including *grounded theory*, posed initially by Glaser and Strauss (1967), use the process of data collection–analysis–feedback very specifically to guide the development of future data collection.

However, some researchers in studies that rely on qualitative materials plan for and collect their data, engaging in little reflection on this until the collection is complete (Sarantakos, 2013).What is most important to remember here is that decisions about the extent of analysis you engage in during data collection must be driven by the epistemology and study design. This, of course, will be tempered by the nature of the issue you seek to understand as well as the participant group from whom you collect data (are they 'elite' and likely to have limited availability for follow up data collection?).

Erlandson et al. (1993) offer relevant and balanced advice; rather than being seen as a one-off event, they see analysis as a progression, which continues on after the conclusion of data collection. They argue that qualitative data require two distinct types of analysis: during collection and after collection. These are qualitatively different processes, with different purposes. As discussed above, early analysis is to inform, revise and shape subsequent data collection, while that done at the conclusion of data collection aims to synthesise your data, seeing patterns and making connections: to develop themes and hypotheses. The aim of this analysis is to turn data into knowledge.

Data analysis: at the conclusion of data collection

There are many approaches to analysing qualitative data. One relatively easy way to think about this is as a hierarchy, from more concrete to more abstract strategies (see Figure 10.1). We describe

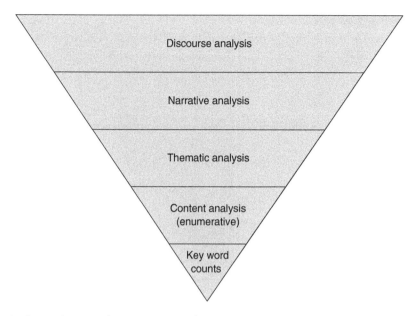

Figure 10.1 Analytic techniques: from concrete to abstract

each approach, beginning with the most concrete, and provide examples, before moving onto a more specific discussion about the practical issue of coding (note, this is not an exhaustive list, but covers the major types of analysis; further resources are provided at the end of the chapter).

Key word count

In your study, do you need an enumerative approach? What we mean by this is, to answer your research question, do you need to analyse and present word frequencies or identify the most dominant (frequently presented) ideas, or the relationships between specific words/concepts? Then a key word count might be appropriate. This approach does exactly as it says: it counts/quantifies key words that occur in your data set. This is clearly a quantitative approach to working with qualitative data. A high count of a particular word indicates that it is an important concept. This approach relies on specific words being used explicitly in the data, as you can only count what is presented (although, as you can see from our example below, you can search for groups of similar or related words). This method tends to be more associated with positivist researchers, given its focus on quantifying and on concrete content. Key word counts are often used in the analysis of *secondary data* (that which exists already – and was not gathered specifically for the purpose of your research) such as media, case files, etc. (e.g. you might want to do a key word count of this book; you would probably find that the words 'research' and 'social work' are used frequently … but we wonder what else …).

We have seen key word counts used very effectively, for example, in the analysis of politicians' speeches; these measurements are then used to make claims about what priority politicians give to specific issues, and therefore, what they 'stand for'. See the case examples.

Case study

Watching their words?

Using political speeches to question political ideas: Austermühl (2014) examined US presidential (State of the Union) speeches from 1789 to 2008, specifically seeking to count the number of times the words 'constitution/al' were used. He observes that there has been a considerable decline in the use of these words over this time, from around 10 mentions per speech in the early days to approximately once in every speech after 1945. This analysis forms part of his argument that 'presidents cast themselves more and more often as the sole agent of American government' (Austermühl, 2014: 86).

In recent years in Australia, Election Watch (2014) has examined budget speeches by a range of politicians. They note that in 2013, while the Labor treasurer's most common words were 'Australia/n' and 'economy', the response from the Liberal (Conservative) opposition had 'government' and 'tax' as the most frequent utterances.

What do you think might be claimed as a result of this trend identified by Election Watch?

To use this strategy you do need to either have reasonably well established ideas of what you are looking for, or to familiarise yourself well with your raw data and begin from the ground up, noting all common words you see. What is attractive about this strategy is that it is very simple to do, even just using basic tools in word processing and related programs. So, it can be an excellent entry point for novice researchers.

Key word in context (KWIC)

This is a related strategy; it is a little more sophisticated as it also captures the surrounding words of the key word being counted. This method seeks to represent the context, and therefore the meaning, more clearly. For example, if you were interviewing individuals in prison about their pre-prison lifestyle, you could simply do a key word count of the word 'drugs'. You might conclude on the basis of the word being used frequently by participants that drugs are a significant problem. However, the situation may be more complex. If you did a KWIC count, you might find that when people talk about drugs, it is the *drug use of others* that they describe, or their own attempts to engage in *drug treatment*. You can see from this brief example how the conclusions you would draw from these analyses would be very different, with a KWIC giving you a more nuanced view of the issue of drug use in your data set.

Both of these strategies, whilst stand-alone processes, can also provide a starting place for some more guided analysis of your data; they can act as a beginning point. See how Alexis engaged in this process.

Case study

Key word in context guides further analysis

You will recall from previous chapters Alexis' study of women's experiences of hospital treatment after miscarriage. In the process of transcribing her data and beginning analysis, she noticed that the word 'baby' seemed to be used a lot by her participants, so she did a KWIC to investigate this initial hunch. A couple of things became clear: (1) women did consider and talk about their 'babies', and (2) examining the context of this key word indicated that this was in considerable contrast to how medical staff spoke. Although Alexis did not use this in her final analysis and write up, it did encourage her to explore women's views on this aspect of treatment (how this experience is considered and spoken about). This became important evidence in the findings, which indicated that whilst women saw the experience as a largely emotional one, they felt that the response was predominantly medicalised, and hence somewhat mismatched.

Content analysis

We would see content analysis (CA) as the next 'step up' from KWIC. Indeed it is described by Liamputtong (2013) as the first level of analysis for qualitative data. Hansen (2006: 147) describes the process of CA as 'selecting units of analysis (i.e. what you are going to look for) and counting the frequency of these units in the data'.

A quick word about terminology here. You will see the terms 'thematic content analysis', 'interpretive content analysis' or even simply 'content analysis' used interchangeably with 'thematic analysis' in much of the material you have come across. While we see these as similar processes, occurring on a spectrum, we have opted for discussing CA and thematic analysis (TA) separately. We will highlight the similarities and differences as we discuss these strategies.

The key similarity is that both approaches seek to move beyond simply counting individual words (on their own or in context) to capturing key ideas in the text. 'Capturing' ideas begins with *coding* (this simply means the grouping and categorising of data containing similar ideas and ascribing a label to these; these ideas are related to your research question). We will discuss specific approaches to coding later in the chapter. Where they differ is that with CA, the focus remains on counting occurrences.

Bryman (2012) suggests that CA should involve coding and categorising in terms of *predetermined categories* (these are 'labels' developed from previous research or theorising; where you have a list of codes and search for them in your text – these are sometimes called *a priori* codes). For example, we could do a CA of the post-release experiences of women exiting prison, either via interviews with these women, or perhaps through an analysis of case notes of those women under community supervision (parole) after release. To do this, we would draw from the existing research to examine our data for the occurrence of previously indicated problems, such as: housing, drugs and alcohol, mental health, violence, etc., as well as perhaps the factors found to be helpful to women (such as family); interestingly there is much less research on what is helpful!

There is considerable variation in views, however, towards the requirement for coding to be predetermined. Grbich (2007) and Liamputtong (2013) take a more flexible approach, arguing that codes can be generated from the data collected. Liamputtong (2013: 247) provides a helpful example of researchers examining print media for reporting on women's health issues. She points out that although the themes that emerge (including abortion, miscarriage and menopause) may not have been what the researchers had 'in mind' before they began the study, they are what is represented and can still be examined for frequency. We agree with these authors and simply suggest that you need to be clear that your chosen strategy (of pre- or post-data collection code development) aligns with your study design. For example, you will recall from Chapter 5 that with exploratory designs you have limited existing research; this would make it less likely that you would have clear pre-existing codes and more likely that codes would be developed from the data collected.

See our example about how CA was used to examine student experiences of preparation for field education placement in Papua New Guinea.

 ## Case study

Mapping student experiences via content analysis

This descriptive study sought to map the placement preparation experiences of social work students at the University of Papua New Guinea (UPNG) after their first placement. Twenty-three students (most of the student cohort – study population) completed a short questionnaire about their experiences. The data, in the form of the written responses to a small number of questions, were analysed using content analysis:

> this is a useful tool for analysing qualitative data, identifying trends and patterns in sets of data, particularly where structured questions are used (Bryman, 2012). The analysis was predominantly enumerative in its focus, given that the aim of the exercise was to 'map' the extent of student preparedness for placement; it is based on the view that the repetition of words/concepts signifies the importance of these ideas (Bryman, 2012). Following Grbich (2007), however, a flexible approach was taken to coding and categorising the data, drawing on ideas generated from the data, rather than predetermined categories. (Flynn et al., 2014: 441)

This was the most appropriate approach, given the lack of pre-existing relevant research on which to base a coding framework. Key ideas identified in this study were that communication was identified as a central valuable skill for field education, but that students typically felt only 'just prepared' for their first placement;

there were notable gaps in their understanding of the nature and role of social work. Participant suggestions for improvements to placement preparation included: curriculum sequencing, to ensure that core learning about relevant intervention skills was covered; and practical preparation, including information about participating agencies, etc.

These findings indicate that when doing content analysis in exploratory studies, it is important to be flexible; whilst some of these themes reflect earlier research findings from western contexts, some are new.

CA is most useful with more sophisticated study designs that involve 'mapping' of study populations, where your aim is to be able to identify, quantify and compare core issues. It is able to be used with a range of data types, and is most appropriately used where there has been a structured approach to data collection. A structured approach generates a response to the same questions for all respondents, allowing you to engage in analysis – measurement and comparison – across your cases. For example, the UPNG case study used a questionnaire – other relevant data/methods include: structured interviews or observations; or structured examination of existing data, including media (as discussed by Liamputtong, 2013 above), texts, images (such as those used in advertising), case files or policy documents (you will recall these methods have been discussed in preceding chapters). CA is less appropriate for less structured approaches to data collection. In these instances, such as unstructured interviews or focus groups, it is much more difficult to meaningfully compare responses across cases because you have not asked all participants the same questions. This means that any attempt to count the frequency of responses is likely to be inaccurate. Just because participants have not raised a particular issue does not mean it is not important to them – perhaps it was just because the researcher had not asked them about it.

Thematic analysis

As noted above, in many ways thematic analysis (TA) is similar to CA. It is described by Braun and Clarke (2012: 57) (two scholars who write well and clearly about this approach) as 'a method for systematically identifying, organising, and offering insight into patterns of meaning (themes) across a data set'. In recent years it has become a very popular method of analysing qualitative data.

Two key differences between CA and TA are that with the latter (1) the focus of analysis may be the manifest/obvious content of the data or it may be the latent meaning behind what is explicitly stated (Braun and Clarke, 2012), and (2) the weight given to concepts/ideas/words is not necessarily defined by repetition of those concepts/ideas/words. Indeed Braun and Clarke (2012: 57) state that '[w]hat is common … is not necessarily in and of itself meaningful or important'. While there is limited guidance on how then to ascertain the importance of ideas and themes in the data, we would suggest consideration of the following; appropriateness of these strategies must be tailored to the specific study being undertaken.

- *Intensity* of the reporting of particular ideas (ideas may not be mentioned by all/majority of participants, but may be associated with a high level of emotion, or may be noted repeatedly within one interview)
- The concept is reported in a particular *sub-group* of your study sample
- A *new* idea/concept is raised that has not been considered before in research in this area
- Occurrence of a particular idea or theme in *extreme* cases
- Occurrence of a particular idea or theme in *typical* cases
- Co-occurrence with *other key ideas*
- What is noticeably *absent* (including, what isn't here that you might expect to be here? What don't people talk about? For example, participants never mention feeling angry or annoyed when it's reasonable to think they could, etc.).

A theme brings together core ideas and patterns in the data; a theme should relate to the study's research question and point to something important about the phenomenon. The process of TA, however, has often been poorly described or discussed quite vaguely. Braun and Clarke (2012: 63) challenge this, particularly the often-used phrase that themes 'emerge' from the data, as if they are simply there, waiting to be found. They argue in contrast that 'Searching for themes is an *active* process, meaning we generate or construct themes rather than discovering them'. You will see that this is similar to the position we have taken throughout this book, that research is based on our observations in practice, our reading of existing research and knowledge; we need to harness and use these resources in a self-aware way, rather than denying them.

Braun and Clarke (2006) present a six-step process for conducting TA. This augments the approach taken by some other authors (see Alston and Bowles, 2012), who summarise the analytic process into three components: data reduction, data organisation and data interpretation. We combine and compare these in Table 10.1, with a focus on practical tasks. Whichever approach you choose, the basic process is all about increasing abstraction: from dense raw data to concepts, ideas and hypotheses with wider application. A general rule of thumb would suggest that around five themes is sufficient in a study relying on qualitative data. There are a range of excellent text books that discuss TA specifically. We provide details of these at the end of the chapter. We would recommend that you read more specifically about this particular method before embarking.

As you can see from the Table 10.1, TA is a broad approach, which makes it suitable for a range of data types and data collection methods, including semi-structured interviews, focus groups and participant observation. It is particularly useful in exploratory studies because of its flexibility.

We will return to a specific discussion about coding towards the end of the chapter.

Narrative analysis

Narrative analysis (NA) is based on the understanding that people use stories to make sense of themselves and their world (Sarbin, 1986, cited in Frost et al., 2010), as well as to represent

Table 10.1 Thematic analysis: a stepped approach

Braun and Clarke (2006)	(Coleman and Unrau, 2008; Alston and Bowles, 2012)	Researcher tasks
1. Familiarisation with the data		• Transcribe (turn any audio files into written documents). The extent to which you need to transcribe 'word for word' depends on: your research design and your method of data collection (unstructured interviews or focus groups seeking rich and detailed data in an emerging area of study are more likely to require verbatim reporting) • Read and re-read transcripts/interview notes
2. Generating initial codes	Data reduction	• Identify 'meaning units' (chunks that encapsulate key ideas in the data) • Group/categorise these • This process may be conducted a number of times as you revisit codes and either broaden or narrow these as you read through the data
3. Searching for themes among codes	Data organisation	• Examine data in relation to categories (separate to individual participants) • Look at the relationships between the categories • Develop themes and hypotheses – propositions
4. Reviewing potential themes		
5. Defining and naming themes		
	Data interpretation	What do these patterns of themes mean, with regard to previous theory and research?
6. Producing the final report		

themselves to others in the world. Viney and Bousfield (1991: 758) emphasise these aspects of narrative when they describe the underpinning concepts in this approach as 'the psychosocial function which narratives fulfil for the narrator: the personal, social and cultural functioning of storytelling itself, as well as the content of the stories told'. Bryman (2012) explains this approach as moving the focus from seeking an account of what happened to seeking an understanding of how an individual has made sense of events/experiences (if you think back to Chapter 2, you will be able to locate this method firmly in the camp of social constructionism).

NA is, however, an umbrella term; a number of different approaches and strategies are situated within this framework (Holstein and Gubrium, 2012). Approaches vary in their focus on the individual's understanding/representation of events (the story content) or on how the events are presented (the story 'plot'). Narrative approaches developed in the 1970s, with Labov being an influential scholar. He defined narrative as 'one method of recapitulating past experience by matching a verbal sequence of clauses to the sequence of events which (it is inferred) actually occurred' (Labov, 1972: 359–60, cited in Franzosi, 1998: 519). His focus was on the effect of stories, in an analysis of the narrative, and how stories are told. Later, Bruner (1991) focused more on examining the role narrative serves in enabling the person to make sense of their life/experience; the emphasis here is more on the person and their interpretation. This formed the basis of more contemporary approaches such as those of Dan McAdams (see McAdams et al., 2006), who is concerned with the construction of the self and identity through stories we tell ourselves. Holstein and Gubrium (2012) explain the different approaches to NA as covering a focus on: the content-stories, the story telling and on the story in its social context.

In some ways, the actual process of NA is not dissimilar to CA: the researcher searches the data for known concepts. However, instead of looking for content, narrative researchers examine key dimensions of the story. Gibbs (2008) describes the analytic process as examining stories for fundamental components, which typically include the following (being aware that the particular focus will be determined by both the specifics of the study and the approach of the researcher):

- Story: actions, characters, events and experiences (including feelings, meanings, reactions) and genre (a question you can ask yourself might be 'where would this story be placed on my bookshelf - action, romance ...?)
- Plot: how the story occurs, the sequence of events, transitions
- Time: when it occurs, and in what order
- Resolution: how this is explained.

How researchers seek to apprehend this narrative will also vary considerably. McAdams (2012: 18) indicates that this can range from an examination of individual words (akin to key word counts or CA) to each utterance, to extended passages from which 'a theme is typically drawn as an inference'.

The most obvious way in which NA varies from CA and TA is that while the latter two seek to focus on the identified themes, abstracted from the individual participant, researchers using a narrative approach do not seek to break up the story or remove it from the individual (Hansen, 2006). They seek a coherent story. Riessman (2002: 695–6) reflects on when she realised that it is also participants who resist researcher efforts to 'fragment their lived experience into thematic (code-able) categories as ... to control meaning'. Gibbs (2008) similarly argues that this narrative structure, with a beginning, middle and end, aligns with how most people order their life history/narrative: chronologically, with key events, such as turning points, and characters. Gibbs (2008) argues that there are some clear benefits to presenting data as a story: it provides relevant context, which in turn provides further evidence for the data; it personalises the data (and allows further exploration for how people tell their stories); it provides a timeframe; participants' voices are clear; and lastly, he suggests that the data are then more relatable. Themes in each story can then be compared across cases. See Carlos' case study for an example of this.

Case study

Using narrative analysis to understand men's desistance from interpersonal violence

Carlos, a PhD student, sought to understand how some men desist from violence in their personal relationships whilst others do not. He interviewed a small number of men, some of whom had been violence-free for an extended period, while others continued to use violence. He asked them to talk about how they understood their life path. All men articulated a narrative plot structured from past to present and extending into an imagined future. The sequencing of critical events of their lives was crucial to give coherence to the personal identity they were claiming in the interview.

Themes, plots and personal identity constructions were derived from the analysis of all of the interviews and have been preliminarily contrasted within and between each group in order to identify common and distinctive features of the narratives and personal identity constructions produced by each group with the purpose of understanding the process of desistance from intimate partner violence.

Men who report persisting with violence claim disparate identities, ranging from claiming the willingness to preserve their couple relationships through the healing of their psychological problems to the positioning of themselves as a victim of adverse and unfair circumstances. For example, one clear storyline presented by men who continue to use violence is of the 'traumatised self'. Those men who characterise their childhood as a bad time of their lives select events where they were victimised or neglected, resulting in the permanent damage to their emotional functioning. They consider those events of their lives to be the root of a set of personal vulnerabilities they use to understand their inability to cope with affective interpersonal problems, adverse life circumstances and their violence against their partner. After accounting for a sequence of events of domestic violence in his family, one participant describes disconnecting from school and becoming aggressive because he was 'hurting'. Although not explicitly stated, he portrays himself as alone in this suffering as no one in his family and school noticed this and offered him support. What he describes after this point is a string of scenes of increased risky and criminal behaviour followed by punitive institutional responses. Selecting sequences of early life negative events allows persisters to build a theory of their inner self as shaped by traumatic circumstances out of their control. Using this theory they understand both their later actions and subjective responses to life events in terms of the expression of a set of lasting nuclear components of their self, which characterise the personal identity they claimed later on during the interview.

This view of the 'traumatised self' from childhood then intersects, for men who continue to use violence, with the 'social self' developed in adolescence. These men complement their identity formation via the socialisation process through which they are indoctrinated into the cultural beliefs and practices of masculinities and gender relations by means of vicarious learning and cultural practices. They story a process through which they were induced into the use of violence and the degradation of women.

In contrast, men who report desisting from violence construct narratives around a story moral that stresses the harmful effects of family violence in general and intimate partner violence in particular. Through their telling, they claim a transformed identity that revolves around bettering their lives through stopping abuse and taking responsibility for the past abusive behaviours they had perpetrated against their partner and/or their children. Their stories emphasise how this occurs alongside recovery/improvement in their psychological problems, including substance abuse.

NA can be applied to data collected in narrative form (perhaps via a life history) or it can be applied to data 'after the fact'. It is an approach that is suitable for semi- or unstructured interviews or observations. Bryman (2012: 584) also suggests that this can be utilised in document analysis (he cites an excellent example (Davis, 2008) examining the narrative of breast cancer in documents produced by the US National Cancer Institute). It is useful for small exploratory studies where you are seeking to uncover processes or issues that are difficult to access or to understand. Carlos' work outlined in the case study is a good example of this: examining how men who engage in violence describe and account for their behaviour; how they understand this and construct their story, noting the key turning points and resolutions.

Discourse analysis

In some writing it can seem that the boundary between narrative and discourse analysis (DA) is a little blurry. The simplest explanation of the difference is that with NA, the focus is on the individual and what the data 'say' (either about the content or the process of the story). With DA the focus is on how the world/experiences are produced in *discourse*: what the data/stories 'do' (where discourse is understood to mean 'socially constructed frameworks of meanings that act upon people like rules, norms or conventions'; Sarantakos, 2013: 331). Similar to NA, there is limited agreement about the scope and process of DA, and a range of approaches sit under the one umbrella term. These include Foucauldian discourse analysis and critical discourse analysis, which both have a focus on uncovering power and inequality through examining language. DA can be applied to a range of data, including 'talk' from interviews, images, existing text, such as newspapers, books, policy documents, etc.

Taylor (2013) describes DA as the study of meanings about a topic which affect how it can be thought and talked about; how meanings are established and challenged. The saying 'One man's terrorist is another man's freedom fighter' is a good example of competing discourses; where understanding of the same set of actions is determined by your point of view, constructed in a particular context. Taylor sees DA as a useful tool to understand the effects of such meanings and ourselves/identity as a core part of that.

Coding and beyond

Whatever analytic approach you choose, before your final analysis can begin, the data must be ready for use – they must be collected and transcribed and then coded. It is not uncommon to see researchers avoid starting analysis (including ourselves!): it can sometimes feel like a leap into the unknown. This is partly why we wanted to provide some guidance on getting started, by talking about coding.

Some things to bear in mind: start with your research question in mind; be clear on the overall approach you are taking and why (are you focusing on the content of what participants say or on how they construct or present the data, or what is implied in their responses; is your research area new and emerging or is there a solid base on which to start coding; do you need to compare across cases or is coherence within each case the focus?). Coleman and Unrau (2014) describe coding as a process of combing through your data and identifying *meaning units* (groups of words important in answering your research question). Once this is done, you need to return to the beginning and allocate each meaning unit a code. You will see that when you begin, you will initially generate many codes, but as you proceed you will be able to fit more data into the existing codes, as well as refine the codes you have developed. An important point also well made by Coleman and Unrau (2014), is that you need to have a clear rationale for grouping and allocating your codes. Remember that the same data can generate very different meaning units, depending on your research question and the lens through which you view your data. Tracking this journey of coding (and re-coding) shows the usefulness of documenting your analytic processes in a coding book; this is also a strategy which provides an excellent audit trail, which will enhance the trustworthiness of your findings. But important first words – do not start this until you are familiar with your data (read, re-read, etc.; this is why we generally suggest students do their own transcribing of any recorded material).

Miles et al. (2014: 73–81) provide an excellent discussion on the types of things we can seek to capture in our codes. We have selected a range of code types to use as examples here in Table 10.2, which we think are useful specifically to social work and social care, but this is not exhaustive, and Miles et al. (2014) describe others.

Table 10.2 Coding qualitative data: types, purposes and usefulness

Type of code	What is it?	When is it useful?
Descriptive	A summary of a chunk of material; most likely manifest (stated in the data)	If seeking to identify *what* participants describe – topics, issues, experiences, etc. Common with content analysis
***In vivo* –** indigenous	A summary that specifically uses the words of the participants	Miles et al. (2014) suggest that these are good for beginning researchers to ensure that the *voice* of participants is clear. Whilst this is good advice, overall we tend to think that the type of coding needs to be driven by the nature of the research problem and the aim of the study
Process	A code that focuses on how something has occurred or been done: likely to be latent (not stated directly in the data)	When seeking to uncover an action, such as *how* decisions are made. This is also relevant when beginning narrative analysis and you are coding data for how the story is told/constructed or presented
Emotive	Emotion that may be named or implied (though you need to be cautious about the latter – can your label be clearly tied back to the raw data?)	Investigations of intra/interpersonal experiences; or with narrative analysis where you want to examine the emotion attached to specific aspects of the story
Holistic	Seeks to summarise large chunks of data. One type of holistic code is 'evaluation', which seeks to summarise and rate the response	When engaging in preliminary coding, to shape further data collection, or when the focus of your study seeks a broad overview
Protocol	Using an established system of pre-existing codes	Where there is established knowledge in the field and clear issues for examination

Miles et al. (2014: 277–92) provide further suggestions for data organisation: moving from codes to knowledge and understanding. Some of those we consider most relevant to social work and social care include: noting recurring patterns; comparing/contrasting participant sub-groups or data sets; clustering participants with similar or different outcomes (seeking common causes); making metaphors; partitioning and exploring one variable in detail; creating a chain of evidence – diagrams can be useful to illustrate links between variables. As should be clear by now, analysing qualitative data is an active and engaged process; it involves you making choices (and being able to defend these). We also like Miles et al.'s general advice: 'Trust your "plausibility" intuitions, but don't fall in love with them' (2014: 278). So remember, keep an open mind – test your ideas out (remember some of the strategies we covered in Chapter 6 – member checking, checking your biases/effect, triangulating the data, checking out alternative explanations)!

Computer-assisted qualitative data analysis (CAQDA)

There has been quite a bit written about CAQDA in recent years: Bryman (2012) provides a comprehensive chapter on using one specific program – NVivo. We give a brief overview here, because we are of the view that the most important learning in analysing qualitative data is understanding the conceptual issues (as discussed above): you need to be clear on these before any type of CAQDA can be useful to you.

That said, there is much to recommend such tools (including NVivo, NUD*IST or Ethnograph). When gathering a lot of data, which is common in studies using qualitative methods, CAQDA helps you to organise and manage your data; the value of this cannot be underestimated! Because you have your data in one place, they can be manipulated much more easily. NVivo for example, has a number of tools with which you can visualise and map your data, for example, generating 'word trees' (from a text search of a specific term you can see the most common contexts in which the word occurs). These are not methods (easily) available by hand (Hansen, 2006). The main benefits of CAQDA, therefore, include the ability to work in a complex way with your data: recording and storing; coding; retrieving and linking – exploring relationships between concepts; displaying in a range of models; developing typologies; and testing ideas (Sarantakos, 2013: 396–7). We have found it particularly useful in allowing comparison of responses across large data sets.

The most important thing to remember, however, is that CAQDA does not analyse the data for you (or even code it for you for that matter!), but it does provide you with the tools to code easily (and re-code or un-code much more simply than via hand with coloured markers). You do need to have the skills and understanding of your chosen analytic method before you can make best use of CAQDA. You then also need to learn to use the specific CAQDA method; some research has shown that the effort and time to learn this is prohibitive to its use (Rodik and Primorac, 2015). The key message here is to ensure that when you want to use CAQDA for the first time, make sure you build in sufficient time to learn your analytic method as well as the practical skills in working with data in such programs. The companies that offer these programs provide excellent online resources (plenty of good YouTube clips). There are now also specific text books that deal with this.

The most common critique of CAQDA is that the structured, compartmentalising and counting approach imposes an essentially positivist framework onto qualitative data. This may be true, and you should be wary of getting too caught up in the micro aspects of data analysis (coding). However, as we have discussed throughout this text, 'there may be an affinity between paradigms and methods, but there is no deterministic link that forces the use of a particular paradigm with a particular set of methods' (Morgan, 2014: 1045) and your choices need to be led by your research goals.

Chapter summary

In this chapter, we have covered a range of analytic approaches, from concrete to abstract: counting key words; content, thematic, narrative and discourse analysis; with some comments about computer-assisted analysis. We have emphasised that qualitative analysis occurs both during and after data collection, and all analysis involves some process of data reduction, organisation and interpretation. Importantly analysis does not end with coding: meaning then needs to be made of the themes and patterns you identify, with reference to existing theory and research.

Key take-home messages

There are a range of methods you can employ to analyse your qualitative data. To make the appropriate choice, be guided by your research question, the purpose of your research, as well as the underpinning theory and/or epistemology. Importantly, continue to be self-aware.

Additional resources

Braun, V. and Clarke, V. (2006) 'Using thematic analysis in psychology', *Qualitative Research in Psychology*, 3 (2): 77–101.
Braun, V. and Clarke, V. (2012) 'Thematic analysis', in H. Cooper (ed.), *APA Handbook of Research Methods in Psychology: Vol. 2. Research Designs*. Washington, DC: American Psychological Association, pp. 57–71.

Braun and Clarke have become key authors in this area, notably for their structured and 'no nonsense' approach to thematic analysis. The 2006 paper presents their first ideas about structuring this approach, while the 2012 chapter provides developed ideas, and a worked illustrative example.

Holstein, J.A. and Gubrium, J.F. (2012) *Varieties of Narrative Analysis.* Thousand Oaks, CA: Sage. This book gives a good account of the range of ways of approaching narrative analysis.

Huddersfield University (n.d.) 'Learning qualitative data analysis on the web', available at: http://onlineqda.hud.ac.uk. This has an excellent range of online resources for qualitative data analysis (QDA): written materials, software, YouTube clips and more.

Miles, M.B., Huberman, A.M. and Saldaña, J. (2014) *Qualitative Data Analysis: a Methods Sourcebook* (3rd edn). Thousand Oaks, CA: Sage. This text has many excellent chapters. We particularly like Chapter 11 on 'Drawing and verifying conclusions', which addresses what do to with the patterns you identify in your material.

Taylor, S. (2013) *What Is Discourse Analysis?* London: Bloomsbury. This is an excellent introduction to this topic.

Viney, L.L. and Bousfield, L. (1991) 'Narrative analysis: a method of psychosocial research for AIDS-affected people', *Social Science and Medicine*, 32 (7): 751–5. This article provides an excellent example of using narrative analysis.

11

Making Meaning from Data[1]

Quantitative Analysis

In this chapter you will learn

- The meaning of quantitative methods and how these differ from qualitative methods
- The importance of the research question in shaping methods and analysis
- The meaning of tests of significance
- How SPSS assists in undertaking quantitative data analysis
- Some of the key data analysis techniques used in quantitative research including frequencies, cross tabs, regression and comparison of means.

Introduction

This chapter provides a brief definition of quantitative methods, their purpose and when these methods are commonly used. It discusses the central role of the research question in deciding on appropriate methods. Again, you can see our pragmatic framework at work. It also discusses SPSS Statistics, the computer program that is commonly used to analyse quantitative data in the social sciences. Tests of significance are then discussed, followed by key methods of quantitative data analysis including: frequencies such as mean, median and mode; cross tabs; regression; and comparison of means (we will define and talk about all of these terms in the chapter). You will see that our approach in this chapter varies somewhat from what we have

---

[1] Co-authored with Chris Trotter

followed in preceding chapters. We are mindful that many people are a bit intimidated by 'stats', so we want to make this material user friendly and accessible. To facilitate this, we have built the chapter around a couple of completed studies – one worked example is examined in particular detail – we use these to illustrate important concepts.

What are quantitative methods?

Research may draw on quantitative, qualitative or a mix of methods and data. Definitions and discussion of the types of approaches involved have been offered elsewhere in this book (Chapters 7, 8 and 9). Suffice to say at this stage that quantitative methods, which you will recall we covered specifically in Chapter 8 'Counting and measuring', involve numbers and generally use tests of statistical significance. Quantitative methods often examine specific outcomes, for example, are particular patients readmitted to hospital, did service users like the intervention, were children removed from their families or did prisoners return to prison? They typically rely on tables and graphs in the presentation of findings.

While quantitative methods focus on specific questions with specific answers, qualitative methods (which you will recall we have discussed in Chapters 7 and 9) on the other hand focus on human experiences and commonly analyse themes that emerge from the analysis of those experiences. We hope that you may find yourself thinking back to Chapter 5 at this point, connecting some of these ideas to the concept of research design. Quantitative methods, and to some extent data, are more likely to be the dominant data type in descriptive or explanatory studies as these design types are most likely to be shaped by specific questions or hypotheses.

Thinking about a current issue you are working on, or the issue you pondered way back in Chapter 1, does this problem lend itself to a quantitative examination?

As discussed in our chapter on research design, however, we are clear that methods and paradigms are not inherently linked, although there is some affinity between particular pairings. As already stated, our pragmatic perspective encourages plurality: matching and 'mixing' methods to the needs of the problem. While quantitative methods may be more commonly thought to be associated with a positivist position, this is not always the case. Spierings (2012) argues that quantitative data and findings can be well used by feminist researchers because they provide improved capacity to engage with diversity, and understand similarities and differences within groups. In addition, researchers working within the critical paradigm may use quantitative data to demonstrate structural inequalities, such as differential access to employment opportunities for disabled people, in order to persuasively argue for policy change.

Quantitative findings can thus be a powerful and effective tool for use in advocacy research, as 'policy makers ... seem to prefer statistics over open-ended interviews and ethnographies' (Spierings, 2012: 343).

By way of comparison, outcome measures are often less specific when using qualitative methods, for example, in an exploratory study of how refugees *experience* discrimination, or how children *experience* foster care. Quantitative methods generally aim to test hypotheses or propositions, whereas qualitative research generally aims to describe situations or develop hypotheses or propositions. Research using a mix of methods often uses quantitative data to test propositions and then gathers qualitative data to give a more detailed picture of the quantitative findings. Creswell and Plano Clark (2011) describe this as an explanatory approach; this compares to what they term an exploratory approach, where qualitative data are collected first and analysed, with the results informing the follow up quantitative phase of data collection.

Alannah, PhD student

At first glance, mothers in prison with or without mental illnesses seem quite similar, in terms of their age, ethnicity, offending and parenting circumstances. It wasn't until I used a quantitative analysis of the data that I uncovered some key differences in the experiences of these two groups. Importantly this analysis showed that mothers with a mental illness were significantly more likely to report having low involvement in planning their children's care compared to the mothers who did not have a mental illness. This knowledge will help us to frame suggestions for improved responses to this group of women and their children.

Using quantitative methods might tell us, for example, if the provision of supported housing after prison leads to lower re-offending, or if the provision of family support services leads to fewer than expected reports of child abuse. Researchers can examine records of offending or child abuse and compare the rates for those who have received housing support or family support with those who did not receive this support. Importantly, these data mean that the researchers can use statistical techniques to explain whether or not the differences might be due to chance or whether they might be significantly related to the support services.

Case study

Using quantitative methods to answer a specific question about satisfaction

Chris and Louise were interested to know whether social work students studying off-campus were receiving an inferior (or superior) form of education compared to students studying on-campus. At the time there was a growth of off-campus courses and students, and some academics argued that this might disadvantage students. One key issue was that off-campus students would not get sufficient access to staff. Using a survey they asked more than 115 on- and off-campus students to rate their satisfaction with access to staff on a 1–5 scale.

Using quantitative methods they analysed the responses in SPSS and found that off-campus students rated their access to staff higher than on-campus students. This was at a statistically significant level. This seemed a puzzling result and qualitative research was able to help make sense of this. They interviewed a sample of on- and off-campus students and found that off-campus students did not expect access to staff other than by phone, whereas on-campus students had higher expectations and were disappointed that staff were often not available (Oliaro and Trotter, 2010).

In this example it was only through quantitative methods that we could judge whether there was a statistically significant difference between the views of on- and off-campus students. However, the use of qualitative methods helped to explain the difference. This is another way of saying that both qualitative and quantitative methods are important in social work and human services research. This chapter is however about quantitative methods and arguably the most important step in doing quantitative research is getting the research question right.

The research question

Research requiring quantitative data should be based on a clear and specific research question (you will recall in Chapter 4 we discussed developing your research question and in Chapter 5 covered material about having a 'loose' versus 'tight' research focus and questions, and increasing sophistication of research designs). In fact it is fair to say that quantitative methods in particular require a specific research question that guides each and every aspect of the research. The research question should guide the researcher in straightforward terms towards what they want to find out. It should be a question worth answering. It should be possible and ethical to collect relevant data to answer the question. And the question should flow from an understanding of the theory and literature available on the topic (Chapter 4 provides a more detailed discussion about research questions).

Returning to your issue of concern, based on your understanding of the literature on this topic, do you think a more quantitative ('tight') or qualitative ('loose') question would best contribute to knowledge?

We now present our worked example, which illustrates the links between the research question, the methods and subsequent coding.

Using quantitative methods to answer a question testing theory for practice

Chris and colleagues conducted a study that aimed to examine the extent to which the skills of youth justice workers related to the re-offending rates for young people under their supervision (Trotter and Evans, 2012).

The issue

A number of studies, mostly done with adults, had already shown that workers with good skills had clients with low re-offending rates. These skills include in particular: role clarification; pro-social modelling; problem solving; and relationship. Our hypothesis or proposition was that if youth justice workers used relevant and appropriate skills the young people under their supervision would offend less often.

The research question

Our research question was, therefore:

> Do youth justice workers in New South Wales, Victoria, assessed as having good skills, have clients who re-offend less often than the clients of youth justice workers assessed as having poor skills?

This is a good research question because it tells you in straightforward terms what the researcher wants to find out. It is a question worth answering – if the answer is positive it has the potential to reduce crime. It is clear and can be answered. Data can be collected to answer the question. It has been developed with an understanding of the theory and literature relevant to the topic.

Some of the terms used in the question did, however, need further definition. Good skills were defined as the worker being scored at 5 or above on the global rating scale completed by the research officers who observed worker/client interviews. Re-offending was defined as any further offence recorded on the police database within 2 years of commencing the supervision order.

The approach

In answering the research question we used the following methodology. After receiving university and juvenile justice ethics approval, juvenile justice staff with responsibility for direct

How would you describe these sampling strategies? Revisit Chapter 6 if you need a reminder.

supervision of young offenders were invited to be involved in the project. Forty-eight staff members initially volunteered. For each worker the next five clients allocated to them became eligible for the study.

Interviews between the staff members and young people were then observed within 3 months of the young person receiving their court order. In total 117 interviews were observed over a period of 4 years. Five interviews were not able to be observed for each worker due to staff and client turnover.

Coding

A *coding manual* was developed. The manual reflected the effective practice skills outlined in Trotter (2015). The manual aimed to define the skills and assist in the accuracy and reliability of the estimates of the extent to which the skills were used in interviews. It was divided into 15 sections including: set up of the interview; structure of the interview; role clarification; needs analysis; problem solving; developing strategies; relapse prevention/cognitive behavioural techniques; pro-social modelling and reinforcement; nature of the relationship; empathy; confrontation; termination; use of referral/community resources; non-verbal cues;

and incidental conversations. Each of the 15 sections contained a number of items that could be rated on a five-point scale (see Chapter 8 for a reminder about using scales). For example, the problem-solving section included: problem survey; problem ranking; problem exploration; setting goals; timeframe; review; developing a contract; developing strategies; ongoing monitoring; and time spent conducting problem solving.

For the skill to be rated highly it needed to be implemented in a way that was consistent with the research about good practice. For example, problem solving would be rated as high if the worker frequently helped clients to identify their own problems and goals and helped clients to identify strategies themselves to address them. It would be rated as low if the worker identified problems with minimal input from the client and then set goals and strategies for the client.

Each of the interviews was coded by the researcher who observed the interview. As discussed later, 20 audiotapes of interviews were also coded by another researcher to examine reliability. When the coding was undertaken from an audiotape the coder also had access to a non-verbal check list, which was completed by the observer following each interview. The non-verbal check list provided information about the body language and non-verbal interactions between the workers/counsellors and the clients.

To sum up, we can say that working with quantitative data relies fundamentally on a clear, focused question. It may be the 'approach of choice' when we want to establish causal links between phenomena, or measure the practical effectiveness of theories for practice, or for measuring the differences between people receiving the same or different services, or in developing a case to advocate for more socially just outcomes. Quantitative methods are methods of measurement using numbers themselves or as proxies for phenomena or variables of interest. These are structured and planned, minimising uncertainty and (in contrast to many qualitative designs) saving data analysis until the conclusion of the data gathering phase.

Data analysis

We have already introduced the general idea of quantitative data, but it is also important to understand the types of quantitative data and *levels of measurement* (this just tells us what type of information is contained in the variable) as this has a flow-on effect to what type/s of analysis you can do. Quantitative data can be broken up into three basic types: nominal/categorical, ordinal and ratio/interval.

- *Nominal/categorical* data: These data are simply categories to which you can apply a numerical code. Examples of this include housing type (public rental, private rental, own home, etc.); relationship status (single, partnered, widowed, etc.); or favourite ice-cream flavour. Importantly these data cannot be put into a ranked order (although we know some of you might argue that ice cream could and should be ordered because chocolate is obviously the best!).

- *Ordinal*: These data can be rank ordered, but the distance between the categories is not equal across the range. These data are useful because they allow you to capture a sense of quality (better/worse or more/less). Examples of ordinal data include: a scale that measures income as low, medium or high. This scale clearly indicates a sense of ranking (more/less), but you could not say that the differences between low and medium or medium and high are the same (each individual within the category would have a different actual income).
- *Ratio/interval*: These are data that are both rank ordered and where the distance between the categories is the same across the range. Some authors differentiate between ratio and interval data. Dudley (2011: 224) gives a good example to explain this difference: interval data do not have a 'true zero' (that is, the absence of the variable), temperature measured in Fahrenheit is a good example of this; while ratio data do have a true zero - for example weight.

In social work and social care, we use descriptive statistics quite a bit. Here is a summary of some key information which will be useful to you.

Descriptive analyses describe or summarise findings. These show us how our sample or population is distributed, or spread, across various factors or variables. These include: frequency distributions; measures of central tendency (mean, mode, median); and measures of dispersion (the spread of responses, including the variation ratio, range, and standard deviation).

Frequency distributions simply show the spread of responses across a sample. See Figure 11.1 for an example. This distribution shows how frequently each type of housing occurs in our sample of prisoners. This tells us quite a bit of information, including that

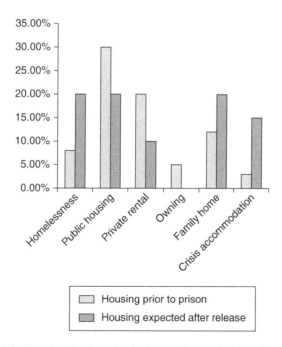

Figure 11.1   Frequency distribution showing housing before and expected housing after prison

whilst public housing is the most common housing type pre-prison, fewer individuals expect to be in such accommodation when they are released (what might this tell us about either losing public housing when you go to prison, or even about family breakdown due to imprisonment?); or that while a small percentage of participants were homeless before prison, it is a commonly expected situation on release.

It is important to remember that these data on their own do not allow us to explain why trends occur. They may give us suggestions (or in the study we may have asked participants to explain their housing circumstances, including the reasons – perhaps seeking some more qualitative data).

Measures of *central tendency* (where the data cluster; often seen in the average or most common response) – the type of data we collect has an impact on what sort of measures are appropriate. So, put quickly and simply:

- *Mean*: Arithmetic mean or average; to calculate this, simply add all responses and divide by the number of responses. This measure is appropriate for interval or ratio data (though some people also use it for ordinal data).
- *Median*: This is the 'mid-point or the number which falls in the middle of the highest and lowest number'; this is best used when there are outlying data, which can skew results, or where you have a small sample size. This measure is appropriate for ordinal, interval or ratio data.
- *Mode*: This just means the most frequently occurring. This is the only measure of central tendency for nominal data, but it doesn't tell you anything about how typical this most common category is. This measure can be used for variables of any level.

When data follow a *normal distribution* (the data are grouped around a central point, with the remaining data tapering off to either extreme end) all of these measures are approximately the same. See Table 11.1, below, as an example of how these three scores can vary.

When reading the research of others you need to know what kind of average they are talking about and when each is appropriate.

For example:

The median is useful if there are some outliers in the data. For example, 10 houses might be sold in one street: nine houses for $1,000,000 and one house for $10,000,000. This would give us a mean value of $1,900,000. Yet the majority of houses actually sold for $1,000,000, so the $1,900,000 is not really the 'average' or typical price. The median and the mode in this case - $1,000,000 - may be more meaningful as it reflects what most houses sold for, or the most likely price. It is also important to know when *not* to use the mean as your average. Continuing with the selling houses theme, let's imagine four real estate agents individually sell five, six, seven and seven houses over a month. Their boss wants to know the average number of houses sold. If you use the mean, this is 6.25, but this is meaningless as you cannot physically sell 6.25 houses!

The mode is the most common or frequently occurring score and is less commonly used in social sciences research. The mode can give quite a skewed picture. For example, in a class of 10 students, two scored 100% on a test, while each of the remaining eight all got different scores, no greater than 60%. In this case the mode (100%) is very misleading. (Rubin and Babbie (2013) provide more detail on frequencies.) But the mode is certainly useful when working with nominal data and you need to know the most common response.

Measures of dispersion: These are used when we wish to know more about how varied our data are, or how widely they are spread (Alston and Bowles, 2012).

- *Range*: This is the difference between highest and lowest values of the variable, for example, we might want to know the age range of people living in a nursing home. We discover that ages range from 99 years to 45 years. This will tell us that there is a range of 54 years. But if only a few people are at the upper or lower range and most closer to the middle, i.e. 79 years, then the range we observe provides a distorted view of the dispersion of ages of residents.
- *Standard deviation (SD)*: This is the average amount of variation around the mean. See Table 11.5 (below) as an example of what the SD can show us.
- *Variation ratio*: This is a measure for nominal data, and simply measures the percentage of those in the sample who fall outside the mode.

Using SPSS

SPSS Statistics is a software package used for statistical analysis. It was originally known as Statistical Package for the Social Sciences, although it is now used more broadly. In the words of the SPSS Statistics Overview 'analysing data with SPSS statistics is easy'. Simply 'open the data editor and enter the data directly into the program', then 'select a procedure from the menu to create statistics or create a chart', then 'select the variables you wish to include in the analysis and then results will be displayed including appropriate tests of significance'. It is not within the scope of this chapter to provide a detailed discussion about the use of SPSS; however, those looking for more detail are referred to the tutorial and coach within the program (IBM SPSS Statistics Version 22). Bryman (2012) provides a detailed chapter on analysing quantitative data with SPSS.

Level of significance

The level of significance is a measure of the extent to which the associations in the data may have occurred by chance. When undertaking correlations or other analysis in SPSS, the program provides the level of significance. Levels of significance can be between 0 and 1, with 1 meaning that there is no significance: in other words the results are purely random. The level at which it is generally accepted that the results are unlikely to have occurred by chance is 0.05. If the level is less than 0.05 then the results are commonly described as *statistically significant*. In this instance the results are likely to have occurred by chance less than 5 times in 100. The 0.05 level is a convention although sometimes it is argued that 0.10 is acceptable if samples are small, if there is a lot of previous research to support the proposition or the results are part of a pattern of results (Weinbach and Grinnell, 2014). Tests may also be one-tailed or two-tailed, which takes into account whether or not the outcome is predicted. A one-tailed test requires a smaller difference to reach statistical significance and may be used when the direction of the results is predicted, whereas a two-tailed test requires a larger difference and may be used when the direction of the results is not predicted. A one-tailed test might be used in our youth justice study, for example, when considering the relationship between worker skills and recidivism by young people under supervision because the numbers are relatively small and previous research has suggested a relationship. Again, Bryman (2012) provides an excellent discussion of tests of statistical significance.

It is also important to understand the limitations of these tests. As Bryman (2012) describes, statistical significance indicates the degree to which you can be confident that the results you have obtained with your study sample (you will recall that we discussed random sampling in Chapter 6) can be generalised or inferred to the study population. Dudley (2011) reminds us that this is why these are often referred to as *inferential statistics*. With that in mind, he also reminds us that in theory these tests should only be used with random samples, but in practice this is often not the case. It is suggested that such tests can be used even with exploratory studies using non-probability samples, provided that the limitations of the sample are acknowledged and the role of the tests is clear – identifying new hypotheses for testing in later more sophisticated research (perhaps descriptive or explanatory designs). It is important that the 'conclusions drawn from such studies, at best, can only be preliminary in nature and recommended for replication in other studies' (Dudley, 2011: 231). See the example from Fiona and Rachel below, which follows from the study they did that we introduced in Chapter 8.

 ## Case study

Using tests of significance in an exploratory way

Rachel and Fiona undertook a study in order to determine whether social work students extended their understanding of evidence based practice following exposure to a research task involving the collection and analysis of systematic reviews relating to health social work practice interventions. Before and after doing this task they completed the EBPPAS, a brief five-point validated scale measuring knowledge of evidence based social work practice. The results, analysing the before and after scores using a two-tailed *t*-test of significance showed no significant change. The level of significance was set at 0.05 and the results from the test recorded 0.1700, indicating that that there was no significant difference in pre- and post-scores. However, many students commented that they had increased their understanding of evidence based practice. This suggested to Rachel and Fiona that a further series of qualitative interviews might assist in understanding why the non-significant outcome was arrived at; for example, did students over-estimate their knowledge base on the first test, or was the understanding gained from doing the task not measured by the scale?

Frequencies

And now back to this chapter's main example ...

In Chris' study the data from the 117 coding forms were entered into SPSS for analysis. First they analysed frequencies, mean, median and mode for the global score. The global score was one of the most important variables in the study. It involved a 1–10 rating scale on overall use of the skills completed by the researcher at the conclusion of the interview (see Figure 11.2).

1	The worker did not utilise any of the effective practice principles
3	The worker used minimal effective practice skills, almost unintentionally
5	The interview showed some use of the effective practice principles
7	The worker used several of the effective practice principles in a deliberate manner
10	The worker deliberately used the effective practice principles in an efficient and successful manner

Figure 11.2   Global score – overall use of skills

The mean is the average score for all of the sample. In other words the score for each person added and divided by the sample size, in this case 117. The median is the mid-point of the scores with half the scores above and half below.

Table 11.1 shows us that the mean or average global score for use of skills in the study is 5.7350, the median, or the mid-point of all the scores is 6.0000 and the mode, the most common score, is 5.0000.

Table 11.1   Global skills scores

	Global score out of 10	
N	Valid	117
	Missing	0
Mean		5.7350
Median		6.0000
Mode		5.0000

This suggests that most of the workers made reasonably good use of the skills whether we consider the mean, median or mode.

Correlations

Before doing further analysis of the data they were interested to know the extent to which the scores given by the research officers were reliable and valid (we have discussed and defined these terms in Chapter 6 when discussing methodological rigour). If the scores by the research officers were heavily dependent on which research officer was observing the interview, then this would compromise the study – it would have a low level of reliability. To test this they did two things, they audio-taped the interviews in addition to observing them. They were then able to code the interviews from the audio-tapes. They also examined the internal consistency of the coding process.

A different research officer to the one who did the original coding coded 20 forms from the audio-tapes. Secondary coding was not a perfect solution to this issue as it missed much of the body language and context of the interview, even though the second coders were given a summary of the context and body language from each interview. Nevertheless it was the best method they had of addressing the issue of reliability of the coding process.

They then wanted to examine *correlations* (the extent to which coding the same interview was consistent between the first and second coders). Correlations provide a measure of the extent to which two things are related and they are expressed as a number between 0 and 1. A perfect correlation is 1, whereas a weak correlation is 0. Correlations can be negative or positive; for example, the hotter it is the fewer clothes people wear is a negative correlation. The hotter it is the more people wear hats is a positive correlation. There are different ways of measuring correlation, including Kendall or Spearman, with the *Pearson correlation coefficient* being the most frequently used in social science research.

In relation to Chris' study, they saw a high correlation between the coders' global ratings of skills. The correlation on the overall global skill score between first and second coders was 0.741. This can be considered a strong correlation (Weinbach and Grinnell, 2014). In other words the workers' coding on the global score was close. The correlation showed a level of significance of 0.000, which suggests that the correlation could not have occurred by chance.

Another way of looking at reliability is to consider the internal consistency. For example, they would expect to see a close correlation between the global skill score as identified by the coders and individual scores on the specific skills of role clarification, pro-social modelling, problem solving and relationship. Table 11.2 shows that each of the skills is positively correlated with the global skills score. Each of the correlations could be considered reasonably strong and all were very unlikely to have occurred by chance.

This does suggest that the global score is a reasonably reliable measure of skills. The internal consistency also helps to show the validity of the scale. As you will recall from Chapter 6, validity refers to the extent to which the measure in fact measures what it intends to measure. There are numerous ways of addressing the issue of validity and there is not sufficient space to discuss them all in this chapter; however, the global score does have some support for its validity. It was developed collaboratively with numerous researchers in this field, it is internally consistent and there were strong correlations with similar measures within the scale, for example, the extent to which clients were engaged in the interviews and estimations of levels of empathy of the workers.

The coding scale they developed had considerable strengths. Ideally, however, they would have used use a pre-developed scale of effective practice skills that had been tested for reliability and validity in numerous studies. In this case such a scale was not available; however, research of this nature would benefit from the development of a scale thoroughly tested for validity and reliability.

Table 11.2 Correlations between the global skill score and score on other skills

		Global score out of 10
Global score out of 10	Pearson correlation	1
	Significance (two-tailed)	
	N (number in sample)	117
Time spent discussing role clarification	Pearson correlation	412
	Significance (two-tailed)	.000
	N	117
Time spent conducting problem solving	Pearson correlation	.553
	Significance (two-tailed)	.000
	N	116
Time spent using pro-social modelling	Pearson correlation	.709
	Significance (two-tailed)	.000
	N	114
Time spent using relationship skills	Pearson correlation	.704
	Significance (two-tailed)	.000
	N	46

Cross tabs

In the youth justice study Chris and his colleagues were interested in the relationship between the use of skills as measured by the global skills score and the recidivism of the young offenders. They anticipated that young people under the supervision of workers who have high global scores would offend less often than young people who have supervisors who are low on the global score. In order to test this we can use cross tabs, which allows for tables identifying frequencies. In this case a 2 by 2 table can be used, which can show the differences in recidivism rates between the two groups and their statistical significance. Table 11.3 shows that 81.3% of the young people supervised by workers with low scores (4 or less) re-offended, whereas only 62.4% of the offenders supervised by workers with high scores (5 or more) re-offended (within 2 years).

To look at this another way, it is apparent that 37.6% of those supervised by workers with poor skills had not re-offended after 2 years compared to 19.7% in the group supervised by workers with good skills. This illustrates the way the presentation of results can lead to different impressions. On the one hand we can say the skilled workers had around 19% reduction in re-offending, yet on the other hand we can say that clients of skilled workers completed 2 years without offending at nearly twice the rate of the less skilled workers (readers sometimes need to study research reports carefully to gain a balanced picture of their findings). Nevertheless the results suggest that workers with good skills do better than workers with poor skills. The results also suggest that we can identify who are the more skilled workers by observing interviews.

Table 11.3 Global score by any further offence in 2 years

| | Reoffended within 24 months total | | Total |
	No	Yes	
Global Score 1–4	6	26	32
	18.8%	81.3%	100.0%
Global Score 5–10	32	53	85
	37.6%	62.4%	100.0%
Total	38	79	117
	32.5%	67.5%	100.0%

$P < .04$ (one-tailed)

Regression

The study found a relationship between use of skills by workers and re-offending by clients. However, it is possible that the relationship between use of skills and client re-offending is not there at all. It might be a factor of something else altogether. It could be, for example, that workers with good skills have caseloads with low risk clients. There could be a tendency for managers to allocate difficult clients to workers who appear tough or punitive, and the tough and punitive workers would have been given low skill scores. *Regression analysis* can help to sort out the extent to which the relationship between two factors is a real relationship and not a factor of some other variable such as risk levels of clients.

Regression analysis puts several variables into an equation and considers which of those variables relate to the dependent variable. Regression analysis can be in the form of multiple regression, where the dependent variable is a continuous variable (e.g. the number of offences committed by each offender), or it can be in the form of logistic regression in which case the dependent variable is dichotomous (e.g. whether or not the young person re-offended).

The logistic regression in Table 11.4 tells us that when we include risk levels of the young offenders as measured by the standard risk assessment measure used in juvenile justice NSW,

Table 11.4 Logistic regression analysis of further offending and risk level, global skills score and age of offender

	B	SE	Wald	Df	Sig.	Exp(B)
Risk score	.112	.030	14.184	1	.000	1.118
Global score	−1.094	.551	3.946	1	.047	.335
Client age	.000	.000	.463	1	.496	1.000
Constant	−38.699	57.804	.448	1	.503	.000

Variable(s) entered on step 1: FR.YLSI_score, gs1to4, Client_DOB.

the Youth Level of Supervision Inventory Revised (YLSIR) plus the age of the young offenders, there remains a significant relationship between the re-offending of those young people supervised by workers who score 5 or more on the global skills scale. We can assert that workers who have a certain level of skill have lower re-offending rates than workers who have lower skill levels regardless of the risk levels or age of the offenders they supervise.

Comparison of means

Another statistical technique that is often used in social work and human services research is comparison of means or the *t*-test. This technique compares the means of two groups to determine whether they are significantly different from each other. This is particularly useful if you have one set of dichotomous data (e.g. used skills/did not use skills) and one set of continuous data (e.g. clients were engaged on a 1–5 scale). In their study they collected data on both of these variables – re-offending by clients and an estimate of the overall engagement of the young person in the interview (see Figure 11.3).

---

1. Client is not engaged in the interview, is non-responsive, giving monosyllabic responses
2. Client is partially engaged in the interview, though responses are still limited
3. Client is occasionally engaged in the interview and is responsive to a proportion of what the worker is saying
4. Client appears engaged in the interview although may appear distracted or disinterested at times
5. Client is actively engaged in the interview, evidenced by taking notice of what the worker is saying, listening, responding to the worker, actively learning

---

Figure 11.3 Overall engagement of the client in the interview

It is clear from Table 11.5 that there was a statistically significant difference between the engagement score of the young people supervised by workers with good skills and the engagement score for young people supervised by workers with poor skills. For workers with good skills the engagement score was 6.6235, whereas for those assessed as having poor skills it was 5.3750. This was statistically significant at 0.000, which suggests that this was very unlikely to have occurred by chance – less than one chance in 10,000. Workers with more skills clearly engaged their clients better as well as having clients with low levels of re-offending.

Table 11.5 Skills of workers by client engagement

Global score	Mean engagement score	N	Standard deviation
Low	5.3750	32	1.47561
High	6.6235	85	1.68308
Total	6.2821	117	1.71628

$P = .000$ significant.

Concluding thoughts

All of the techniques referred to are about associations and/or differences between groups. This may suggest causation; however, statistical analysis of this nature can only tell us that factors are associated, not that one factor necessarily leads to another. In other words, it seems likely that good skills lead to or cause lower offending among young offenders who are exposed to them. However, the results of this study can only say that it is likely that they are associated. There could be some unknown variable operating which is actually causing the association.

In reaching conclusions from the quantitative data analysis it is important that the results of the study are considered alongside the previous research and the theory about the particular topic. Regarding the study that we have focused on in this chapter, there have now been at least eight different published research studies from several countries which have found that when probation officers and others who supervise offenders have good skills their clients offend less – at statistically significant levels (Trotter, 2013). These studies have used different methodologies. Some have trained probation officers in skills, others have observed and/or taped interviews, then coded them for skills and then examined re-offending. The findings of this study are consistent with findings from earlier research. The findings are also consistent with theories of human behaviours and motivation, including learning theory, which suggests that people change in response to positive feedback and rewards. This increases our confidence in saying that there is a relationship between workers' skills and client re-offending even though there may be some limitations in methodology.

Chapter summary

In this chapter several statistical techniques have been outlined. These include means, medians and modes, cross tabs, regression and comparison of means. There are of course many other statistical techniques, although these are perhaps the most commonly used in social work and social care research. As noted at the outset, we have tried to present the techniques by using a case study that shows how the techniques can be used in practice to answer a specific research question.

Key take-home messages

A research design using quantitative methods begins with a clear, succinct question with a focus on identifying the causal links between well-defined variables. Perhaps more so than with qualitative research, the extent to which quantitative research delivers answers that are valid and reliable is highly dependent on addressing design and methodological issues which exclude, or at the least limit, the possibility that the answers arrived at may be influenced by other extraneous factors. However, in concert with the pragmatic approach advocated here, many social/care researchers are likely to combine both quantitative and qualitative elements in order to extend understanding and account for the complex nature of social reality.

Additional resources

Dudley, J.R. (2011) *Research Methods for Social Work: Being Producers and Consumers of Research*. Boston, MA: Allyn & Bacon/Pearson. His chapter on quantitative analytic techniques is a great introductory read.

Lane, D. (n.d.) 'Online statistics education: an interactive multimedia course of study', available at: http://onlinestatbook.com (accessed 25 April 2016). This online resource is very comprehensive and well indexed to help you on your journey through quantitative data.

Trotter, C. and Evans, P. (2012) 'An analysis of supervision skills in youth probation', *Australian and New Zealand Journal of Criminology*, 45 (2): 255–73. This article gives an excellent example of how counting and measuring can be useful in understanding practice.

12

Writing and Sharing Your Findings

Creating Knowledge for Practice

In this chapter you will learn

- About dissemination of research findings as a core component of the research process
- To present your findings for particular audiences
- Creative ways of sharing your research
- Some strategies for getting started on writing.

Introduction

We are definitely of the view that: 'It's not research til it's shared!'. But we are also very aware that 'research utilization sits within the messy and complex worlds of policymaking and practice' (Morton, 2015: 405).

It is vital that social work research not simply collect data and observe it; it must take 'action, [pursue] social justice and [collect] systematic information in order to make a difference in people's lives' (Alston and Bowles, 2012: 9). Researching in the fields of social work and social care, much time is spent trying to share our findings widely and strategically; seeking to inform practice, management/organisational action and policy-making. Yet, the challenges of not just disseminating but implementing and utilising what has been found are well known.

In this, our concluding chapter for the book, we encourage you to reflect on any findings you may have from your own projects. We focus on the purpose/s of research dissemination – including as evidence to inform our practice, outlining the possible audiences for your research, and sharing some tips for writing and making use of your findings.

What is the purpose of sharing your findings?

The purpose of sharing your findings will determine both your writing style and the platform you choose. This may include a range of academic or other, more open source media; organisational working papers; conference presentations; journal articles; media opinion pieces; blogs, etc.

These are all very important sites for accessing knowledge – and undoubtedly in the course of your research project you have accessed and made use of many of them. So now you need to think of them as places where your own work can contribute and be used by others to assist them in carrying out research, developing policy and effecting change for the people, projects and issues that you as a social/care worker really care about.

Evidence for practice: it has sometimes been said that there is limited research that informs social work and social care practice, but this is not the case. Thyer (2015), for example, found 750 primary social work studies that used experimental methodology published in the past 65 years. Clearly, there is much evidence for practice 'out there', and this is not including the many theses, evaluations and qualitative studies done by or useful for practitioners in our field.

More importantly, perhaps, is the ongoing debate about the evidence based practice movement and the sometimes-noted reluctance of social workers to embrace empirical and experimental studies as a source of knowledge. A number of scholars have studied the factors that create barriers as well as facilitate the use of evidence in practice settings, such things as time, resources, support (see, for example, Parrish and Rubin, 2011; Gray et al., 2012, 2013; Bender et al., 2013; Cheung et al., 2014).

We also know that social/care workers have a history of valuing their 'practice wisdom', which might also be thought of as their 'tacit knowledge' (as discussed in Chapter 1) about how to practice. Explorations of the nature of this 'tacit knowledge' suggest that this may be a source of evidence for everyday intervention that practitioners readily draw on (Gordon et al., 2009). But, as with other professions, social/care workers need to be able to account for the practice decisions and interventions they make.

Social/care workers like yourselves, who are likely to be undertaking research, are crucial to the development, accountability and progression of our professions, and making your research findings available and accessible is a key part of so doing. In this chapter we offer suggestions for how you might do this. In synchrony with the pragmatic approach taken in this book, getting your findings into the wider domain means acting strategically – identifying your audience, writing to/for them, and making your work engaging and easily understood.

What do we mean by findings?

We often consider 'research findings' to refer to the final outcomes or results from a research study. But it is very important to consider that there are a range of findings that can be significant to communicate to others. These 'others' may be those who participated in the research, or other researchers who are tackling similar problems, or organisations and policy bodies. Useful and relevant findings are produced at every stage of the research process: indeed, the chapters in this book can provide a guide to those stages: context, ethics, literature review, methodology, method and data analysis.

Here are some examples of researchers who published either before their research was completed, or who took findings from particular aspects of their research process as the focus for their publication.

Context: Bawden (2015) describes the micro, meso and macro contextual factors in relation to researching and understanding health issues for Australian Indigenous people; and Flynn (2013) critically examines the knowledge context – how we have constructed and understood the risks to children whose parents have experienced imprisonment.

Literature review: Peters et al. (2013) report on the literature underpinning their study of palliative care nurses' death anxiety, while Reed and Harding (2015), social work practitioners, conducted a systematic review of family meetings.

Research design and its ethical implications: Haines et al. (2014) describe an innovative research methodology for studying health service disinvestment and the ethical issues raised by the design prior to the commencement of the study.

Methodology and methods: Flynn (2010) reflects on the methodological challenges of engaging in research with children whose mothers have been in prison and shares her learning.

Research process: McAlinden (2015) describes the cyclical process of undertaking Action Learning and Action Research in order to analyse elder abuse policy in a health network.

Emerging thematic findings: Proudley (2013) reports on the early themes arising from her ongoing qualitative study of bushfire survivors.

Research dissemination[1]

Research dissemination is a broad term. It can be understood to simply mean 'the diffusion or spread of ideas that stem from research studies out to those who need and can use them' (Thyer, 2001: 501). It is increasingly understood that this needs to move beyond publication in traditional journals to involve targeted and tailored messages to different groups of stakeholders.

---

[1]This section is taken from Rose and Flynn (in press) 'Animating social work research findings: a case study of research dissemination to benefit marginalised young people' *Visual Communication*.

Often, however, when we talk about 'research dissemination', 'research utilisation' or 'research translation', this typically focuses on how to bring together what are seen as the three disparate 'cultures' of research (science), policy and practice (Shonkoff, 2000). There are, however, far more stakeholders involved in the process of research use (Davies and Powell (2012). While Thyer (2001) suggests that this sometimes should include service users, McArthur and Winkworth (2013) describe the consumer voice as largely absent in any of this discussion. This lack of emphasis on sharing research with service users/research participants seems somewhat surprising, given the values and goals of social work and social care, and that these are the very people we are seeking to work in partnership with and empower (International Federation of Social Workers, 2012).

In recent years, particularly in the area of qualitative research, Bartlett (2013: 215) argues that there have been growing attempts to connect with non-academic audiences, with researchers '[experimenting] with alternative ways of disseminating scholarly findings'. Such experimentation has been aided by the rapid growth in information technology, where we can now see the use of social media and platforms such as YouTube to both process and transmit research findings. For example, the Economic and Social Research Council in the UK have a dedicated YouTube channel (www.youtube.com/user/theesrc) that has over 80 videos related directly to their research funding. More recently the Social Services Research Unit (London School of Economics and Political Science), in seeking to bring research and practice closer together, has presented *Tales from Social Care* (Brimblecombe et al., 2014) – research findings in the form of a comic. The target audience for many of these initiatives is practitioners, who are argued to be time poor (Brimblecombe et al., 2014) and not inclined to read research journals or research focused articles (Thyer, 2001). And as we saw in Chapter 9, the use of visual images in research provides a highly engaging and accessible means of conveying knowledge and understanding of particular social phenomena (we will discuss this further later in the chapter).

Creative strategies for sharing and encouraging knowledge use

Davies and Powell (2012: 216) make a strong argument for social researchers to expand their current strategies for communicating research findings; they emphasise the incorporation of a broader repertoire of more innovative methods to move beyond simply sharing information to creating influence. They propose a range of strategies:

- Narratives and stories: encouraging researchers to reflect on the power of a story to challenge and change how we see situations; they highlight the impact of case studies
- Language choice and metaphors: reminding us how what we think is shaped by the language we have available to us (e.g. 'drug addict' vs. 'substance user')
- Advertising and marketing: they highlight that researchers would benefit from being aware of the psychology of how intended audiences take on information
- Journeying together: co-producing knowledge
- Immersion and experiential learning
- Creativity and the arts.

Three recent projects provide excellent examples of using creativity and the arts. Bartlett (2013), in her examination of the social activism of people with dementia, made use of cartoons to represent and present findings, while Sligo and Tilley (2011) used visual composites to present data from participants about their experiences of literacy and an adult literacy programme. There were limitations noted with both of these visual approaches, respectively: people often have strong reactions to cartoons, or question the role of humour in talking about a sensitive or difficult issue; visual methods may not be seen as sufficiently formal or rigorous for funders or policy-makers; or pictures may be interpreted in many ways. More recently Rose and Flynn (in press) involved Catherine collaborating with a visual arts academic (Cameron Rose) and his students, to work with existing data gathered from children who had experienced maternal imprisonment. See case study below.

 Case study

Thinking outside the box

Catherine was motivated to ensure that her research into the experiences of young people who had experienced maternal imprisonment had wider impact than just her getting a PhD! She was committed to wide dissemination, and had presented at conferences, written academic journal articles, as well as for magazines and other open access media. She knew, however, that this was unlikely to reach an audience of young people. Working with SHINE for Kids (an Australian national children's charity who work with and for young Australians affected by family member involvement in the criminal justice system) they came up with a mutually beneficial idea: the provision of individual stories outlining the research participants' experiences, to be provided via the organisation's website. Eight narratives were produced. All highlighted one key theme, with links to relevant support services provided at the conclusion. Despite this achievement, all parties involved were aware of the likely low literacy levels of many of the young people they were hoping would ultimately benefit from these stories. A new plan was developed – to turn the stories into short animations (this is where Cameron and his students got involved!). Using this medium had lots of benefits: it provided 'bite sized' findings in a way that is engaging for children, as well as protecting the anonymity of possibly vulnerable young people. These documentaries are publicly available via the SHINE for Kids YouTube channel: https://www.youtube.com/user/SHINEforKids.

As well as considering *how* to present your findings (in what format), you also need to have a plan for *how* to get most use out of your findings, whilst remaining realistic (we have heard it suggested (Morton et al., 2012) that politicians pay more attention to the views of taxi drivers than to research findings!).

Realistic aims for impact

Morton et al. (2012, citing Weiss, 1979) remind us that research use occurs on a continuum, from more conceptual use – such as raising awareness of, or changing perceptions about an issue, through to direct, instrumental use – such as changing how we provide a service, introducing an intervention or developing and implementing a policy. Much of what we do in social work and social care is at the more conceptual end of the spectrum. These authors (2012: 245–7, citing Nutley, 2007) present some strategies for ways to improve research use:

1. Set realistic expectations and ambitions about research use (see what you do as informing rather than determining).
2. Improve the supply of relevant, accessible and credible evidence but do not stop there (put effort into related areas: making research accessible; building collaborations and ways to co-produce knowledge; consider synthesising existing research rather than trying to 'reinvent the wheel').
3. Shape – as well as respond to – the demand for evidence in policy and practice settings (develop relationships and work with those in advocacy roles to get particular areas of concern onto the public agenda).
4. Develop multi-faceted strategies to address the interplay between supply and demand (make use of the interaction between different types of knowledge, including tacit knowledge/practice wisdom; be aware that research use is a social interaction – relationships are important).
5. Recognise the role of dedicated knowledge broker organisations and networks.
6. Target multiple voices to increase opportunities for evidence to become part of policy discourse (relationships again!).
7. Evaluate (knowledge exchange) strategies to improve research use and learn from this.

If you have embarked on a piece of research, do any of these strategies seem useful to you? What steps could you take to incorporate this strategy/ies into your research plan?

As has been evident throughout this book, we consider participation to be a key strategy to empowering and useful research; you also need to consider participation at the stage of dissemination.

Participatory dissemination

MacKenzie et al. (2015: 113) contend that the dissemination involved with participatory approaches, such as 'writing policy reports and delivering community feedback workshops are not prioritised to nearly the same degree in conventional academic culture as peer reviewed journals and conference presentations'. Hence it is more typical in social work and social science research, for 'participation' to be minimal, with participants offered access to the research results/final report, if they ask for it.

However, the process-focused nature of participatory research, especially Participatory Action Research (PAR), which we described in Chapter 2, places high importance on good, clear and purposeful communication. Indeed, to ensure improvements in the lives of those involved in a study means that their unique knowledge of what will work for them, or in their community, needs to be integrated into information-sharing and problem-solving processes synonymous with adopting a participatory approach. By enabling participants to claim a larger share of decision-making for their community, it is more likely too that the findings can be applied to address health and social issues raised by them. The potential that participating and ongoing communication around findings hold for increasing people's control over their own lives through developing and supporting community strengths and problem-solving abilities embedded in participatory research also should not be underestimated (Viswanathan et al., 2004). Here are two key considerations for ensuring effective communication:

- Report findings to the community in appropriate, relevant and sensitive formats, which may be visual, oral, dramatic or written. Reported findings should address the original research questions or focus; be disseminated and explained to participants; applied to develop interventions or policy changes within the community; and used to sustain research-related actions by the community. Thus, working to ensure participating groups or communities remain involved with making decisions about what, where, to whom and how to disseminate findings and apply them in action is essential to effective participatory research (MacLean et al., 2009). A taskforce of community members to study any recommendations, prior to their release, may sometimes be desirable
- Foster collaboration in co-authoring communications about findings. To do this might require technical training and skill development, support and information about how community collaborators can be involved in the dissemination of information and findings (Viswanathan et al., 2004; de Wolff et al., 2009). For example, Fossey developed and presented conference papers and publications with her research participants (Fossey et al., 2002; Fossey, 2009). This process facilitated establishing and maintaining the authenticity of the research process, and the credibility of the research within the wider community of interest through providing a space for responses and commentary within public forums.

Be aware, however, that in other fields, there may be a very different focus. Ferris and Sass-Kortsak (2011) argue that in the broader, specifically clinical, literature there is no consensus about sharing research results with participants. Discussion centres more on the ethics of whether or not to share results than on accepting this as a given and focusing on how we can do this respectfully and effectively. For social work and social care researchers, there is a greater ethical and professional imperative to share our results with study participants.

Research impact?

It is all very well to share your findings, but how will you know if these have been used or useful to your intended audience? Morton (2015: 406) helpfully distinguishes between research uptake, use and impact. She defines uptake as the audience having engaged somehow with the research and suggests that you can gauge this by looking at changes in their awareness and any reactions to this awareness. Research use is seen to involve the audience acting upon the research (such as discussing, presenting, adapting, etc.); Morton suggests that you can understand about research use by examining changes in skills or knowledge of the research users. It has been noted (Marshall, 2014: 4) that '[w]hilst some academics, particularly those earlier and later in their careers, like the idea of being more immediately useful to front-line decision-makers, the reward systems in most academic institutions have not in the past encouraged [these] kinds of approaches [academic and practice collaborations]'. Shojania and Levinson (2009: 768) argue in relation to clinical research, that where research leads to beneficial changes in clinical practice it should be documented, examined in relation to the extent to which the findings or outcomes of the activity have been emulated elsewhere and reviewed via written attestations regarding the effect of the activity or its influence.

If you have completed a project, or are planning a study, what would be evident if your research had impact? (For example, changes in knowledge, skills, or behaviours.)

For those of us who work within practice settings, these kinds of impacts are often noted anecdotally, but perhaps rarely result in publications. Finally, research impact is seen to encompass 'changes in awareness, knowledge and understanding, ideas, attitudes and perceptions, and policy and practice as a result of research'. Morton (2015) suggests that you can assess the impact of your work by examining changes in the behaviours or practices of those you were seeking to influence.

See our example below for an example about how a focus on something seemingly small can have a beneficial impact.

Case study

Easily overlooked but of significant impact

Gait physiotherapists (Davies et al., 2016) examined the impact of different kinds of footwear on the propensity for older women to fall. They found that lace-up shoes rather than slippers or bare feet reduced falls, offering a simple but very easily implemented strategy for potentially leading to significant improvements in the health of older women, which, as we know, can so easily deteriorate once a fall has occurred.

Sharing your findings requires you to 'translate' these into a format that is accessible and meaningful to your audience. In social work and social care this will typically involve some writing, even if you use more visually informed methods. Writing can be challenging for most of us (we are all a lot slower than we anticipate!) but there are some good strategies for getting going on this.

Strategies for writing

Suggestions for writing strategies are almost as numerous as the people who write them but, in general, they advise that writers develop a structure and begin with an outline that follows the structure. It is often a good idea to begin by writing an abstract, which requires you, in less than 500 words, to summarise the main argument you will be making in your paper. You can refer again and again to the abstract to make sure that you are keeping on track. An abstract or summary requires that you focus on:

- The purpose of the paper
- The main findings from your study
- The evidence that supports or challenges your findings
- The implications of your findings for policy or practice or programme development.

Getting started: this is always a challenge – sitting at a keyboard and not knowing what to write. Here are some tips for 'breaking the ice' and getting going:

Journal writing group:

- Set up a small group of fellow students or practitioners who also want to write
- Meet often and always go along even if you haven't written anything
- Plan what you will have written by what dates
- Ask group members to read and comment
- Be prepared to read and comment on other group members' work.

Co-authorship: many of us benefit from working collaboratively with others. Not only does this share the writing task but often leads to a better product when the minds of two or more people combine. Co/multi authors do spur each other on and are a ready-made critical audience. Our experience in writing this book is an excellent example.

Supervision: work with a more experienced writer, perhaps your research supervisor. Set a timeframe for completing your report or paper; schedule regular meetings; meet without fail, even if you have not written anything.

Present at a conference: this can be a great strategy for getting you writing a paper or preparing a poster. The conference timeline will ensure that you 'get going' quickly in order to meet it.

Once you have presented, you may have received valuable feedback which can assist in revising your paper. Some conferences also provide the option of publishing your paper once you have presented it, provided that it is accepted by reviewers. If you work in a large organisation, such as a hospital, it is likely that an annual research week offers opportunities for papers and presentations.

Journals: Many journals offer advice to would-be contributors which is helpful and informative. The home pages for journals always include a section offering 'information for authors'. Some journals also have separate sections for academic and practice focused articles. See, for example, *Australian Social Work* (https://www.aasw.asn.au/publications/australian-social-work) or *Health and Social Work* (www.oxfordjournals.org/our_journals/hsw/for_authors/msprep_submission.html).

One important point to bear in mind, is that there is almost no one who has submitted an article to a journal that has not been returned with (in the best case scenario) advice for revisions and resubmission. Writing for publication requires a thick skin, so be prepared to write, revise and resubmit.

Chapter summary

In this chapter we have emphasised the core role of dissemination in the research process, encouraging you to consider who your audience may be and how you can share your findings in ways that have an impact.

Key take-home messages

The communication of research findings is a key part of the research process, not an add-on. Incorporate a dissemination strategy into your research plan (who needs to know, how might they best know and who needs to be involved?). Build in time (and use your social work and social care skills) to build relationships, to share ideas, write, think creatively. Be prepared for knock-backs when you submit papers for publication, and see these as opportunities to hone your writing skills. And be patient with yourself. Research takes time.

A few final words

This book has emerged out of our (Catherine and Fiona's) practice, teaching and research experience. We see the development of 'research-mindedness' beginning in the classroom and being stimulated by experiences in the field as a student and as a practitioner. Our activities as students and practitioners in the social work and social care field bring us directly into contact with the everyday 'problems in living' that service users encounter. Practising well means being able to draw on the best available evidence in combination with skills and understanding in order to improve all our lives. And we as social/care workers are far better placed than almost anyone to identify and bridge the gaps in knowledge, understanding and intervention strategies that can contribute to better practice. In this book we have outlined various approaches, methods and strategies for asking the right, researchable questions and answering them through collecting data in ethical and pragmatic ways. Research is often hard work but it is also intellectually stimulating. Very importantly, to arrive at better ways of working with our service users is always central to our endeavours. Doing good research because we always need to know more about what will work or work better is at the heart of the social work and social care professions. We trust that this book will be a useful guide in so doing.

Additional resources

Green, W. and Simon, B.L. (2012) *The Columbia Guide to Social Work Writing*. New York: Columbia University Press. This resource has excellent chapters on writing for different audiences and different fields of practice.

Healy, K. and Mulholland, J. (2012) *Writing Skills for Social Workers* (2nd edn). London: Sage. These authors discuss a range of areas where writing matters, including journal articles and research proposals.

References

Abma, T.A., Nierse, C.J. and Widdeershoven, G.A.M. (2009) 'Patients as partners in responsive research: methodological notions for collaborations in mixed research teams', *Qualitative Health Research*, 19 (3): 401–13.

Ackerly, B. and True, J. (2010) *Doing Feminist Research in Political and Social Science*. New York: Palgrave Macmillan, St. Martin's Press LLC.

Adams, K.B., Matto, H.C. and LeCroy, C.W. (2009) 'Limitations of evidence-based practice for social work education: unpacking the complexity', *Journal of Social Work Education*, 45 (2): 165–86.

Alston, M. and Bowles, W. (2012) *Research for Social Workers*. St. Leonards, NSW: Allen & Unwin.

Argyris, C. and Schon, D. (1974) *Theory in Practice: Increasing Professional Effectiveness*. San Francisco, CA: Jossey-Bass.

Armstrong, E.M. (2014) 'Shared subjects, divergent epistemologies: sociology, social work, and social problems scholarship', *Qualitative Social Work*, 13 (6): 757–65.

Arnd-Caddigan, M. (2010) 'Evidence based practice and the purpose of clinical social work', *Smith College Studies in Social Work*, 80 (1): 35–52.

Australian Bureau of Statistics (2012) 'Australian Health Survey: First results, 2011–12' (cat.no. 4364.0. 55.00). Canberra: Australian Bureau of Statistics.

Austermühl, F. (2014) *The Great American Scaffold. Intertextuality and Identity in American Presidential Discourse*. Philadelphia, PA: John Benjamins Publishing.

Aveyard, H. (2010) *Doing a Literature Review in Health and Social Care: A Practical Guide* (2nd edn). Milton Keynes: Open University Press/McGraw-Hill.

Bagnoli, A. (2009) 'Beyond the standard interview: the use of graphic elicitation and arts based methods', *Qualitative Research*, special issue 9 (5): 547–70.

Bailliard, A. (2015) 'Visual methodologies in research: unlocking the complexities of occupation', *Canadian Journal of Occupational Therapy*, 82 (1): 35–43.

Ballenger, B. (2007) *The Curious Researcher* (5th edn). New York: Pearson/Longman.

Banks, M. (1995) 'Visual research methods', *Social Research Update*, 11 (3). Available at: http://sru.soc.surrey. ac.uk/SRU11/SRU11.html (accessed 26 April 2016).

Banks, M. (2001) *Visual Methods in Social Research*. London: Sage Publications.

Baranek, G.T., Barnett, C.R., Adams, E.M., Wolcott, N.A., Watson, L.R. and Crais, E.R. (2005) 'Object play in infants with autism: methodological issues in retrospective video analysis', *American Journal of Occupational Therapy*, 59: 20–30.

Barrett, C. (2008) *My People: Exploring the Experiences of Gay, Lesbian, Bisexual, Transgender and Intersex Seniors in Aged Care Services*. Melbourne: Matrix Guild Victoria Inc. and Vintage Men Inc. Available at: www.matrixguildvic.org.au/docs/MyPeople_Exploring-Experiences-2008.pdf (accessed 26 April 2016).

Bartlett, R. (2013) 'Playing with meaning: using cartoons to disseminate research findings', *Qualitative Research*, 13 (2): 214–27.

Baum, F., MacDougall, C. and Smith, D. (2006) 'Participatory action research', *Journal of Epidemiology and Community Health*, 60: 854–7.

Bawden, G. (2015) 'Australia's indigenous people', in E.M.P. Schott and E.L. Weiss (eds), *Transformative Social Work Practice*. London: Sage, pp. 513–23.

Bawden, G. and McDermott, F. (2012) 'Project Discovery: social work research at Southern Health', *Australian Social Work [P]*, 65 (1): 136–44.

Bell, J. (2005) *Doing Your Research Project* (4th edn). Milton Keynes: Open University Press.

Bellamy, J.L., Mullen, E.J., Satterfield, J.M., Newhouse, R.P., Ferguson, M., Brownson, R.C. and Spring, B. (2013) 'Implementing evidence based practice education in social work: a transdisciplinary approach', *Research on Social Work Practice*, 23 (4): 246–56.

Benatar, S.R. and Singer, P.A. (2000) 'A new look at international research ethics', *British Medical Journal*, 321 (7264): 824–6.

Bender, K., Altschul, I., Yoder, J., Parrish, D. and Nicke, S.J. (2013) 'Training social work graduate students in the evidence-based practice process', *Research on Social Work Practice*, 24 (3): 339–48.

Berg, B. (2014) 'Visual ethnography, entry', in L. Given (ed.), *The Sage Encyclopedia of Qualitative Research Methods*. Thousand Oaks, CA: Sage.

Berger, P.L. and Luckman, T. (1966) *The Social Construction of Reality*. London: Penguin.

Berger, R. (2010) 'Practitioners in search of evidence', *Journal of Social Work*, 10 (2): 175–91.

Bhaskar, R. (2008) *A Realist Theory of Science*. New York: Routledge.

Bigby, C. and Frawley, P. (2010) 'Reflections on doing inclusive research in the "Making Life Good in the Community" study', *Journal of Intellectual and Developmental Disability*, 35 (2): 53–61.

Bishop, F.L. (2015) 'Using mixed methods research designs in health psychology: an illustrated discussion from a pragmatist', *Journal of Health Psychology*, 20: 5–20.

Boddy, J., Le Bon, G. and Lakhani, A. (2014,)'"I don't like seeing 'land sold' signs!": using Photovoice to elicit children's views about their community', *Communities, Children and Families Australia*, 8 (1): 81–93.

Bodie, G.D. (2011) 'The understudied nature of listening in interpersonal communication: introduction to a special issue', *International Journal of Listening*, 25 (1–2): 1–9.

Borden, W. (2013) 'Experiments in adapting to need: pragmatism as orienting perspective in clinical social work', *Journal of Social Work Practice*, 27 (3): 259–71.

Bowling, A. and Windsor, J. (2008) 'The effects of question order and response-choice on self-rated health status in the English Longitudinal Study of Ageing (ELSA)', *Journal of Epidemiology and Community Health*, 62: 81–5.

Boyatzis, R.E. (1998) *Transforming Qualitative Information: Thematic Analysis and Code Development*. Thousand Oaks, CA: Sage.

Braun, V. and Clarke, V. (2006) 'Using thematic analysis in psychology', *Qualitative Research in Psychology*, 3 (2): 77–101.

Braun, V. and Clarke, V. (2012) 'Thematic analysis', in H. Cooper (ed.), *APA Handbook of Research Methods in Psychology: Vol. 2. Research Designs*. Washington, DC: American Psychological Association, pp. 57–71.

Brewer, J. and Hunter, A. (2006) *Foundations of Multi-Method Research: Synthesizing Styles*. Thousand Oaks, CA: Sage.

Brimblecombe, N.S., Stevens, B. and Hu, M. (2014) 'Tales from social care', Personal Social Services Research Unit, London School of Economics and Political Science. Available at: http://issuu.com/pssrulse/docs/tales_from_social_care (accessed 26 April 2016).

British Association of Social Workers (BASW) (2012) 'Code of ethics'. Available at: http://cdn.basw.co.uk/upload/basw_112315-7.pdf (accessed 26 April 2016).

Brophy, L. and McDermott, F. (2013), 'Using social work theory and values to investigate the implementation of community treatment orders', *Australian Social Work*, 66 (1): 72–85.

Bruner, J. (1991) 'The narrative construction of reality', *Critical Inquiry*, 18 (1): 1–21.

Brydon, K. and Flynn, C. (2014) 'Expert companions? Constructing a pedagogy for supervising honours students', *Social Work Education: The International Journal*, 33 (3): 365–80.

Bryman, A. (2012) *Social Research Methods* (4th edn). South Melbourne: Oxford University Press.

Burgess, A. and Flynn, C. (2013) 'Supporting imprisoned mothers and their children: a call for evidence', *Probation Journal*, 60: 73–81.

Byrne, D. (1998) *Complexity Theory and the Social Sciences: an Introduction*. London: Routledge.

Caldwell, K., Coleman, K., Copp, G., Bell, L. and Ghazi, F. (2007) 'Preparing for professional practice: how well does professional training equip health and social care practitioners to engage in evidence-based practice?', *Nurse Education Today*, 27 (6): 518–25.

Carroll, K., Iedema, R. and Kerridge, I. (2008) 'Reshaping ICU ward round practices using video-reflexive ethnography', *Journal of Qualitative Health Research*, 18: 380–90.

Catalani, C. and Minkler, M. (2010) 'Photovoice: a review of the literature in health and public health', *Health Education Behavior*, 37 (3): 424–51.

Chalfen, R. and Rich, M. (2007) 'Combining the applied, the visual and the medical: patients teaching physicians with visual narratives', in S. Pink (ed.), *Visual Interventions: Applied Visual Anthropology*. Oxford: Blackwell, pp. 53–70.

Charles, C. (1997) 'Research as part of everyday practice: a finishing student's experience', *Australian Social Work*, 50 (2): 57–9.

Charmaz, C. (2006) *Constructing Grounded Theory: a Practical Guide through Qualitative Analysis*. Thousand Oaks, CA: Sage.

Cheung, M., Ma, A., Thyer, B.A. and Webb, A.E. (2014) 'Research–practice integration in real practice settings: issues and suggestions', *Research on Social Work Practice*, 25 (4): 1–8.

Choi, B.C.K. and Pak, A.W.P. (2006) 'Multidisciplinarity, interdisciplinarity and transdisciplinarity in health research, services education and policy', *Clinical & Investigative Medicine*, 29 (6): 351–64.

Clark, C.D. (1999) 'The autodriven interview: a photographic viewfinder into children's experience', *Visual Sociology*, 14: 39–50.

Clark-Ibanez, M. (2004) 'Framing the social world with photo-elicitation interviews', *American Behavioural Scientist*, 47: 1507–27.

Cleary, P.D., Mechanic, D. and Weiss, N. (1981) 'The effect of interviewer characteristics on responses to a mental health interview', *Journal of Health and Social Behavior*, 22 (2): 183–93.

Coleman, H. and Unrau, Y. (2014) 'Qualitative data analysis – a step-by-step approach', in R.M. Grinnell and Y. Unrau (eds), *Social Work Research and Evaluation: Foundations of Evidence-Based Practice* (10th edn). New York: Oxford University Press, pp. 554–72.

Cossar, J. and Neil, E. (2015) 'Service user involvement in social work research: learning from an adoption research project', *British Journal of Social Work*, 45: 225–40.

Creswell, J.W. (2003) *Research Design: Qualitative, Quantitative, and Mixed Methods Approaches* (2nd edn). Thousand Oaks, CA: Sage.

Creswell, J. and Plano Clark, V. (2011) *Designing and Conducting Mixed Methods Research* (2nd edn). Thousand Oaks, CA: Sage.

Crowe, L., Quinn, V., Chenoweth, L., Kularatna, S., Boddy, J. and Wheeler, A.J. (2015) 'Advance care planning for older Australians living in the community: the impact of a group education session', *SAGE Open*. DOI: 10.1177/2158244015593117.

Crowne, D.P. and Marlowe, D. (1960) 'A new scale of social desirability independent of psychopathology', *Journal of Consulting Psychology*, 24 (4): 349–54.

Csiernik, R., Birnbaum, R. and Pierce, B.D. (2010) *Practising Social Work Research: Case Studies for Learning*. Toronto: University of Toronto Press.

Cummings, E., Robinson, A., Courtney-Pratt, H., Cameron-Tucker, H., Wood-Baker, R. and Walters, E. (2010) 'Pathways home: comparing voluntary IT and non-IT users participating in a mentored self management project', *Studies in Health Technology and Informatics*, 160: 23–7.

Cummings, S.R., Browner, W.S. and Hulley, S.B. (1988) *Designing Clinical Research: an Epidemiologic Approach*. Baltimore, MD: Williams & Wilkins.

Curtis, K., Roberts, H., Copperman, J., Downie, A. and Liabo, K. (2004) 'How come I don't get asked no questions? Reaching hard to reach children and teenagers', *Child and Family Social Work*, 9 (2): 167–75.

Daley, K. (2012) 'Gathering sensitive stories: using care theory to guide ethical decision making in research interviews with young people', *Youth Studies Australia*, 31 (3): 27–34.

Davies, A.M., Galna, B., Murphy, A.T., Williams, C.M. and Haines, T.P. (2016) 'Effect of footwear on minimum foot clearance, heel slippage and spatiotemporal measures of gait in older women', *Gait and Posture*, 44: 3–47.

Davies, H.T.O. and Powell, A.E. (2012) 'Communicating research findings more effectively: what we can learn from other fields', *Evidence and Policy*, 8 (2): 213–33.

Davis, R.E., Couper, M.P., Janz, N.K., Caldwell, C.H. and Resnicow, K. (2010) 'Interviewer effects in public health surveys', *Health Education Research*, 25 (1): 14–26.

Davison, J. (2004) 'Dilemmas in research: issues of vulnerability and disempowerment for the social worker/researcher', *Journal of Social Work Practice: Psychotherapeutic Approaches in Health, Welfare and the Community*, 18 (3): 379–93.

D'Cruz, H. and Jones, M. (2004) *Social Work Research: Ethical and Political Contexts*. Thousand Oaks, CA: Sage.

de Koning, K. and Martin, M. (1996) 'Participatory research in health: setting the context', in K. de Koning and M. Martin (eds), *Participatory Research in Health: Issues and Experiences*. London: Zed Books, pp. 1–18.

de Wolff, A. and Associates and the Dream Team advocacy group (2009) 'The creation of "We are neighbours": participatory research and recovery', *Canadian Journal of Community Mental Health*, 28 (2): 61–72.

Derry, S., Pea, R., Barron, B., Engle, R., Erickson, F., Goldman, R. and Sherin, B. (2010) 'Conducting video research in the learning sciences: guidance on selection, analysis, technology, and ethics', *Journal of the Learning Sciences*, 19 (1): 3–53.

Dijktstra, W. (1983) 'How interviewer variance can bias the results of research on interviewer effects', *Quality and Quantity*, 17: 179–87.

Dodds, S.J. and Epstein, I. (2012) *Practice Based Research in Social Work: a Guide for Reluctant Researchers*. New York: Routledge.

Dominelli, L. and Holloway, M. (2008) 'Ethics and governance in social work research in the UK', *British Journal of Social Work*, 38 (5): 1009–24.

Dudley, J. (2011) *Research Methods for Social Work: Being Producers and Consumers of Research*. Boston, MA: Allyn & Bacon/Pearson.

Dwyer, S.C. and Buckle, J.L. (2009) 'The space between: on being an insider-outsider in qualitative research', *International Journal of Qualitative Methods*, 8 (1): 54–63.

Eakin, J. and Mykhalovskiy, E. (2003) 'Reframing the evaluation of qualitative health research: reflections on a review of appraisal guidelines in the health sciences', *Journal of Evaluation in Clinical Practice*, 9 (2): 187–94.

Edmond, T., Megivern, D., Williams, C., Rochman, E. and Howard, M. (2006) 'Integrating evidence-based practice and social work field education', *Journal of Social Work Education*, 42 (2): 377–96.

Election Watch (2014) 'Visualising the budget speeches'. Available at: http://electionwatch.edu.au/australia-2013/analysis/visualising-budget-speeches (accessed 26 April 2016).

Engel, R.J. and Schutt, R.K. (2014) 'Survey research', in R.M. Grinnell and Y. Unrau (eds), *Social Work Research and Evaluation: Foundations of Evidence-based Practice* (10th edn). New York: Oxford University Press, pp. 414–54.

Engin, M. (2011) 'Research diary: a tool for scaffolding', *International Journal of Qualitative Methods*, 10 (3): 296–306.

Epstein, I. (2010) *Clinical Data-mining: Integrating Practice and Research, Pocket Guides to Social Work Research Methods*. New York: Oxford University Press.

Epstein, I. and Blumenfield, S. (2001) *Clinical Data-mining in Practice-based Research: Social Work in Hospital Settings*. New York: Haworth Social Work Practice Press.

Epstein, P., Coates, P. and Wray, L. (2006) *Results that Matter: Improving Communities by Engaging Citizens, Measuring Performance and Getting Things Done*. San Francisco, CA: Jossey-Bass.

Erlandson, D.A., Harris, E.L., Skipper, B.L. and Allen, S.D. (1993) *Doing Naturalistic Inquiry: a Guide to Methods*. Newbury Park, CA: Sage.

Evans, T. and Hardy, M. (2010) *Evidence and Knowledge for Practice*. Cambridge: Polity.

Ferris, L.E. and Sass-Kortsak, A. (2011) 'Sharing research findings with research participants and communities', *International Journal of Occupational and Environmental Medicine*, 2 (3): 172–81.

Fine, M., Weis, L., Weseen, S. and Wong, L. (2000) 'For whom? Qualitative research, representations, and social responsibilities', in N.K. Denzin and Y.S. Lincoln (eds), *Handbook of Qualitative Research* (2nd edn). Thousand Oaks, CA: Sage, pp. 107–32.

Finestone, S. and Kahn, A.J. (1975) 'The design of research', in N.A. Polansky (ed.), *Social Work Research*. Chicago, IL: University of Chicago Press, pp. 38–67.

Flynn, C. (2010) 'Young people who have experienced maternal imprisonment: ensuring their well-being and voice in research', *Advances in Social Work and Welfare Education*, 12 (1): 53–72.

Flynn, C. (2013) 'Understanding the risk of offending for the children of imprisoned parents: a review of the evidence', *Children and Youth Services Review*, 35 (2): 213–17.

Flynn, C. and Lawlor, J. (2008) 'Building a therapeutic care team – foster care intervention when a mother is imprisoned – case study', *Children Australia*, 33 (4): 24–30.

Flynn, C. and Saunders, V. (2015) 'Research with children of prisoners: bringing them in from the margins', in S. Bastien and H.B. Holmarsdottir (eds), *Youth at the Margins: Experiences from Engaging Youth in Research Worldwide*. Rotterdam: Sense Publishers, pp. 219–40.

Flynn, C., Kamasua, J., Brydon, K., Lawihin, D., Kornhauser, T. and Grimes, E. (2014) 'Preparedness for field education placement: social work students' experiences in Papua New Guinea', *Social Work Education*, 33 (4): 435–50.

Flynn, C., Naylor, B. and Fernandez Arias, P. (2015) 'Responding to the needs of children of parents arrested in Victoria, Australia: the role of the adult criminal justice system', *Australian and New Zealand Journal of Criminology*. DOI: 10.1177/0004865815585390.

Fossey, E. (2009) *Participating as Resisting: Everyday Life Stories of People Experiencing Mental Health Issues*. PhD Thesis, The University of Melbourne.

Fossey, E., Epstein, M., Findlay, R., Plant, G. and Harvey, C. (2002) 'Creating a positive experience of research for people with psychiatric disabilities by sharing feedback', *Psychiatric Rehabilitation Journal*, 25 (4): 369–78.

Fox, M., Martin, P. and Green, G. (2007) *Doing Practitioner Research*. New York: Sage.

Franzosi, R. (1998) 'Narrative analysis – or why (and how) sociologists should be interested in narrative', *Annual Review of Sociology*, 24: 517–54.

Fritz, H. and Lysach, C. (2014) '"I see it now": using photo elicitation to understand chronic illness self-management', *Canadian Journal of Occupational Therapy*, 81 (4): 247–55.

Frost, N., Nolas, S.M., Brooks-Gordon, B., Esin, C., Holt, A., Mehdizadeh, L. and Shinebourne, P. (2010) 'Pluralism in qualitative research: the impact of different researchers and qualitative approaches on the analysis of qualitative data', *Qualitative Research*, 10 (4): 441–60.

Gerstl-Pepin, C. and Patrizio, K. (2009) 'Learning from Dumbledore's Pensieve: metaphor as an aid in teaching reflexivity in qualitative research', *Qualitative Research*, 9 (3): 299–308.

Gibbs, G.R. (2008) *Analysing Qualitative Data*. London: Sage.

Gilgun, J.F. and Abrams, L.S. (2002) 'The nature and usefulness of qualitative social work research', *Qualitative Social Work*, 1 (1): 39–55.

Glaser, B.G. and Strauss, A.L. (1967) *Discovery of Grounded Theory: Strategies for Qualitative Research*. Chicago, IL: Aldine.

Goldkuhl, G. (2012) 'Pragmatism vs interpretivism in qualitative information systems research', *European Journal of Information Systems*, 21: 135–46.

Goodrich, J. and Cornwell, J. (2008) *Seeing the Person in the Patient: the Point of Care Review*. London: The Kings Fund.

Gordon, J., Cooper, B. and Dumbleton, S. (2009) *How Do Social Workers Use Evidence in Practice?* Milton Keynes: The Open University.

Goulding, D. (2004) *Severed Connections: an Exploration of the Impact of Imprisonment on Women's Familial and Social Connectedness*. Perth: Murdoch University.

Grant, L. and Fine, A. (1992) 'Sociology unleashed: creative directions in classical ethnography', in A. LeCompte, W. Milroy and J. Preissle (eds), *Handbook of Qualitative Research in Education*, Academic Press, San Diego, pp. 406–46.

Gray, M., Joy, E., Plath, D. and Webb, S.A. (2012) 'Implementing evidence-based practice: a review of the empirical research literature', *Research on Social Work Practice*. DOI: 1049731512467072.

Gray, M., Joy, E., Plath, D. and Webb, S.A. (2013) 'What supports and impedes evidence-based practice implementation? A survey of Australian social workers', *Research on Social Work Practice*, 23 (2): 157–66.

Gray, M., Sharland, E., Heinsch, M. and Schubert, L. (2015) 'Connecting research to action: perspectives on research utilisation', *British Journal of Social Work*, 45 (7): 1952–67.

Grbich, C. (1999) *Qualitative Research in Health: an Introduction*. Thousand Oaks, CA: Sage.

Grbich, C. (2007) *Qualitative Data Analysis: an Introduction*. Thousand Oaks, CA: Sage.

Green, D. and McDermott, F. (2010) 'Social work from inside and between complex systems: perspectives on person-in-environment for today's social work', *British Journal of Social Work*, 1 (17). DOI:10.1093/bjsw/bcq056.

Green, L., Morris, H., Bawden, G. and McDermott, F.M. (2015) '"You'll need to go to hospital in Melbourne!" The experience of country patients and families in the city: an evaluation of a supported

accommodation service for rural patients attending hospital', *Practice Reflexions*. Available at: www.
acwa.org.au/resources/Referreed-article-You-ll-need-to-go-to-hospital.pdf (accessed 26 April 2016).

Greig, A., Taylor, J. and MacKay, T. (2013) *Doing Research with Children: a Practical Guide* (3rd edn).
London: Sage.

Guillemin, M. and Gillam, L. (2004) 'Ethics, reflexivity, and "ethically important moments" in research',
Qualitative Inquiry, 10 (2): 261–80.

Haaken, J. and O'Neill, M. (2014) 'Moving images: psychoanalytically informed visual methods in documenting the lives of women migrants and asylum seekers', *Journal of Health Psychology*, 19 (1): 79–89.

Hadorn, G.H., Pohl, C. and Bammer, G. (2010) 'Solving problems through transdisciplinary research', in
J. Frodeman, J. Thompson Klein and C. Mitcham (eds), *The Oxford Handbook of Interdisciplinarity*. New
York: Oxford University Press.

Haines, T.P., O'Brien, L.J., McDermott, F.M., Markham, D., Mitchell, D., Watterson, D.M. and Skinner, E.
(2014) 'A novel research design can aid disinvestment from existing health technologies with uncertain effectiveness, cost-effectiveness, and/or safety', *Journal of Clinical Epidemiology [P]*, 67 (2): 144–51.

Hampson, R. and McDermott, F. (2004) 'Ethics, ethics and more ethics ... Passing the hurdle', *Contributing
to an Ageing Agenda*, 105. Available at: www.academia.edu/975656/ETHICS_ETHICS_AND_MORE_
ETHICS_PASSING_THE_HURDLE (accessed 26 April 2016).

Hansen, E.C. (2006) *Successful Qualitative Health Research: a Practical Introduction*. Crows Nest, NSW: Allen
& Unwin.

Hardwick, L. and Worsley, A. (2011) *Doing Social Work Research*. London: Sage.

Harper, D. (2002) 'Talking about pictures: a case for photo elicitation', *Visual Studies*, 17 (1): 13–26.

Harvey, D., Plummer, D., Pighills, A. and Pain, T. (2013) 'Practitioner research capacity: a survey of social
workers in Northern Queensland', *Australian Social Work*, 66 (4): 540–54.

Harvey, W.S. (2011) 'Strategies for conducting elite interviews', *Qualitative Research*, 11 (4): 431–41.

Heal, L.W. and Sigelman, C.K. (1995) 'Response biases in interviews of individuals with limited mental
ability', *Journal of Intellectual Disability Research*, 39 (4): 331–40.

Heenan, M. and Murray, S. (2006) 'A study of reported rapes in Victoria: 2000–2003'. Available at: www.
dhs.vic.gov.au/__data/assets/pdf_file/0004/644152/StudyofReportedRapes.pdf (accessed 26 April 2016).

Heisley, D. and Levy, S. (1991) 'Autodriving: a photoelicitation technique', *Journal of Consumer Research*,
18: 257–72.

Heppner, P.P. and Heppner, M.J. (2004) *Writing and Publishing Your Thesis, Dissertation and Research: a
Guide for Students in the Helping Professions*. Belmont, CA: Thomson/Brooks-Cole.

Hernandez-Albujar, Y. (2007) 'The symbolism of video: exploring migrant mothers' experiences', in
G.C. Stanczak (ed.), *Visual Research Methods: Image, Society and Representation*. London: Sage, pp. 281–306.

Hiscock, H., Bayer, J.K., Hampton, A., Ukoumunne, O.C. and Wake, M. (2008) 'Long-term mother and
child mental health effects of a population-based infant sleep intervention: cluster-randomized,
controlled trial', *Pediatrics*, 122 (3): 621–7.

Hoey, B. (2008) 'American dreaming: refugees from corporate work seek the good life', in E. Rudd and
L. Descartes (eds), *The Changing Landscape of Work and Family in the American Middle Class: Reports from
the Field*. Plymouth, MA: Lexington Books.

Hoeyer, K., Dahlager, L. and Lynöe, N. (2005) 'Conflicting notions of research ethics: the mutually challenging traditions of social scientists and medical researchers', *Social Science and Medicine*, 61 (8):
1741–9.

Holbrook, A., Bourke, S., Fairbairn, H. and Lovat, T. (2007) 'Examiner comment on the literature review
in Ph.D. theses', *Studies in Higher Education*, 32 (3): 337–56.

Holliday, A. (2001) *Doing and Writing Qualitative Research*. London: Sage.

Holosko, M. (2006) *Primer for Critiquing Social Research: a Student Guide*. Belmont, CA: Thomson Wadsworth.

Holstein, J.A. and Gubrium, J.F. (2012) *Varieties of Narrative Analysis*. Thousand Oaks, CA: Sage.

Hounslow, B., Stephenson, A., Stewart, J. and Crancher, J. (1982) *Children of Imprisoned Parents*. Sydney: NSW Department of Youth and Community Services.

Hugman, R., Pittaway, E. and Bartolomei, L. (2011) 'When "do no harm" is not enough: the ethics of research with refugees and other vulnerable groups', *British Journal of Social Work*, 41 (7): 1271–87.

Humphrey, C. (2013) 'Dilemmas in doing insider research in professional education', *Qualitative Social Work*, 12: 572–85.

Iedema, R., Mesman, J. and Carroll, K. (2013) *Visualising Health Care Practice Improvement: Innovation from Within*. Milton Keynes: Radcliffe Publishing.

International Federation of Social Workers (2012) 'Global standards on social work education'. Available at: http://ifsw.org/policies/global-standards (accessed 26 April 2016).

International Practice Research Conference (2008) 'Salisbury Statement'. Available at: www.socsci.soton.ac.uk/spring/news/int-prac-res2008 (accessed 26 April 2016).

Isaacs, A.N., Pepper, H., Pyett, P., Gruis, H.A., Waples-Crowe, P. and Oakley-Browne, M.A. (2011) 'What you do is important but how you do it is more important', *Qualitative Research Journal*, 11 (1): 51–61.

Israel, M. and Hay, I. (2006) *Research Ethics for Social Scientists*. London: Sage.

Jernigan, V., Salvatore, A.L., Styne, D.M. and Winkleby, M. (2012) 'Addressing food insecurity in a Native American reservation using community based participatory research', *Health Education Research*, 27: 645–55.

Jesson, J.K., Matheson, L. and Lacey, F.M. (2011) *Doing Your Literature Review: Traditional and Systematic Techniques*. Thousand Oaks, CA: Sage.

Johnson, T., Kulesa, P., Cho, Y.I. and Shavitt, S. (2005) 'The relation between culture and response styles: evidence from 19 countries', *Journal of Cross-Cultural Psychology*, 36 (2): 264–77.

Kellehear, A. (1993) *The Unobtrusive Researcher*. St. Leonards: Allen & Unwin.

Kerstetter, K. (2012) 'Insider, outsider, or somewhere in between: the impact of researchers' identities on the community-based research process', *Journal of Rural Social Sciences*, 27 (2): 99–117.

Kessler, R.C., Andrews, G., Colpe, L.J., Hiripi, E., Mroczek, D.K., Normand, S.L.T., Walters, E.E. and Zazlavsky, A.M. (2002) 'Short screening scales to monitor population prevalences and trends in non-specific psychological distress', *Psychological Medicine*, 32: 959–76.

Khanlou, N. and Peter, E. (2005) 'Participatory action research: considerations for ethical review', *Social Science and Medicine*, 60: 2333–40.

Lal, S., Donnelly, C. and Shin, J. (2015) 'Digital storytelling: an innovative tool for practice, education and research', *Occupational Therapy Health Care*, 29 (1): 54–62.

Lambert, M.J. (2013) 'The efficacy and effectiveness of psychotherapy', in M.J. Lambert (ed.), *Bergin and Garfield's Handbook of Psychotherapy and Behavior Change* (6th edn). New York: Wiley, pp. 169–218.

Lapenta, F. (2011) 'Some theoretical and methodological views on photo-elicitation', in E. Margolis and L. Pauwels (eds), *The Sage Handbook of Visual Research Methods*. London: Sage, pp. 201–213.

Latham, A. (2003) 'Research, performance and doing human geography: some reflections on the diary-photograph, dairy-interview method', *Environment and Planning A*, 35 (11): 1993–2017.

Lawrence, R.J. and Despres, C. (2004) 'Introduction: futures of transdisciplinarity', *Futures*, 36: 397–405.

Leavy, P. (2012) 'Transdisciplinarity and training the next generation of researchers. Problem-centered approaches to research and problem-based learning', *International Review of Qualitative Research*, 5 (2): 205–23.

Lee, D.-C.A, Day, L., Hill, K., Clemson, L., McDermott, F. and Haines, T.P. (2015) 'What factors influence older adults to discuss falls with their health-care providers?', *Health Expectations*, 18 (5): 1593–609.

Lee, J. and Ingold, T. (2006) 'Fieldwork on foot: perceiving, routing, socializing', in S. Coleman and P. Collins (eds), *Locating the Field: Space, Place and Context in Anthropology*. Oxford: Berg.

Leigh, J.T. (2014) 'The process of professionalisation: exploring the identities of child protection social workers', *Journal of Social Work*, 14 (6): 625–44.

Liamputtong, P. (2013) *Qualitative Research Methods* (4th edn). South Melbourne: Oxford University Press.

Lincoln, Y. and Guba, E.G. (1985) *Naturalistic Enquiry*. Newbury Park, CA: Sage.

Lofland, J. (2006) *Analyzing Social Settings: a Guide to Qualitative Observation and Analysis* (4th edn). Belmont, CA: Wadsworth.

Lomax, H. (2012) 'Contested voices? Methodological tensions in creative visual research with children', *International Journal of Social Research Methodology*, 15 (2): 105–17.

Lomax, H., Fink, J., Singh, N. and High, C. (2011) 'The politics of performance: methodological challenges of researching children's experiences of childhood through the lens of participatory video', *International Journal of Social Research Methodology*, 14 (3): 231–43.

Lunt, N., Shaw, I. and Mitchell, F. (2009) 'Practitioner research in CHILDREN 1st: cohorts, networks and systems', Institute for Research and Innovation in the Social Services. Available at: www.iriss.org.uk/sites/default/files/iriss-practitioner-research-children1st-report-2009.pdf (accessed 26 April 2016).

Luttrell, W. (2010) '"A camera is a big responsibility": a lens for analysing children's visual voices', *Visual Studies*, 25 (3): 224–37.

Mackenzie, C.A., Christensen, J. and Turner, S. (2015) 'Advocating beyond the academy: dilemmas of communicating relevant research results', *Qualitative Research*, 15(1): 105–21.

MacLean, S., Warr, D. and Pyett, P. (2009) 'Was it good for you too? Impediments to conducting university-based collaborative research with communities experiencing disadvantage', *Australian and New Zealand Journal of Public Health*, 33 (5): 407–12.

Mannay, D. (2010) 'Making the familiar strange: can visual research methods render the familiar setting more perceptible?', *Qualitative Research*, 10 (1): 91–111.

Mannay, D. (2013) '"Who put that on there … why why why?": power games and participatory techniques of visual data production', *Visual Studies*, 28 (2): 136–46.

Marshall, C. and Rossman, G.B. (1989) *Designing Qualitative Research*. Newbury Park, CA: Sage.

Marshall, M. (2014) 'Bridging the ivory towers and the swampy lowlands: increasing the impact of health services research on quality improvement', *International Journal for Quality in Health Care*, 26 (1): 1–5.

McAdams, D.P. (2012) 'Exploring psychological themes through life-narrative accounts', in J.A. Holstein and J.F. Gubrium (eds), *Varieties of Narrative Analysis*. Thousand Oaks, CA: Sage, pp. 15–32.

McAdams, D.P., Josselson, R. and Lieblich, A. (2006) *Identity and Story: Creating Self in Narrative*. Washington, DC: American Psychological Association.

McAlinden, F. (2015) 'Using Action Research and Action Learning (ARAL) to develop a response to the abuse of older people in a healthcare context', *Journal of Work-Applied Management*, 7 (1): 38–51.

McAlinden, F., McDermott, F. and Morris, J. (2013) 'Complex patients: social workers' perceptions of complexity in health and rehabilitation services', *Social Work in Health Care*, 52: 899–912.

McArthur, M. and Winkworth, G. (2013) 'Powerful evidence: changing policy and practice through research', *Developing Practice: The Child, Youth and Family Work Journal*, 35: 41–53.

McCrystal, P. and Wilson, G. (2009) 'Research training and professional social work education: developing research-minded practice', *Social Work Education: The International Journal*, 28 (8): 856–72.

McDermott, F. (1996) 'Social work research: debating the boundaries', *Australian Social Work*, 49 (1): 5–10.

McDermott, F. (2002) *Inside Groupwork: A Guide to Reflective Practice*. Crows Nest, NSW: Allen & Unwin.

McDermott, F.M. (2014) 'Complexity theory, trans-disciplinary working and reflective practice', in A. Pycroft and C. Bartollas (eds), *Applying Complexity Theory: Whole Systems Approaches to Criminal Justice and Social Work*. Bristol: Policy Press, pp. 181–98.

McFadden, P., Taylor, B.J., Campbell, A. and McQuilkin, J. (2012) 'Systematically identifying relevant research: case study on child protection workers' resilience', *Research on Social Work Practice*, 22: 626–63.

McLean, A. and Flynn, C. (2013) '"It's not just a pap-smear": women speak of their experiences of hospital treatment after miscarriage', *Qualitative Social Work*, 12 (6): 782–98.

Meadows, D. (2003) 'Digital storytelling: research based practice in new media', *Visual Communication*, 2 (2): 189–93.

Mendes, P. (2010) 'Moving from dependence to independence: a study of the experiences of 18 care leavers in a leaving care and after care support service in Victoria', *Children Australia*, 35 (1): 14–21.

Miles, M.B., and Huberman, A.M. (1994) *Qualitative Data Analysis: An Expanded Sourcebook*. Thousand Oaks, CA: Sage.

Miles, M.B., Huberman, A.M. and Saldaña, J. (2014) *Qualitative Data Analysis: a Methods Sourcebook* (3rd edn). Thousand Oaks, CA: Sage.

Mitchell, F., Lunt, N. and Shaw, I. (2010) 'Practitioner research in social work: a knowledge review', *Evidence and Policy*, 6(1): 7–31.

Morgan, D.L. (2014) 'Pragmatism as a paradigm for social research', *Qualitative Enquiry*, 20 (8): 1045–53.

Morton, S. (2015) 'Progressing research impact assessment: a "contributions" approach', *Research Evaluation*, 24: 405–19.

Morton, S., Phipps, D. and Nutley, S. (2012) 'Using research to influence family services and policies: issues and challenges', *Families, Relationships and Societies*, 1 (2): 243–53.

Mullen, E.S., Bledsoe, S.E. and Bellamy, J.L. (2008) 'Implementing evidence based social work practice', *Research on Social Work Practice*, 18: 325–38.

National Health and Medical Research Council (NHMRC) (2003) 'Values and ethics: guidelines for ethical conduct in Aboriginal and Torres Strait Islander health research'. Available at: www.nhmrc.gov. au/_files_nhmrc/publications/attachments/e52.pdf (accessed 26 April 2016).

Neuman, W.L. (2014) *Social Research Methods: Qualitative and Quantitative Approaches* (7th edn). Harlow: Pearson New International.

Newhouse, R.P. and Spring, B. (2010) 'Interdisciplinary evidence-based practice: moving from silos to synergy', *Nursing Outlook*, 58: 309–17.

Nutbrown, C. (2011) 'Naked by the pool? Blurring the image?: ethical and moral issues in the portrayal of young children in arts-based educational research', *Qualitative Inquiry*, 17 (1): 3–14.

Oakley, A. (2005) *The Ann Oakley Reader: Gender, Women and Social Science*. Bristol: Policy Press.

O'Callaghan, C.C. (2015) 'Therapeutic opportunities associated with the music when using song writing in palliative care', *Psychology of Music*, 43 (1): 122–39.

Office for Human Research Protections (OHRP) (2009) *Code of Federal Regulations – Protection of Human Subjects*, US Department of Health and Human Services. Available at: www.hhs.gov/ohrp/policy/ohr pregulations.pdf (accessed 26 April 2016).

O'Leary, Z. (2005) *Researching Real-world Problems: a Guide to Methods of Inquiry*. London: Sage.

O'Leary, Z. (2010) *The Essential Guide to Doing Your Research Project*. London: Sage.

Oliaro, L. and Trotter, C. (2010) 'On campus and off campus social work education', *Australian Social Work*, 63 (3): 324–40.

Parrish, D.E. and Rubin, A. (2011) 'Validation of the evidence-based practice process assessment scale short version', *Research on Social Work Practice*, 21 (2): 200–11.

Patton, M.Q. (2015) *Qualitative Research and Evaluation Methods. Integrating Theory and Practice* (4th edn). Thousand Oaks, CA: Sage.

Peters, L.A., Cant, R.P., Payne, S.L., O'Connor, M.M., McDermott, F.M., Hood, K.L., Morphet, J.N. and Shimoinaba, K. (2013) 'How death anxiety impacts nurses' caring for patients at the end of life: a review of literature', *The Open Nursing Journal*, 7 (1): 14–21.

Phelan, S. and Kinsella, E.A. (2013) 'Picture this … safety, dignity and voice – ethical research with children: practical considerations for the reflexive researcher', *Qualitative Inquiry*, 19 (2): 81–90.

Pierce, D. (2005) 'The usefulness of video methods for occupational therapy and occupational science research', *American Journal of Occupational Therapy*, 59: 9–19.

Pink, S. (2006) *The Future of Visual Anthropology: Engaging the Senses*. Oxford: Routledge.

Pink, S. (2011) 'Images, senses and applications: engaging visual anthropology', *Visual Anthropology*, 24 (5): 437–54.

Plath, D. (2012) 'Evidence-based practice', in M. Gray and S. Webb (eds), *Social Work Theories and Methods* (2nd edn). London: Sage.

Prosser, J., Clark, A. and Wiles, R. (2008) *Visual Research Ethics at the Crossroads*. Working Paper. Manchester: National Centre for Research Methods, Realities.

Proudley, M. (2013) 'Place matters', *Australian Journal of Emergency Management*, 28 (2): 11–16.

Pycroft, A. and Bartolas, C. (2014) *Applying Complexity Theory: Whole Systems Approaches to Criminal Justice and Social Work*. Bristol: Policy Press.

Pyett, P. (2002) 'Working together to reduce health inequalities: reflections on a collaborative participatory approach to health research', *Australian and New Zealand Journal of Public Health*, 26 (4): 332–6.

Pyett, P., Waples-Crowe, P. and Van der Sterren, A. (2009) 'Engaging with Aboriginal communities in an urban context: some practical suggestions for public health researchers', *Australian and New Zealand Journal of Public Health*, 33 (1): 51–4.

Pyett, P., Waples-Crowe, P. and Van Der Sterren, A. (2013) 'Collaborative participatory research with disadvantaged communities', in P. Liamputtong (ed.), *Research Methods in Health. Foundations for Evidence Based Practice* (2nd edn). Oxford: Oxford University Press, pp. 344–62.

Rapley, T. (2007) *Doing Conversation, Discourse and Document Analysis*. London: Sage.

Reed, M. and Harding, K.E. (2015) 'Do family meetings improve measurable outcomes for patients, carers, or health systems? A systematic review', *Australian Social Work*, 68 (2): 244–58.

Reinharz, S. (1992) *Feminist Methods in Social Research*. Oxford: Oxford University Press.

Riessman, C.K. (2002) 'Analysis of personal narratives,' in J.F. Gubrium and J.A. Holstein (eds), *Handbook of Interview Research: Context and Method*. Thousand Oaks, CA: Sage, pp. 695–710.

Rodik, P. and Primorac, J. (2015) 'To use or not to use: computer-assisted qualitative data analysis software usage among early-career sociologists in Croatia', *Qualitative Social Research*, 16 (1): Art. 12.

Rose, G. (2001) *Visual Methodologies*. London: Sage.

Rose, G. (2015) 'Keynote address', Visual Methods Conference, Sept. 16–18, Brighton, UK.

Rose, C. and Flynn, C. (in press) 'Animating social work research findings: a case study of research dissemination to benefit marginalised young people', *Visual Communication*.

Rubin, A. and Babbie, E.R. (2011) *Research Methods for Social Work* (7th edn). Belmont, CA: Brooks/Cole, Cengage Learning.

Rubin, A. and Babbie, E.R. (2013) *Essential Research Methods for Social Work* (3rd edn). Belmont, CA: Brooks/Cole, Cengage Learning.

Rubin, A. and Bellamy, J. (2012) *Practitioner's Guide to Using Research for Evidence-based Practice*. Richmond, VA: John Wiley & Sons.

Rubin, A. and Parrish, D.E. (2007) 'Challenges to the future of evidence-based practice in social work education', *Journal of Social Work Education*, 43 (3): 405–28.

Sack, W.H., Seidler, J. and Thomas, S. (1976) 'The children of imprisoned parents: a psychosocial exploration', *American Journal of Orthopsychiatry*, 46 (4): 618–28.

Sanger, M. and Giddings, M.M. (2012) 'Teaching note: a simple approach to complexity theory', *Journal of Social Work Education*, 48 (2): 369–75.

Sarantakos, S. (2013) *Social Research*. London: Palgrave-Macmillan.

Sayer, A. (2000) *Realism and Social Science*. Thousand Oaks, CA: Sage.

Schofield, I., Tolson, D. and Fleming, V. (2012) 'How nurses understand and care for older people with delirium in the acute hospital: a critical discourse analysis', *Nursing Inquiry*, 19 (2): 165–76.

Schwartz, D. (1989) 'Visual ethnography: using photography in qualitative research', *Qualitative Sociology*, 12 (2): 119–54.

Shaw, I. (2005) 'Practitioner research: evidence or critique', *British Journal of Social Work*, 35: 1231–48.

Shaw, I. (2007) 'Is social work research distinctive?', *Social Work Education*, 26 (7): 659–69.

Shaw, I. (2008) 'Ethics and the practice of qualitative research', *Qualitative Social Work*, 7 (4): 400–14.

Shaw, I. and Faulkner, A. (2006) 'Practitioner evaluation at work', *American Journal of Evaluation*, 27: 44.

Shojania, K.G. and Levinson, W. (2009) 'Clinicians in quality improvement: a new career pathway in academic medicine'. *Journal of the American Medical Association*, 30: 766–8.

Shonkoff, J.P. (2000) 'Science, policy and practice: three cultures in search of a shared mission', *Child Development*, 71 (1): 181–7.

Sligo, F.X. and Tilley, E. (2011) 'When words fail us: using visual composites in research reporting', *Visual Communication*, 10 (1): 63–85.

Spierings, N. (2012) 'The inclusion of quantitative techniques and diversity in the mainstream of feminist research', *European Journal of Women' Studies*, 19 (3): 331–47.

Spradley, J. (1980) *Participant Observation*. Belmont, CA: Wadsworth.

Sunderland, N., Bristed, H., Gudes, O., Boddy, J. and Da Silva, M. (2012) 'What does it feel like to live here? Exploring sensory ethnography as a collaborative methodology for investigating social determinants of health in place', *Health and Place*, 18(5): 1056–67.

Sunderland, P. and Denny, R. (2007) *Doing Anthropology in Consumer Research*. Walnut Creek, CA: Left Coast Press.

Sweetman, P. (2009) 'Revealing habitus, illuminating practice: Bourdieu, photography and visual methods', *Sociological Review*, 57 (3): 491–511.

Talbot, L. and Verrinder, G. (2008) 'Turn a stack of papers into a literature review: useful tools for beginners', *Focus on Health Professional Education: a Multi-disciplinary Journal*, 10 (1): 51–8.

Taylor, S. (2013) *What Is Discourse Analysis?* London: Bloomsbury.

Thomas, S.A. (2000) *How to Write Health Science Papers, Dissertations and Theses*. New York: Churchill Livingston.

Thomson, P. (2013) 'Not all literature reviews are the same' (patter: research education, academic writing, public engagement, funding, other eccentricities). Available at: http://patthomson.wordpress.com/2013/05/23/not-all-literature-reviews-are-the-same (accessed 26 April 2016).

Thyer, B.A. (2001) *The Handbook of Social Work Research Methods*. London: Sage.

Thyer, B.A. (2015) 'A bibliography of randomized controlled experiments in social work (1949–2013): solvitur ambulando', *Research on Social Work Practice*, 25 (7): 753–93.

Timmins, F. and McCabe, C. (2005) 'How to conduct an effective literature search', *Nursing Standard*, 20 (11): 41–7.

Tomaino, J., Ryan, S., Markotić, S. and Gladwell, J. (2005) 'Children of prisoners project; Steering committee's report to the Justice Cabinet Committee', Attorney General's Department, South Australia.

Tri-Council Policy Statement 2 (TCPS2) (2014) 'Ethical conduct for research involving humans', Canadian Institutes of Health Research, Natural Sciences and Engineering Research Council of Canada, Social Sciences and Humanities Research Council of Canada, Government of Canada. Available at: www.pre. ethics.gc.ca/pdf/eng/tcps2-2014/TCPS_2_FINAL_Web.pdf (accessed 26 April 2016).

Tripodi, T. (1985) 'Research design', in R. Grinnell Jr (ed.), *Social Work Research and Evaluation* (2nd edn). Itasca, IL: F.E. Peacock, pp. 231–59.

Trotter, C. (2013) 'Reducing recidivism through probation supervision – what we know and don't know from four decades of research', *Federal Probation*, 77 (2): 9–15.

Trotter, C. and Evans, P. (2012) 'An analysis of supervision skills in youth probation', *Australian and New Zealand Journal of Criminology*, 45 (2): 255–73.

Trotter, C. (2015) *Working with Involuntary Clients* (3rd edn). Sydney: Allen & Unwin.

Truman, C. and Raine, P. (2001) 'Involving users in evaluation: the social relations of user participation in health research', *Critical Public Health*, 11 (3): 215–39.

Tudball, N. (2000) *Doing It Hard: a Study of the Needs of Children and Families of Prisoners in Victoria*. Melbourne: VACRO.

Unrau, Y.A. and Grinnell, R.M. (2005) 'The impact of social work research courses on research self-efficacy for social work students', *Social Work Education*, 24 (6): 639–51.

Viney, L.L. and Bousfield, L. (1991) 'Narrative analysis: a method of psychosocial research for AIDS-affected people', *Social Science and Medicine*, 32(7): 751–65.

Viswanathan, M. et al. (2004) 'Community-based participatory research: assessing the evidence', Agency for Health Care Research and Quality (US). Available at: http://archive.ahrq.gov/downloads/pub/ evidence/pdf/cbpr/cbpr.pdf (accessed 26 April 2016).

Wade, K. and Neumann, K. (2007) 'Practice based research: changing the professional language of social work', *Social Work in Health Care*, 44 (4): 49–64.

Wadsworth, Y. (1991) *Everyday Evaluation on the Run*. Melbourne: Action Research Issues Association.

Wadsworth, Y. (2001) 'Becoming responsive – and some consequences for evaluation as dialogue across distance', *New Directions in Evaluation*, 92: 45–58.

Wadsworth, Y. and Epstein, M. (1998) 'Building-in dialogue between consumers and staff in acute mental health services', *Systemic Practice and Action Research*, 11 (4): 353–79.

Wallerstein, N. and Duran, B. (2003) 'The conceptual, historical and practice roots of community based participatory research and related participatory traditions', in M. Minkler and N. Wallerstein (eds), *Community-based Participatory Research for Health*. San Francisco, CA: Jossey-Bass, pp. 27–51.

Wang, C., Cash, J. and Powers, L. (2000) 'Who knows the streets as well as the homeless? Promoting personal and community action through Photovoice', *Journal of Health Promotion Practice*, 1: 81–9.

Warr, D.J. and Pyett, P.M. (1999) 'Difficult relations: sex work, love and intimacy', *Sociology of Health and Illness*, 21 (3): 290–309.

Weinbach, R.W. and Grinnell, R.M. (2014) *Statistics for Social Workers* (9th edn). New York: Pearson.

Wiles, R., Prosser, J., Bagnoli, A., Clark, A., Davies, K., Holland, S. and Renold, E. (2008) *Visual Ethics: Ethical Issues in Visual Research*. Southampton: ESRC National Centre for Research Methods Review Paper, National Centre for Research Methods. Available at: http://eprints.ncrm.ac.uk/421 (accessed 26 April 2016).

Wiles, R., Coffey, A., Robison, J. and Heath, S. (2010) *Anonymisation and Visual Images: Issues of Respect, 'Voice' and Protection*, NCRM Working Paper Series, ESRC National Centre for Research Methods, NCRM Hub, University of Southampton, WISERD, University of Cardiff. Available at: http://eprints.ncrm.ac.uk/1804/1/anonymisation_and_visual_methods_working_paper.pdf (accessed 26 April 2016).

Williams, M., Grinnell, R.M. and Tutty, L.M. (1995) *Research in Social Work: an Introduction*. Itasca, IL: F.E. Peacock.

Wolf-Branigin, M. (2009) 'Applying complexity and emergence in social work education', *Journal of Social Work Education*, 28 (2): 115–27.

Wolf-Branigin, M. (2013) *Using Complexity Theory for Research and Program Evaluation*. Bristol: Policy Press.

Zea, M.C., Reisen, C.A. and Diaz, R.M. (2003) 'Methodological issues in research with Latino gay and bisexual men', *American Journal of Community Psychology*, 31: 281–91.

Index

Tables and Figures are indicated by page numbers in bold print. The abbreviation '*bib*' after a page number refers to bibliographical information in the 'Additional resources' sections.